Information Investigation

Information Investigation

Exploring Nonfiction with Books Kids Love

Laura Turner Pullis

fulcrum resources
Golden, Colorado

*This book is dedicated to my ever-supportive husband and my two precious ones.
And to every curious young mind who has made teaching so wonderful for me.*

Book design by Bill Spahr

Library of Congress Cataloging-in-Publication Data

Pullis, Laura Turner.
    Information investigation : exploring nonfiction with books kids love / Laura Turner Pullis.
        p. cm.
    Includes bibliographical references.
    ISBN 1-55591-955-3 (paperback)
    1. Children's literature—Study and teaching (Elementary)—United States. 2. Education, Elementary—Activity programs—United States. 3. Interdisciplinary approach in education—United States. 4. Children—Books and reading. I. Title.
    LB1575.5.U5P85   1998
    372.64—DC21   97-43288
                                                                 CIP

Printed in the United States of America
0 9 8 7 6 5 4 3 2 1

Fulcrum Publishing
350 Indiana Street, Suite 350
Golden, Colorado 80401-5093
(800) 992-2908 • (303) 277-1623
e-mail: fulcrum@fulcrum-resources.com
website: www.fulcrum-resources.com

Table of Contents

Acknowledgments

I would like to express my appreciation to the staff at Woodbury Library in Denver, Colorado, especially Mildred, Bertha, and Theresa. I am truly grateful for all their assistance throughout this writing project.

I would also like to thank the entire Denver Public Library and to compliment its staff and the millions of fabulous books that they make available to all of us.

Finally, I would like to express my sincere appreciation and gratitude to my brother Paul Turner who is responsible for all of the artwork within these pages.

Introduction

WHY WAS THIS BOOK WRITTEN?

As a third-grade teacher, one of the things I loved most was planning and gathering resources for a theme unit. However enjoyable, this was always a very time-consuming task. This book is designed to help teachers spend less time planning and more time involving students in the learning process.

As a book lover, I have noticed an enormous improvement in the number and quality of nonfiction books available for children during the past seven to ten years. Coupled with schools' increased interest in getting more nonfiction books in the classrooms for students, I believe that the idea of teaching themes with excellent nonfiction literature is more than logical; it is exciting and energizing for curriculum. Nonfiction books offer a vast array of meaningful topics that can help children acquire numerous skills in all of the content areas and learn more about the world around them. For more information on the value of nonfiction literature and how to choose excellent nonfiction books for your students, I recommend *A Matter of Fact* by Pamela Green.

As a parent, I have often thought about how I can be involved in what my daughters do at school. I strongly believe that parents always have something to contribute to what is happening at their child's school. This book provides parents with suggestions on the many different opportunities to do just that. Who knows? This may be the "jump start" toward a true partnership with parents in the education of their children.

WHO IS THIS BOOK WRITTEN FOR?

This book is designed for teachers of grades 3 through 6 who continually seek out new topics for students to really sink their teeth into as they learn and practice the skills they need. It is for teachers who take pleasure in helping students work together to learn about their worlds from different angles. This book may also provide an excellent opportunity for regular classroom teachers, special education teachers, art teachers, music teachers, and others to team together in their teaching approaches.

This book has been designed with many different types of students in mind. The books represented here and accompanying investigations can be adapted to many different ability levels and offer a variety of activities to match the variability in student interests. Most of the investigations are designed for students to work in cooperative groups, which, in my experience, is one of the best methods to get students involved in their own learning as well as to provide opportunities for social and emotional growth. For further information on the benefits and methods of cooperative learning, I recommend *Cooperation in the Classroom* by David W. Johnson, Roger T. Johnson, and Edythe Johnson Holubec.

WHAT IS IN EACH UNIT?

This book contains twelve separate units on a wide variety of topics, each of which includes numerous activities for developing and strengthening skills in math, language, reading, social science, and the arts. Each unit begins with a short description of the featured book, the themes to be addressed, and the skills that will be focused on throughout the unit. In the "investigations" section are new words investigations that result in a display of the unit vocabulary. Then the investigating activities are described in detail for before reading, during reading, and after reading the featured book. In addition, each unit suggests strategies for reading the featured book. I often suggest at least three separate read alouds of a book in different contexts, because each reading becomes increasingly enjoyable for children as it becomes more familiar and understandable. Following the investigations is a letter to parents that informs them of what their child is going to learn about in the upcoming weeks, as well as invites their involvement on several different levels. Each unit then offers a "unit appendix," in which investigation sheets, patterns, and a student evaluation can be found that pertain specifically to that unit. Finally, each unit provides a "supporting library," which is an annotated bibliography of additional resources to support the investigations and to provide for further reading material on the unit topic.

TIPS FOR USING THIS BOOK

First, you must consider your students' interests (and your own as well) and select a unit. Also, consider the time of year, special events happening at your school, and so on.

Once you have chosen a unit, visit your local library with your list of supporting library books. In my experience, I have found librarians to be exceptionally helpful to teachers in gathering materials. Ask them to help you find or order the books you need, including multiple copies of the featured book. Also, always check with the media specialist in your school or district for additional resources on your chosen unit topic. Once you have the books you need, keep them on display and accessible for group work and independent reading throughout the unit.

Before you begin the unit, schedule special events and reserve field trip transportation if applicable. Determine places, dates, and times. Adjust information to suit your specific needs on the parent letter and make copies. Then check the materials list, gather what you can, and determine what you can ask parents to lend or donate to your class. (Encourage and welcome all types of involvement. Remember, parental involvement empowers you as well as

the parents and students.) Write these items on the "Wanted" sheet and make copies. Attach the "Wanted" sheet to the parent letter and send them home with students before actually beginning the unit.

Once you start the unit, the description of activities will guide you through before reading investigations (including new words investigations), during reading investigations, and after reading investigations. Do not feel, however, that you must attempt all of the activities described. Choose the ones that will best suit the needs of your students and yourself.

I recommend that students designate a folder to use for each unit to keep maps, notes, drawings, letters, stories, responses, and investigation sheets in. Students can make a new folder for each unit by folding large pieces of construction paper in half. Challenge students to look for and share any newspaper or magazine articles that relate to the unit topic and have them keep the various clippings in the folder.

At the close of the unit, provide each student with the evaluation and ask them to evaluate their own performance during the unit. Students may want to look at the evidence available in their unit folders. This is a critical element because not only is it important for young people to think critically about their own progress and the outcomes of their attitudes and actions, but it will help you in your own evaluation of the unit and each student. There is a unit evaluation in the Main Appendix for teacher use only that will also help determine the effectiveness of the unit for your students. Other helpful resources can be found in the Main Appendix that can be used in several of the units, including reading responses, the "Wanted" sheet, group checklists, field trip permission forms, and more.

It is my hope that *Information Investigation* finds you ready and willing to embark on a series of exciting learning adventures with your students, and that it guides your curiosity and enthusiasm with confidence into the wide world of fascinating nonfiction literature for children. Have fun!

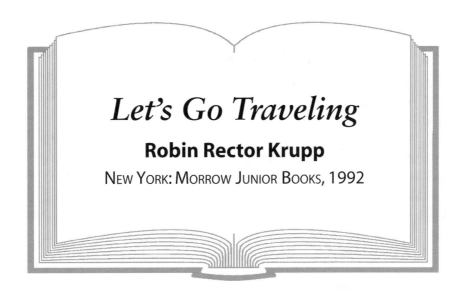

Let's Go Traveling

Robin Rector Krupp

NEW YORK: MORROW JUNIOR BOOKS, 1992

ABOUT THE BOOK

Let's Go Traveling takes us to six different countries to explore ancient and mysterious monuments such as famous rock formations, pyramids, caves, temples, and ancient cities. We journey along with a young traveler named Rachel, who keeps an entertaining diary, writes letters and postcards throughout her trip, and adds to a new word list at each destination. The illustrations are a treasure trove of maps, drawings, and photographs as well as an interesting collection of little odds and ends that Rachel gathers along the way.

INVESTIGATIONS

Investigative Themes

World Travel
Geography
Ancient Ruins/Past Civilizations
Foreign Customs, Languages, and Currency
Writing: Letters, Postcards, Diary, Pen Pals

Investigative Skills

using maps
planning
making lists
making decisions
writing letters
making books
researching
comparing costs
using numbers
following directions

sequencing
working cooperatively
listening/speaking
writing creatively
making models
journal writing
using money
hypothesizing
defining words
reading for information

Investigative Materials

1 copy of *Let's Go Traveling* for every three or four students
supporting library books
encyclopedias

travel brochures, magazines, newspaper ads from travel sections, books
large world wall map
overhead transparencies of world, continent, and/or country maps
student copies of world, continent, or country maps
several globes
camera and film for taking passport photos
"diaries" or travel journals premade or purchased
potatoes, knives, and stamp pads for passport stamps
6 pillow cases, brushes, newspaper, safety pins, and paints for flags
6 postcards (4 x 6 index cards) for each student to "send" from each country
6 calculators
watercolor paints
markers
menus from different restaurants
plastic spoons and forks, cups, bowls
hot tea, ingredients and tools for making English Toffee Bars
rice, chopsticks, fortune cookies
peanuts, juice
Kleenex boxes (empty)
clay, sugar cubes, large pieces of brown and white butcher paper, rocks, glue, cardboard,
     tagboard, papier-mâché, cardboard tubes/boxes, yarn or string, and other materials for
     making models of monuments

New Words for *Let's Go Traveling*

France
Paleolithic—the earliest part of the Stone Age; 500,000 B.C.–10,000 B.C.
prehistoric—before recorded history
Rouffignac—one of many prehistoric caves in France
stalactite—limestone rock that hangs like an icicle from the ceiling
stalagmite—limestone rock that builds up from the floor of a cave like a cone

England
Great Britain—an island made up of England, Scotland, and Wales
megalith—a huge stone
Neolithic—the last part of the Stone Age; 3700 B.C.–2000 B.C.
Stonehenge—a famous circle of ancient, giant standing stones in England
trilithon—a prehistoric archway of two standing stones with another across the top

Egypt

hieroglyph—a picture or symbol used in ancient writing
pharaoh—an ancient Egyptian ruler
pyramid—a solid form with equal triangular sides
sphinx—an imaginary creature with the body of a lion and the head of a man, ram, or hawk
tomb—a place of burial usually above ground

China

archeologist—a scientist who studies the remains of ancient civilizations and cultures
bronze—a hard, strong mixture of copper, tin, and other metals
calligraphy—the art of elegant handwriting
dynasty—a line of rulers who are all part of the same family
excavate—to dig out carefully

Mexico

equinox—two times of the year when the hours of day equal the hours of night
Maya—ancient people of Central America and Mexico
mural—a wall painting or carving
tourist—a person who takes a journey for pleasure
Uxmal—an ancient Mayan Pyramid with a temple on top

Peru

Inca—ancient people of the Cuzco Valley in Peru
Machu Picchu—an ancient city of steps built by the Inca
Milky Way—faint band of light stretching across the night sky, composed of millions of distant stars
Nazca—ancient people of southwestern Peru
souvenirs—objects collected on a trip in memory of that journey

Investigations for Before Reading

(*Note:* Take passport photos now and ask students to obtain six addresses for people they will write to during the journey.)

Investigating Travel Journals

Purchase some examples of travel journals and examine them together and/or read *Stringbean's Trip to the Shining Sea* by Vera Williams. Talk about the reasons for keeping a journal and make a list of the things that one might write in a travel journal. Provide travel journals for each student to write in at each destination. These can be small spiral notebooks or ones that are handmade by stapling blank paper together.

Investigating the World Map and Globe

Using a large wall map and the cover of the book, ask students to locate each of the six countries to be visited. They could mark it with a miniature flag as shown in the book (premade, of course). This demonstrates the larger picture of where our travels will take us. Now is a good time to introduce the concept of the time zones that will be traveled through on this journey. To further use their map-reading skills, students should work in small groups and locate the same countries on globes, labeling them with removable stickers. Depending on their experience with globes and maps, you may want to leave the wall map visible to students or you may want to make their task more difficult by covering it. Finally, provide students with their own copies of world maps and, using an overhead map or large wall map, have them identify continents and oceans and draw a compass rose. This map will be referred to and used "on route" to mark each destination during reading.

Investigate Book's Beginning

In groups, have students examine the title page. Ask them to try to guess in which country each photograph was taken and the reasons for their guess. Have them look at the copyright pages and ask for their interpretations of the drawings and what they think they might see on their journey. Next, have students look at the world map pages. Discuss each country, where it is in the world, what they will see exactly, and its place in the timeline. This would be a good time to introduce or review the terms "B.C." and "A.D." and each country's flag.

Investigation and Production of Country Flags

Following the previous activity, students will need to form six groups to research and produce a flag for each country. Provide students with resource books and encyclopedias to get a better look at their country's flag and to gather information on its development. Students should cooperatively write a short description about the flag's development to share with the class when they present their country's flag. To make the actual flag, provide students with an old white pillowcase that has been donated, newspapers, paints, and brushes. Before handing out materials, talk about drawing in pencil first to avoid mistakes and firmly discuss proper painting procedures so as not to have a huge mess on your hands. Hang all six flags on the wall within reach in order to attach new words to the bottoms (see Investigating New Words).

Investigating New Words

Provide groups with five new words from one country and ask them to cooperatively hypothesize as to their definitions. Students should write their guesses on the New Words Investigation sheet (see unit appendix) in the appropriate spot. Then they should locate actual definitions of each word from a variety of sources, while comparing their guesses with the actual definitions. When all of the groups have finished this, give each group the word/definition strips for their country, which can be made by students or premade by writing one word and its definition on each strip. Individual students should safety pin the strips onto the bottom of their country's flag like streamers. As group members pin the fabric or paper streamers on, they should orally present each word and definition to the whole class. (See illustration below.)

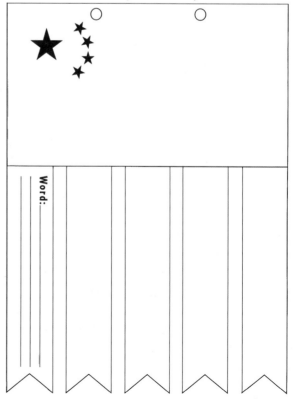

Example: China Flag

Word:

Investigating the Art of Packing

As a whole group, brainstorm the things that one would need to pack for a trip such as this (considering the variety of weather and activities) and make a list of everything. Bring in as many of the items that are on the list (or ask students to bring them) and a standard-sized suitcase. Put check marks next to each item that has been brought for packing. Ask students to predict if everything will fit. Ask individual students to help pack the suitcase. Students may decide to adjust their list for various reasons. As an exercise in decision making it is important that students state reasons for any adjustments. You could make baggage tickets for each destination to display on the suitcase once it is packed and ready to go. Another option for this activity is to have students bring in their own packed suitcases from home and compare what each person has packed and then create a list from there.

Investigating Travel Options and Costs

Provide groups of students with several travel brochures, books, newspaper advertisements for travel, magazine articles, and so on for them to investigate. Ask each group to write a list of six things that they would like to see or do in each of the six countries. Rotate brochures so that each group gets to investigate options for each country. After discussion, groups should try to estimate the cost of a visit to one of the countries using the Investigation Estimation sheet (see unit appendix). Add group estimations for a grand total.

As this may be overwhelming for young children, this activity could be done as a whole group activity, using a travel video such as the one on Mexico that is as referenced in the supporting library at the end of this chapter. The important thing is to get them thinking about money and what things cost.

To give older students a further sense of finances, provide each group with play money or make fake traveler's checks that correspond to the grand total and ask them to decide on a safe place to keep them. Refer to estimation sheets and take the money away as they "spend" it at each destination. It also may be interesting to discuss ways in which students might be able to save money to take a trip such as this.

Passport Investigation

Assemble passports (see unit appendix) ahead of time by stapling pages together and have students' photographs ready. Students should paste their photo on the appropriate page and fill in the information in the front. As they go from country to country students should fill in the information for each country and stamp the page. Upon arriving in each different country, students could create their own designs for six different passport stamps and carve them into potatoes with butter knives. For example, students could carve an ancient sign when visiting France or a trilithon when visiting England. Then they could use the potato stamps with an ink pad and stamp their own passports.

Investigations for During Reading

Suggestions for Reading Let's Go Traveling

Plan on spending one to two days in each country. After reading pages 6 and 7 together, begin each journey by looking back at pages 4 and 5. Students should locate each destination on their own world maps and mark it with words, pictures, flags, coloring—whatever seems age appropriate. They should also identify the capital. Practice the helpful phrases together and invite students to use these words during their visit. Students should read each section cooperatively in their groups, then participate in a short whole-group discussion, after which they should proceed with the activities for that country. Before departing from each country, students should write at least one entry in their travel diary, write one postcard to someone (addresses obtained earlier), and design a postage stamp as well as a picture of the country or the attraction on the blank side. It may be necessary to review placement of addresses, message, and stamps the first time around. Also, if using play money or traveler's checks, be sure to collect money for each expense.

France

- After reading, ask students to make a list of the things that were seen inside the cave. Provide each group with a large piece of brown bulletin board or butcher paper. Ask students to use their imagination and draw the things that they might have seen if they were really there. Drawings should include several items from their list, but encourage their own ideas as well. They could look for additional ideas in books like *Prehistoric Rock Art* by Marinella Terzi. Suggest sketching drawings on scrap paper first and deciding who will draw what. They could paint in minimal color (i.e., browns, grays, black, earth red).

- Share the book *Caves* by Jenny Wood, especially the story of the boys finding the famous Lascaux Cave and what has happened to it since then.

England

- After reading, ask students to design their own model of Stonehenge in groups. Encourage them to look at additional resources for photographs and diagrams to guide their design. Provide each group with a sturdy base, cardboard boxes or tubes, newspaper, and papier-mâché. (See recipe in Main Appendix.) If papier-mâché is too messy for you, students could use clay instead. Review cooperative decision making and problem solving and let them create their own design. Encourage students to

talk about who they think could have built Stonehenge and why.

- Invite students to English tea. Serve hot tea and English Toffee Bars (see unit appendix for recipe). Invite students to take part in making this treat to eat. Ask each group to present their finished model and their theories on who built the real Stonehenge and why. The remainder of the class should be free to ask questions of the presenting group in regard to their design and/or theories.

Egypt

- After reading, invite students in small groups to examine books on pyramids, tombs, pharaohs, and ancient Egypt. Ask them to think of questions that they would like to ask an archeologist who uncovers ancient things. Send these letters to the natural history museum in your area.

- Show the video *Pyramid* to give students a better view of some of the ancient artifacts and of one possible story of the building of a pyramid. Invite questions, comments, reactions, and/or ask students to write personal responses. Also read Macauley's book *Pyramid* and compare/contrast the story in the video with the story in the book.

- Challenge groups to make their own model of a pyramid using tagboard or sugar cubes. Together they should decide on the type of pyramid, the year it was built, and who it was built for. They should provide that information on a small card made to stand in front of the model for display. Specific instructions for making Khufu's Great Pyramid can be found in *Ancient Egypt: A Civilization Project Book* by Susan Gold Purdy.

- Provide groups with copies of different books of hieroglyphics. Students should practice spelling their name in hieroglyphic pictures. Then give them oval cards (precut from tagboard) on which to make their own cartouche (official name seal) like Tutankhamen's. They could be made by drawing directly on the card or by covering the card with heavy crayon and scraping the designs into the crayon. They could also be made from plaster of paris as instructed in Susan Purdy's book. Students can wear their cartouches by punching a hole in one end and tying a string to fit around their neck.

China

- After reading, provide each student with clay so that each person can make their own soldier. Put all of the soldiers together to form the army that guards Qin's tomb. Students could use their imaginations to attach speech bubbles to each soldier saying what they think that soldier would say if he could talk. Speech bubbles could be made out of blank index cards with toothpicks glued onto the back, then attached by poking the toothpick into the clay.

- Read aloud *Talking Walls* by Margy Burns Knight for information about other famous walls. Also, share *The Great Wall of China* by Leonard Everett Fisher for more information on the building of the Great Wall and an introduction to a few Chinese characters.

- Using *Long Is a Dragon* by Peggy Goldstein as a resource, give a lesson in writing Chinese characters. Provide students with black markers or black watercolor paint and brushes and paper. Allow students to experiment with Chinese number formation. When they feel comfortable invite them to make a book of numbers for a young child. Each page should have a Chinese number drawn with the corresponding number represented with colorful pictures of familiar objects. Books can be stapled or bound, then shared with classmates or a class of kindergarten students. A further challenge for students could be to have them learn how to pronounce each number so that their books could be read aloud in Chinese.

- Serve rice with chopsticks. If possible, have a guest show children exactly how to use the chopsticks and let them experiment. Follow with fortune cookies. Compare fortunes in groups. Why aren't there any bad fortunes? Do people believe in fortunes? Can they still make someone smile even if they don't believe? Can the fortunes be put into categories like money fortunes, love fortunes, travel fortunes, and so on? Ask students to pick someone in their family or a neighbor to write a good fortune for. They should write it on a small piece of white paper, roll it, tie it into a scroll, and secretly slip it someplace where they will find it.

Mexico

- After reading, show the video *Sentinels of Silence* to give students a better picture of the ancient ruins of Mexico. While viewing, students should try listing the seven ruins mentioned in the film, including the two mentioned in the book. During and/or afterward, they should write down any questions and reactions they had while watching the video.

- Share *The Maya* by Robert Nicholson to find out more about the ancient ball court game mentioned in the book. Ask students in small groups to write rules or instructions for the ball game as they think it might have been played in its time.

- Prepare and share a traditional Mayan lunch. There is a simple recipe for bean stew to follow in *The Maya*. Invite the office staff to share your meal.

- In groups, ask students to examine several sources showing ancient ruins of civilizations of Mexico, such as *The Mayas* and *City of the Gods* and the encyclopedia. Ask students to design any artifact or structure of their choosing that could tell us more about the ancient civilization, using clay, fabric, or other materials. They should write down all important information, including when and who the artifact comes from, on a small card to be placed next to their projects upon completion.

- Ask students to try using the Maya number system using the Investigation into Maya Math sheet (see unit appendix). For more information see *The Maya* by Robert Nicholson.

Peru

- Before the students begin reading this section, draw or trace Nazca shapes from the book and provide copies for each student. Ask them to write down their best guesses (invite more than one guess) as to what each drawing is. Then have them compare their own guesses to the guesses of experts in the book.

- After reading, invite students to make their own Nazca line drawings in small groups. Suggest brainstorming and sketching first. Then, using a poster board, students can design their picture with a light-colored crayon. When the drawing is complete, they can use a thin, water-based, brown- or gray-colored paint to cover the entire poster board. The paint signifies the darker-colored desert ground, while the crayon, which will resist the paint, will be the lighter-colored ground underneath.

- Share *The Grandchildren of the Incas* by Matti Pitkanen to illustrate the remains of an ancient civilization. Make a large Venn diagram showing similarities and differences between the Quechua Indians of today and ourselves. Older students could do their own diagrams in pairs.

- Provide groups with clay and butter knives for carving. Ask each student to cut "stones" in rectangular/cubed shapes of different sizes. When each student has made about ten stones, ask the group to work together to build a wall or a street made up of their stones. Groups should try to make stones fit together as puzzle pieces for a wall or street that will last as long as the fine Inca designs. Students may want to consult resources if they wish to construct a model of a specific Inca wall or structure.

Conclusion

After reading the last several pages and during discussion, have students identify the pictures and souvenirs and from which country they were taken during the journey. Identify the countries that Rachel would like to go to next and locate them on the large world wall map. Talk about places that they would like to visit some day. Older children could select one destination to research.

Investigations for After Reading

A Postcard Book

Using the postcards from the trip, invite students to put together their own book using *Stringbean's Trip to the Shining Sea* as a model. Or they could design their own book about their favorite place or places, including informative text and illustrations. This could be a place we visited together during *Let's Go Traveling* or a place they have actually visited or a place that they have researched and would like to visit.

Around the World Mural

Create a class mural from pieces of large butcher paper depicting all of the sights visited during the journey, including sidebars that provide information about what it is and where it was seen. It could also include foreign language phrases or writing. Students could choose which portion of the mural they would like to work on. In order to give groups of students space to work, pieces could be connected later to form one long hallway mural. Once the pieces are put together, the bottom of the mural could be left open to add a timeline, such as the one in the beginning of the book.

Take Off!

A.) Take students to your local airport for a tour to investigate what it might be like to really go on a trip in an airplane. They could bring bags to be "checked," which could mean attaching name and address tags to their bag. They could experience going through security and finding a specific gate. If the tour allows, they may be able to board a real plane and meet a flight attendant. They could also go to baggage claim to see bags being returned to passengers. Call your local airport to see what other wonderful things they may have in store for children in terms of learning about an airport.

B.) Take students to a local museum that offers exhibits and tours of ancient artifacts relating to the ancient ruins discussed in *Let's Go Traveling*.

Presenting … A Trip Around the World!

Invite parents for a trip around the world. Use the form in the unit appendix or have students create their own. Students will need to form six groups and choose jobs, prepare, and practice before parents arrive. Set up chairs in the classroom similar to airplane seats. Before the plane takes off, provide each parent with passports such as the ones the students used. Flight attendants will serve juice and peanuts during the trip. The pilots will announce the departure and arrival from and to in each country. Passports will be stamped upon arrival to each country by passport agents. Tour guides will draw a running line from the point of takeoff and identify locations on an overhead map

throughout the trip. Upon arrival at each destination, they will point out the country's flag, provide a few facts about the country, and give a brief foreign language lesson. Experts will present pictures, posters, projects, and models to demonstrate their knowledge of a particular attraction (ancient ruin) within the country. Flight crew could also be responsible for presenting "Bon Voyage" and "Welcome Home" banners to signify the beginning and ending of the trip around the world. If possible, play a recording of a plane in takeoff and flight while students rotate jobs and prepare for their presentations. An additional challenge for older students may be to design travel brochures to photocopy and distribute to parents upon their arrival to each country.

Pen Pals

Invite students to begin correspondence with a pen pal from a different country. For information and addresses, write to one of the following:

International Pen Friends
P.O. Box 290065
Brooklyn, NY 11229

Worldwide Pen Friends
P.O. Box 39097
Downey, CA 90241

When writing, students should include their full name, address, and age, and what country they would like a pen pal from.

Extensions

As one possible extension of this travel unit, students may be interested in exploring the art of photography and photojournaling. I recommend investigating the book *My Camera* by George Ancona.

PARENT LETTER

Dear Parents,

We will soon be embarking on a most amazing journey to six different countries around the world. Our journey is based upon the book *Let's Go Traveling* by Robin Rector Krupp. We will visit many mysterious and wondrous places along the way, while investigating several ancient civilizations and what they have left behind.

We will visit France, England, China, Egypt, Mexico, and Peru during the next several weeks. If you have any artifacts, souvenirs, currency, postage stamps, post-cards, pictures, information, language background, travel stories, or something else from any of these countries that you would be willing to share with our class, please let me know as soon as possible.

We will be working on many projects during our travels. Please see the attached "Wanted" sheet for any items that you might be able to help out with. Thanks a million!

At the end of our journey we will be taking a field trip to the airport to investigate what it might be like to embark on such a journey. We would love to have you join us. Be looking for the permission slip sometime next week. Please sign and return it as soon as you can.

Lastly, you are cordially invited to take a shortened version of our trip around the world, once we have returned. Your trip is scheduled for_____ at _____. We hope that you will be able to join us in this adventurous travel presentation. Mark your calendar now! You will be receiving an invitation from your child in approximately two weeks. Please R.S.V.P. as soon as possible.

Bon voyage!

Investigation Estimation

How much will it cost?

Names: _____

Country: _____

Attraction #1 _____   Attraction #4 _____

Cost _____   Cost _____

Attraction #2 _____   Attraction #5 _____

Cost _____   Cost _____

Attraction #3 _____   Attraction #6 _____

Cost _____   Cost _____

Transportation to countries and attractions

Airfare _____   Train fare _____   Bus fare _____

Lodging

First night _____   Second night _____   Third night _____

Meals

3 breakfasts _____   3 lunches _____   3 dinners _____

One souvenir _____   One gift _____

One postcard and postage stamp _____

One long-distance phone call _____

Emergency cash _____   Other _____

Total trip cost for a three-day visit _____

Student Name: _____'s

PASSPORT

United States
of America

PASSPORT
PHOTO

PHOTO

NAME:_____

ADDRESS:_____

_____

CITIZEN OF:_____

TRAVEL DATES:_____

FROM:_____UNTIL:_____

COUNTRY YOU
ARE VISITING:_____

REASON FOR
YOUR VISIT:_____

DATES OF YOUR VISIT:_____

OFFICIAL STAMP:

COUNTRY YOU
ARE VISITING:_____

REASON FOR
YOUR VISIT:_____

DATES OF YOUR VISIT:_____

OFFICIAL STAMP:

Investigation into Maya Math

Name: _____

Key

👁	●	▬	👁̇
0	**1**	**5**	**20**

Using the ancient Maya number system (above) try to figure out these numbers:

●●●● _____   ●●●
                              ▬▬▬ _____

●●   ▬
▬▬ _____   ▬
                              ▬
                              ▬ _____

▬   ●●●●
▬ _____   👁 _____

How would you write the following using the Maya number system?

Your age: _____   Your grade: _____

The number of books in your desk:

The number of pencils in your desk:

How many brothers do you have?

How many sisters do you have?

The number of stripes on the American flag:

New Words Investigation

From (name of country) _____

Names _____

Definition Guess (Word)	**Actual Definition**
1.) _____	_____
_____	_____
2.) _____	_____
_____	_____
3.) _____	_____
_____	_____
4.) _____	_____
_____	_____
5.) _____	_____
_____	_____

Using these words as a hint, what do you predict we will be seeing in this country? _____

_____

English Toffee Bars

Ingredients

1 cup butter or margarine
1 cup packed brown sugar
1 egg yolk
1 teas. vanilla
2 cups flour
1 6-oz. pkg. (1 cup) semisweet chocolate chips
1 cup finely chopped walnuts or pecans

Directions

Beat butter for 30 seconds. Add brown sugar and beat until fluffy. Add egg yolk and vanilla. Gradually add flour to mixture, beating constantly. Press evenly into an ungreased 9 x 13-inch baking pan. Bake at 350°F. 15 to 18 minutes. After removing from the oven immediately sprinkle chocolate pieces over the top and let stand until softened. Spread out chocolate evenly and sprinkle nuts on top. Cut into bars while still warm. Makes 48 bars.

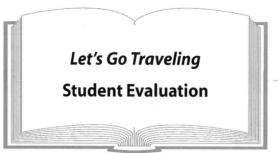

Let's Go Traveling
Student Evaluation

Name:_____

1.) During the unit, I worked cooperatively in my groups

      not at all   sometimes   most of the time

2.) During the unit, I tried my best

      not at all   sometimes   most of the time

3.) During the unit, I completed

____ a letter   ____ an invitation   ____ a cost estimation
____ several postcards   ____ a recipe   ____ a flag
____ a world map   ____ models of monuments   ____ a passport
____ a travel journal   ____ a mural   ____ a group presentation
____ a list   ____ a postcard book
____ writing in a different language
____ speaking in a different language

4.) Something new that I learned about ancient civilizations is:_____

_____

5.) Something new that I learned about traveling is:_____

_____

6.) Something new that I learned about another country is: _____

_____

7.) One thing that I worked on that I am especially proud of is: _____

_____

8.) My favorite things about this unit were: _____

_____

9.) A place that I would like to travel to next is:_____

Supporting Library

France

Bendick, Jeanne. *Caves!* (Underground Worlds). New York: Henry Holt, 1995.
Describes many aspects of caves, including the ancient Lascaux Cave.

Gans, Roma. *Caves* (Let's-Read-and-Find-Out Science Book). New York: Thomas Y. Crowell, 1976.
Provides an introduction to caves, their features, how they were formed, and their uses.

Gibbons, Gail. *Caves and Caverns.* New York: Harcourt Brace, 1993.
Describes physical features of caves, types of caves, and spelunking.

Kramer, Stephen. *Caves.* Minneapolis, Minn.: Carolrhoda Books, 1995.
Describes spelunking, how caves were formed, types of caves, and life within.

Ruspoli, Mario. *The Cave of LASCAUX: The Final Photographs.* New York: Harry N. Abrams, 1987.
Includes numerous large-sized photographs of prehistoric cave art. Adult text.

Sturges, Jo. *Discovering France.* New York: Crestwood House, 1993.
Describes modern-day France and all it has to offer.

Terzi, Marinella. *Prehistoric Rock Art* (The World Heritage Series). Chicago: Childrens Press, 1992.
Descriptions and photographs of prehistoric rock art in seven different sites including France.

Wood, Jenny. *Caves: Facts, Stories, Projects.* New York: Puffin Books, 1990.
Describes caves, their formation, cave paintings and dwellers, and exploring caves.

England

Abels, Harriette. *The Mystery of Stonehenge.* Mankato, Minn.: Crestwood House, 1987.
Provides descriptions and photographs of Stonehenge and the theories behind its construction and
    purposes.

Lyon, Nancy. *The Mystery of Stonehenge.* New York: Contemporary Perspectives, 1977.
Provides a description of Stonehenge, its mystery, and its meaning. Includes photographs and drawings.

Martin, Ana. *Prehistoric Stone Monuments* (The World Heritage Series). Chicago: Childrens Press, 1993.
Describes several ancient stone monuments, including Stonehenge and Avebury. Many photographs.

China

Fisher, Leonard Everett. *The Great Wall of China.* New York: Macmillan Publishing, 1986.
Tells the story of the building of the original wall. Accompanied by Chinese characters throughout.

Goldstein, Peggy. *Long Is a Dragon.* San Francisco: China Books and Periodicals, 1991.
Shows how to write numerous Chinese characters representing numbers and words.

Haskins, Jim. *Count Your Way Through China.* Minneapolis, Minn.: Carolrhoda Books, 1990.
Illustrates the numbers one through ten in Chinese along with facts about China and its people.

Knight, Margy Burns. *Talking Walls.* Gardiner, Maine: Tilbury House Publishers, 1992.
Describes and illustrates fourteen well-known walls, including the Great Wall of China, the Wailing Wall, the Berlin Wall, and others.

Nicholson, Robert, and Claire Watts. *Ancient China.* New York: Chelsea House Publishers, 1994.
Examines ancient Chinese civilization, including the Great Wall and the Forbidden City.

Egypt

Bendick, Jeanne. *Egyptian Tombs.* New York: Franklin Watts, 1989.
An in-depth look at ancient Egyptians, tombs, pyramids, and customs. Includes a section on how to build a pyramid, photos, and drawings.

Crosher, Judith. *Ancient Egypt* (See Through History Series). New York: Viking/Penguin Books, 1992.
Complete look at ancient Egyptian civilization.

DerManuelian, Peter. *Hieroglyphs from A to Z.* Boston: Museum of Fine Arts, 1991.
An ABC book of facts, with symbols to copy. Includes a chart and stencils.

Haskins, Jim. *Count Your Way Through the Arab World.* Minneapolis, Minn.: Carolrhoda Books, 1991.
A counting book from one to ten in Arabic with informative text about the Arab people.

Katan, Norma Jean. *Hieroglyphs: The Writing of Ancient Egypt.* New York: Atheneum, 1984.
Includes description, photographs, and examples of the hieroglyph alphabet.

Macaulay, David. *Pyramid.* Boston: Houghton Mifflin, 1975.
Tells one possible story of how a pyramid was built.

Macaulay, David (host). *Pyramid* (Video). Washington, D.C.: Unicorn Projects, 1988.
Animated version of Macaulay's book of the same name. Includes documentary and footage of real pyramids and ancient artifacts. 60 minutes.

Morley, Jacqueline. *An Egyptian Pyramid.* New York: Peter Bedrick Books, 1991.
Provides a look at how pyramids were built and their purposes in ancient Egyptian life.

Pitkanen, Matti A. *The Children of Egypt.* Minneapolis, Minn.: Carolrhoda Books, 1991.
Realistic introduction to modern Egyptian life with a focus on children. Includes map and many photographs.

Purdy, Susan Gold. *Ancient Egypt: A Civilization Project Book.* New York: Franklin Watts, 1982.
Readers learn how to make an ancient board game, a plaster name cartouche, frieze paintings, and a model of the Great Pyramid.

Reeves, Nicholas. *Into the Mummy's Tomb.* New York: Scholastic, 1992.
An in-depth look at Howard Carter's discovery of Tutankhamen's tomb. Includes many large color photographs.

Sabuda, Robert. *Tutankhamen's Gift.* New York: Atheneum, 1994.
Tells the story of Tutankhamen as a boy and his becoming pharaoh.

Terzi, Marinella. *The Land of the Pharaohs* (The World Heritage Series). Chicago: Childrens Press, 1988.
Examines pyramids, temples, and other ancient Egyptian monuments.

Mexico

Amram, Robert (director and writer). *Sentinels of Silence* (Video). La Jolla, Calif.: ALTI Publishing, 1990.
Presents views of seven ancient civilizations of Mexico and their ruins, including Chichen Itza, Uxmal, and Teotihuacan. Narrated by Orson Wells. 18 minutes.

Arnold, Caroline. *City of the Gods.* New York: Clarion Books, 1994.
Provides a look at the ancient city and civilization of Teotihuacan in Mexico. Large color photographs and map.

Haskins, Jim. *Count Your Way Through Mexico.* Minneapolis, Minn.: Carolrhoda Books, 1989.
Teaches the numbers one through ten in Spanish while providing facts about the land and people of Mexico.

Nicholson, Robert. *The Maya* (Journey into Civilizations Series). New York: Chelsea House Publishers, 1994.
Full easy-to-read description of the Mayan civilization.

Odijk, Pamela. *The Mayas* (The Ancient World Series). Englewood Cliffs, N.J.: Silver Burdett Press, 1990.
Complete look at the Mayan civilization, their legends, laws, customs, palaces, and other ruins.

Rand McNally. *Mexico* (Video Traveler Collection). San Ramon, Calif.: International Video Network, 1992.
Briefly looks at ancient and modern-day Mexico and its tourist attractions. 35 minutes.

Peru

Baquedano, Elizabeth. *Aztec, Inca and Maya* (Eyewitness Books). New York: Dorling Kindersley, 1993.
Examines the civilizations and history of the ancient Aztec, Maya, and Inca people.

Clark, Ann Nolan. *Secret of the Andes.* New York: Penguin Group, 1952.
Classic children's fiction about a modern Inca boy living in the Andes.

Ford, Dr. Robert E. *Andes Mountains* (Wonders of the World). Austin, Tex.: Raintree/Steck-Vaughn, 1995.
Describes the Andes Mountain regions of South America.

Gonzales, Christina. *Inca Civilization* (The World Heritage Series). Chicago: Childrens Press, 1990.
An in-depth description of the Inca civilization including ancient Machu Picchu.

Lepthien, Emilie. *Enchantment of the World: Peru.* Chicago: Childrens Press, 1992.
An in-depth look at Peru's history, geography, people, and government. Includes chapter on Inca civilization.

Pitkanen, Matti A. *The Grandchildren of the Incas.* Minneapolis, Minn.: Carolrhoda Books, 1991.
Describes the ancient Incas and their modern-day descendants, the Quechua Indians.

Steele, Philip. *The Incas: Machu Picchu* (Hidden World Series). New York: Macmillan Publishing, 1993.
Examines the city of Machu Picchu, its building, its fall to European power, and its discovery in 1911.

Other

Ancona, George. *My Camera.* New York: Crown Publishers, 1992.
Provides child-friendly information on cameras and the art of photography.

Avi-Yonah, Michael. *Dig This! How Archeologists Uncover Our Past.* Minneapolis, Minn.: Runestone Press, 1993.
Discusses methods of excavation, ancient civilizations around the world, and preserving the treasures of the past.

Caselli, Giovanni. *Wonders of the World.* New York: Dorling Kindersley, 1992.
A look at many wonders of the world, including Stonehenge, the Great Wall of China and the terra-cotta army, the pyramids of Egypt, the Statue of Liberty, and the Eiffel Tower.

Jaspersohn, William. *A Week in the Life of an Airline Pilot.* Boston: Little, Brown, 1991.
Reader flies to India with a 747 pilot and learns about the duties of the job.

King, Celia. *Seven Mysterious Wonders of the World.* San Francisco: Chronicle Books, 1993.
A pop-up book of seven wonders, including the Nasca Lines and Stonehenge.

Lobel, Anita. *Away from Home.* New York: Greenwillow Books, 1994.
An ABC book of children doing things in places around the world.

Priceman, Marjorie. *How to Make an Apple Pie and See the World.* New York: Alfred A. Knopf, 1994.
An ambitious little baker travels around the world to gather ingredients to bake her pie when she finds the market closed.

Putnam, James. *Pyramid* (Eyewitness Books). New York: Dorling Kindersley, 1994.
Contains abundant pyramid facts. Includes discussion of Egyptian, Mayan, and Aztec pyramids.

Waterlow, Julia. *Journeys* (Young Geography Series). New York: Thomson Learning, 1993.
Looks at different modes of transportation and the reasons why people travel.

Wilkinson, Philip, and Michael Pollard. *Mysterious Places—Master Builders.* New York: Chelsea House Publishers, 1994.
Discusses ten ancient places, including Stonehenge, Machu Piccu, and Chichen Itza. Great resource for examining places less commonly mentioned.

Williams, Vera B. *Stringbean's Trip to the Shining Sea.* New York: Greenwillow Books, 1988.
A young boy's travel journal of postcards written along the way.

Ziegler, Sandra. *A Visit to the Airport.* Chicago: Childrens Press, 1988.
Reader accompanies children on a tour of an airport.

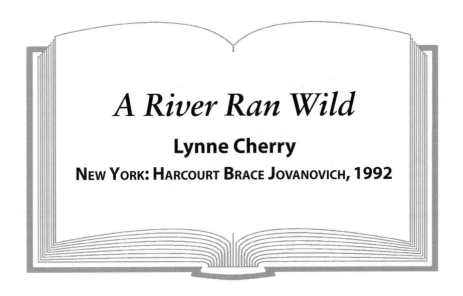

A River Ran Wild

Lynne Cherry

New York: Harcourt Brace Jovanovich, 1992

About the Book

A River Ran Wild is the true story of the evolution of the Nashua River in Massachusetts. Its story begins with the natural environment of the river and is part of a Native American settlement. The story moves through the Industrial Revolution and the river's almost complete death due to pollution. The Nashua is finally brought back to life through the passing of new laws and the unrelenting efforts of people who cared.

Investigations

Investigative Themes

Industrial Revolution and Inventions
Immigration and Colonization
River Ecology
Environment
Pollution and Environmental Policy
Native Americans
Massachusetts

Investigative Skills

using numbers
working cooperatively
defining words
using maps
predicting
making models
problem solving
writing letters
observing
writing creatively

reading for information
listening/speaking
comparing/contrasting
planning
researching
sequencing
experimenting
thinking critically
recording

Investigative Materials

1 copy of *A River Ran Wild* for every three or four students
supporting library books

large U.S. wall map
student copies of Massachusetts map
large, clear, shallow plastic container with pebbles to simulate a river
clay for making model animals, trees, and a dam
Popsicle sticks, Styrofoam pieces, a large rock, yarn, food coloring, vinegar, and tissues for
    introducing changes to the river
small glass jars with lids
strainer, gravel, sand, coffee filters, and bleach for water filtration and purification
pieces of window screens and frames, food coloring, paper scraps, a blender, old bath
    towels, rags, a rolling pin, and possible parent volunteers for making homemade paper
brown paper grocery bags
markers, crayons, colored pencils, and paints
green and blue bulletin board paper
large construction paper for posters
small scales for weighing
trash bags, cleaning supplies, and refreshments

New Words for *A River Ran Wild*

dam—a structure in a river meant to hold back or redirect water

immigrant—a person who comes from another country to live in a new one

decomposition—the chemical breakdown of a substance

industry—the business of manufacturing products

dumping—putting waste into an inappropriate or illegal place

pelt—the skin and fur of an animal

environment—everything that surrounds us

pollution—anything that has a negative effect on our land, air, or water

epidemic—a sickness or disease that spreads rapidly and kills many people

settlement—a new place where no one has lived before, where many people choose to make their homes together

generations—groups of people born at about the same time

textiles—products made with fibers; fabrics

Investigations for Before Reading

Investigating New Words

Prepare a green bulletin board with a large blue river flowing through it. Have groups of students make "skins" (twelve altogether) by tearing large pieces from a brown paper grocery bag in skin shapes. They can make it look more skinlike by taking turns wrinkling and flattening over and over again until the paper is soft like fabric. Assign one word for each group to write across the top of the skin and then tack it on, above, or below the river. (See illustration below.) Then give each group a set of definition cards on which to write their names, initials, or some other identifying symbol. Groups cooperatively decide which definition goes with which word by using all available resources and discussion. When they have reached a consensus they should tack the definition card underneath the word (facedown) on the skin. When all groups have their cards up, go over each word with the whole group. Whenever a group is correct with their card placement, they get to keep the card. The group with the most cards wins. After all words have been discussed, each group should write the correct definition directly onto their skins for display along the river.

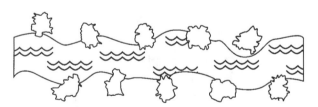

Map Investigation

A.) Look at a wall map of the United States. Ask students to locate the state of Massachusetts, the Nashua River, and the cities in the Nashua River valley. Provide each student with a copy of a blank map of Massachusetts to label. In addition, they should include the Atlantic Ocean, the state capital, bordering states, a compass rose, and whatever else they think might provide important information. More information can be added throughout the unit.

B.) Look at the two map drawings on the inside cover of *A River Ran Wild*. Compare the drawings with real maps. Compare the map from the 1500s with the map from the 1900s. Together, discuss and list the similarities and differences and speculate reasons for the changes.

Investigate Title Page

Look at the many small pictures on the title page. Ask students to think about and discuss with their groups what each picture could mean, and why the author/illustrator included them on the title page. What predictions can be made from the title page and the cover? Other questions to ponder ... How many years does this story cover? What is an environmental history? How does the author know all of these facts? (*Note:* Set time and date for neighborhood cleanup [see Investigations for After Reading].)

Investigations for During Reading

Suggestions for Reading A River Ran Wild

A whole group reading may be in order to start off with so that children can become familiar with the words and concepts and be given ample time to closely examine the many bordering illustrations that tell their own story. The whole group reading should be broken up into several days to utilize the "during reading activities." Afterward, groups of two to three children could read aloud to one another in a manner agreed upon by all group members.

River Simulation Investigation

Have students as a whole group construct a pebble-bottomed river by using a large, long, shallow, clear plastic container, pebbles (maybe from a pet supply store), and clean water. Students can add and subtract things to the river and its surroundings as the story moves along. They could begin with adding wildlife and trees (made of clay or other materials).

Ideas for additions that lead to pollution of the Nashua River:

- floating logs (Popsicle sticks or twigs)
- a dam (a big rock or made from other materials)
- pulp (shredded facial tissues)
- fibers (yarn pieces)
- dye (food coloring—change colors a few times)
- stinky chemical (vinegar)
- Styrofoam pieces
- signs
- houses and mills

Toward the end of the book, these things can all be removed one by one to illustrate the beginnings of cleaning up the Nashua (see Purification Investigation).

The River Changes

Ask students to compare the illustrations on the first pages, pages 15 and 16, and the last pages. Discuss how they are similar and how they are different. In groups of three, ask students to design their own illustration layout (three illustrations that will sit side by side) depicting the changes that the Nashua River valley went through and have them write a sentence or two about each illustration. Invite students to hypothesize reasons for the changes in the pictures.

Wildlife Investigation

In pairs or individually, ask students to examine the wildlife represented in the story, espe-cially on page 3. They should choose one animal (including birds or fish) to investigate further using the questions on the Wildlife in a River Wild sheet (see unit appendix) and all available resources. They should also design a poster depicting the animal in its habitat. A 3-D clay design may also be desired to add to the river (see above). Students could share their findings with a class of younger students on a designated day toward the end of the unit.

Purification Investigation

Once the students can no longer see the pebbles in their simulated river, and they can agree that it is gross and smelly, it is time to talk about how to clean up the mess. Discuss what it will take to continue the cleanup process. The discussion should lead them to think about the need for money and governmental support. As an exercise in activism, have each student or pair of students put a sample of the polluted water into a small clear jar with a secure lid. Then give them the Pretend Petition (see p. 32) for our river cleanup (or design one as a whole group) to get signatures of people who agree that the water is polluted and should be cleaned up. Their job is to get as many signatures on their petition as they can in twenty-four hours. It will be important to discuss what kinds of problems the children had in getting people to sign the petition and how they solved those problems. After the petitions are all filled out and returned, this is a neat opportunity to work out some logical mathematical problems together.

Here are some suggestions to get the ball rolling:

A.) Ask how many signatures each child gathered; estimate, then add to find total (maybe using a calculator if you add by groups)
B.) Figure out how many names the boys obtained versus the girls
C.) Estimate the number of females/males who signed; count to find out and determine whether more males or females signed
D.) Do the same for adults and children
E.) Figure out percentages from the information gathered above

F.) Pose problems such as "If each person who signed contributed $5.00 to a cleanup fund, how much money would that be?" or "If each person who signed also volunteered two hours of their time to helping with the cleanup, how many hours of help would that be?"

Using the book *The Magic Schoolbus at the Waterworks* by Joanna Cole, lead children to discover what they might be able to do to clear up the water. They can experiment by pouring water through a strainer, sand, gravel, and cof-fee filters to extract debris. They may try bleach to improve the smell and color. It may be a point of discussion that some chemicals used to purify are still harmful, especially to animals. Note that some new water may be added to show that a river flows and can help clean itself when the pollution stops. The goal, of course, is the return of the original, clean pebble-bottomed river with its wildlife and trees. Students may even want to add evidence of restored recreation and wildlife in the restored river (i.e., canoes, anglers, etc.).

Investigations for After Reading

In groups of two or three students, give them the following choices for an antipollution project:

A.) Think of a place in your neighborhood that needs cleaning up. Write and present a speech that you would give to the public to get them to join you in cleaning up this area.
B.) Write a letter to an environmental organization such as the one below asking for information on what the organization is doing for our planet and/or how you can help.

Kids for a Clean Environment
c/o Trish Poe
P.O. Box 158254
Nashville, TN 37215

C.) Imagine that you are a politician and write three laws that would protect our environment (one for air, one for water, one for land). Then present as a speech to the class.
D.) Write a letter to Marion Stoddard asking two questions about being an environmentalist, thanking her for her efforts in protecting the environment, and saying why you think she did such a great thing in helping to clean up the Nashua River.

Make a Human Timeline

Using the information on the inside cover of *A River Ran Wild* and/or the author's note, write significant pieces of historical information (the number and difficulty will depend upon the age level) on large individual papers, leaving space at the top of each to write the date later. The print should be large enough for the class to read at their seats. Ask students to line up facing the class and hold papers in front of them while individuals in the class try to direct them into order according to when they occurred in history. When the correct sequence is acquired have students write in the appropriate dates. This timeline can be displayed in the classroom, hanging clothesline style with illustrations on the flip side, or made into a class book with corresponding illustrations on opposite pages.

Guest Speaker

Read aloud *Letting Swift River Go* by Jane Yolen and invite students to respond with discussion or a Reading Response page (see Main Appendix) to the changes that took place, how the author felt about them, and how they would have felt. Invite an elderly community member (perhaps a grandparent) who would be willing to share stories and pictures of how their community has changed over the years. If possible, a walking tour to point out actual changes would probably be the most meaningful for the children. Students should prepare questions ahead of time and follow up immediately with a thank-you note.

River Field Trip

Visit a nearby accessible stream or river (with adequate supervision!) and do some firsthand investigating of wildlife and the influence of people and other changes. (See River Field Trip Observation Sheet in the unit appendix.) Upon return and after questions and discussion, have a long piece of bulletin board paper ready for children to turn into a mural by drawing the things that they observed.

Project Cleanup

Plan a neighborhood or schoolyard cleanup. Students should select a time and date (as well as a rain date) when parents and community members would be able to join in at the beginning of the unit. In groups, children could decide to make posters, write letters to community members or the superintendent, or write a newspaper article telling the community about the cleanup. Another group of students could write to a local store to ask for donations of trash bags and perhaps refreshments for participants. Arrange to have a scale to weigh the trash collected. Invite students to create sculptures out of usable trash. Write a follow-up news article reporting on the success of the cleanup day. Send copies of the reports along with the thank-you notes to places who donated supplies. Depending on the cleanup site, cleaners or paint may be required for getting rid of graffiti. Also, depending on funds, it may be an opportunity to beautify the site as well with newly planted trees, flowers, or a fresh coat of paint. Be sure to have all supplies ready for participants and a place to put collected trash.

Investigate Inventions

Provide groups of students with one or two of the suggested books on inventions and the In-vention! Invention! Read All About It! sheet (see unit appendix). Ask each group to choose one invention that they think is interesting and answer the questions cooperatively. Each group should share the information about their chosen invention along with a picture of it with the whole group.

The Breakdown

Invite students to observe decomposition in two ways:

A.) Place an orange, a tomato, and an apple on dishes in a sunny window. Students should predict what will happen, then observe and record their observations in an observation log (several pieces of blank paper stapled together or use the booklet pages from *Caves and Caverns*.)

B.) Fill three glass jars with water. In one add a piece of bread. In another add a tissue. In the third add a piece of plastic from a grocery bag. Students should predict what will happen and record their observations in their observation log.

After you deem the observations complete enough to draw some conclusions, ask students to share their thoughts in a class discussion.

Environmental ABC

Share several environmental books such as *Every Kid's Guide to Saving the Earth* by Joy Berry, *Recycle!* by Gail Gibbons, and *50 Simple Things Kids Can Do to Save the Earth* by John Javna. Challenge students to create an ABC book of things to help the Earth. This could be done as a whole group activity for younger students or several books can be created by different groups of students. Or allow students to design their own bulletin board depicting "what I can do for my environment."

Homemade Paper Project

This will probably be a whole class project unless additional supplies and adult volunteers can be obtained.

1.) Put torn paper scraps and water into a blender and blend until mushy. Then place mixture in a plastic container or tub—you will need to do this several times depending on the number of sheets you want to make—this is also the time to add bleach.

2.) Dip framed screen into mush and lift out—mush should cover screen and be about a $\frac{1}{2}$ inch thick—water should drip out slowly.

3.) Squish out more water by pressing the mush with a rag. Place newspaper underneath to catch the drips.

4.) Wrap an old towel around the screen and gently flip the screen so the wet paper is released; remove the screen.

5.) Use a rolling pin to squeeze out more water and flatten the paper while it is still inside the two layers of towel—here you may want to add a drop or two of food coloring to make fancier, more colorful paper.

6.) Peel off the top layer of towel and gently flip wet paper onto a hard, flat table or countertop, and let it dry for twenty-four hours.

Extensions

Try additional experiments with water using the book *Environmental Experiments About Water* by Thomas R. Rybolt and Robert C. Mebane.

PARENT LETTER

Dear Parents,

During the next couple of weeks we will become historians, ecologists, researchers, reporters, environmental activists, and maybe even inventors as we share the book *A River Ran Wild* by Lynne Cherry. This is a true story about the pollution and cleanup of the Nashua River in Massachusetts, which was at one time an Indian settlement.

We will be working on many exciting projects during this unit, including cleaning up our own classroom river and a neighborhood cleanup scheduled for_____. You will be hearing lots more about that soon.

We will be going on a field trip to _____ on _____. We hope that you will be able to join us as it is our goal to have one adult for every two children so that we will all be safe. Be looking for the permission slip in the next day or two. Please sign it and note if you will be able to attend and return it as soon as possible so that we can plan accordingly.

Also, our classroom will become a paper factory (nonpolluting, of course) on _____ at _____. If you would like to assist in the manufacturing and/or would be able to help out with a few supplies, please see the attached "Wanted" sheet for the items we need. We would love to have you! Let me know by _____ if you will be joining us for this project.

You are encouraged to discuss and plan things that you and your family can do to help our environment. And we would love to hear about them! Drop by or drop us a line to share what you are doing for our Earth.

Keep it green!

River Field Trip Observation Sheet

Name: _____

Write or draw your observations:

Animals I saw …

Bugs I saw …

Birds I saw …

Fish I saw …

Special plants or trees I saw …

Evidence of people near the river … _____

_____

Evidence of changes that have taken place over the last 100 years … _____

_____

Some things I wonder about this river … _____

_____

Pretend Petition

Name: _____

This is a pretend petition to save our classroom river that has become dirty, smelly, and polluted. (Look at the jar and see for yourself!) If you would be in favor of the cleanup of our classroom river, please print your full name below.

_____   _____

_____   _____

_____   _____

_____   _____

_____   _____

_____   _____

_____   _____

_____   _____

_____   _____

_____   _____

_____   _____

_____   _____

_____   _____

Wildlife in a River Wild

Name:_____

Name of animal:_____

Description:_____

_____

Where this animal is found in the United States:_____

_____

How does this animal use the river?_____

_____

What would happen to this animal if its river becomes polluted? What could you do to help?

_____

_____

_____

Besides water pollution, what other dangers are there for this animal?_____

_____

_____

_____

Why did you choose this animal to investigate?_____

_____

_____

Invention! Invention! Read All About It!

Names: _____

Answer all questions by consensus with your group.

1.) What is it? _____

2.) When was it invented? _____

3.) Who invented it? _____

4.) What prompted its invention? _____

_____

5.) How did it change our lives? _____

_____

6.) Where would we be without this invention? _____

_____

7.) Has anyone in your group ever thought that something needed inventing?
What was it? Why is there a need for it? _____

_____

_____

8.) What kind of personality characteristics might you need and what kinds of things would you
need to think about in order to become a successful inventor? _____

_____

_____

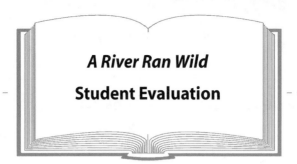

A River Ran Wild

Student Evaluation

Name:_____

1.) During the unit, I worked cooperatively with my groups

      not at all   sometimes   most of the time

2.) During the unit, I tried my best

      not at all   sometimes   most of the time

3.) During the unit, I completed

____ a letter/note   ____ a speech   ____ a wildlife sheet

____ a poem/story   ____ a poster   ____ an ABC book

____ a pollution petition   ____ a river observation   ____ a map of Massachusetts

____ a group presentation   ____ contributions to river simulation

4.) Something new that I learned about rivers is:_____

_____

5.) Something new that I learned about industry and invention is:_____

_____

6.) Something new that I learned about Native Americans is: _____

_____

7.) Something new that I learned about our environment is:_____

_____

8.) One thing that I completed during the unit that I am proud of is:_____

_____

9.) My favorite things about this unit were: _____

_____

10.) The things that helped me learn the most are:_____

_____

SUPPORTING LIBRARY

Books on Inventions and the Industrial Revolution

Bender, Lionel. *Invention* (Eyewitness Books). New York: Dorling Kindersley, 1991.
Covers inventions and inventors from simple tools to the silicon chip.

Clare, John D., ed. *Industrial Revolution* (Living History Series). New York: Gulliver Books, Harcourt Brace, 1994.
An in-depth look at the Industrial Revolution, the people it affected, and its major catalysts. Excellent reference for teachers.

Hockman, Hilary, ed. *Great Inventions* (What's Inside Series). New York: Dorling Kindersley, 1993.
A look at eight significant inventions and what makes them work inside.

Jeffries, Michael, and Gary A. Lewis. *Inventors and Inventions.* New York: Smithmark Publishers, 1992.
Organized by sections such as "communications" and "weapons and warfare." Mentions several important inventors and their inventions within each section.

Lafferty, Peter, and Julian Rowe. *The Inventor Through History.* New York: Thomson Learning, 1993.
Provides a focus on the major inventors organized by ages in invention (the steam age, the electronic age, etc.). Includes a timeline of major inventions.

Langley, Andrew. *The Industrial Revolution* (See Through History Series). New York: Penguin Books, 1994.
A colorful look at everything that made the Industrial Revolution come about and how it affected society. Includes a section on immigration.

Platt, Richard. *Smithsonian Visual Timeline of Inventions.* New York: Dorling Kindersley, 1994.
Organized in timeline fashion from 600,000 B.C. to the year A.D. 2000. Countless tidbits of information on inventors and inventions.

Wilkinson, Philip. *Incredible Inventions* (Snapshot Series). New York: Covent Garden Books, 1995.
Inventions are organized by categories (power, air travel, etc.). Questions and answers. Easy reading.

Wilkinson, Philip, and Michael Pollard. *Ideas That Changed the World: The Industrial Revolution.* New York: Chelsea House Publishers, 1995.
Discusses the major ideas that occurred during the Industrial Revolution.

Books on the Environment and Rivers

Amos, Janine. *Pollution* (First Starts Series). Austin, Tex.: Steck-Vaughn, 1993.
An easy reader on all types of pollution.

Baker, Jeannie. *Where the Forest Meets the Sea.* New York: Scholastic, 1987.
After a special day, a boy wonders whether the forest will be there the next time he and his dad want to visit. Easy reading. Unique pictures. Fiction.

Berry, Joy. *Every Kid's Guide to Saving the Earth.* Nashville, Tenn.: Ideals Children's Books, 1993.
Provides facts and ideas for conserving resources, stopping pollution, and preserving nature.

Cherry, Lynne. *The Great Kapok Tree.* Orlando, Fla.: Harcourt Brace Jovanovich, 1990.
Animals of the rain forest whisper into the ear of a sleeping tree cutter. Fiction.

Chinery, Michael. *Questions and Answers About Freshwater Animals.* New York: Kingfisher Books, 1994.
Includes interesting questions and answers about wildlife and a short section on rivers in danger.

Cole, Joanna. *The Magic Schoolbus at the Waterworks.* New York: Scholastic, 1986.
A class of children led by Ms. Frizzle takes a trip to a water purification plant and learns lots of wet facts firsthand.

Dorros, Arthur. *Follow the Water from Brook to Ocean* (Let's-Read-and-Find-Out Science Book). New York: HarperCollins, 1991.
Explains the different paths water takes on a long journey to reach the ocean.

Gibbons, Gail. *Recycle!* Boston: Little, Brown, 1992.
Talks about how glass bottles, paper, cans, plastics, and polystyrene are made and how they can be re-cycled.

Hester, Nigel. *The Living River* (Watching Nature Series). New York: Franklin Watts, 1991.
Examines all types of river life.

Hoff, Mary, and Mary M. Rodgers. *Our Endangered Planet: Rivers and Lakes.* Minneapolis, Minn.: Lerner Pub-lications, 1991.
An in-depth look at freshwater bodies, the life they support, how they are polluted, the effects, and how we can help.

Holmes, Anita. *I Can Save the Earth.* New York: Simon & Schuster, 1993.
A collection of simple experiments and things kids can do to help save our Earth.

Javna, John. *50 Simple Things Kids Can Do to Save the Earth.* Kansas City, Mo.: Andrews and McMeel, 1990.
Contains facts, experiments, and things that kids really can do for their environment.

May, Julian. *Blue River.* New York: Holiday House, 1971.
Tells the story of the Blue River based on the history of an actual stream from the time its banks were inhabited by Native Americans to the development of factories.

Rybolt, Thomas R., and Robert C. Mebane. *Environmental Experiments About Water.* Hillside, N.J.: Enslow Publishers, 1993.
Numerous experiments using water including several on water pollution, acid rain, and water purifica-tion.

Schwartz, Linda. *Earth Book for Kids.* Santa Barbara, Calif.: The Learning Works, 1990.
Includes facts, experiments, creative writing ideas, projects, and math activities in the areas of energy, natural resources, and plant/animal habitats.

Showers, Paul. *Where Does the Garbage Go?* New York: HarperCollins, 1994.
Addresses landfills, incinerators, recycling, and reducing waste.

Stains, Bill. *River.* New York: Viking-Penguin Books, 1994.
An illustrated song inspired by an ever-changing river.

Taylor, Barbara. *River Life* (Look Closer Series). New York: Dorling Kindersley, 1992.
Describes wildlife and plant life in and around a river.

VanAllsburg, Chris. *Just a Dream*. Boston: Houghton Mifflin, 1990.
A boy dreams of a very polluted world and decides to change some of his ways.

Yolen, Jane. *Letting Swift River Go*. Boston: Little, Brown, 1992.
A story of the town of Dillon being moved to purposefully flood the Swift River in order to create reservoirs to provide water for the city of Boston.

Books on Massachusetts

Fradin, Dennis Brindell. *Massachusetts* (From Sea to Shining Sea Series). Chicago: Childrens Press, 1991.
Provides specific information about the state then and now. Includes map.

Books on/by Native Americans

(focus on tribes of the northeastern United States)

Amon, Aline. *The Earth Is Sore*. New York: Atheneum, 1981.
A collection of Native American poetry in celebration of nature and the abuse of our Earth.

Bierhorst, John. *On the Road of Stars*. New York: Macmillan Publishing, 1994.
A collection of simple Native American night poems and sleep charms.

Caduto, Michael J., and Joseph Bruchac. *Keepers of the Earth*. Golden, Colo.: Fulcrum Publishing, 1989.
A collection of Native American stories and environmental activities for children. An excellent resource for teachers.

Cohlene, Terri. *Little Firefly: An Algonquian Legend*. Mahwah, N.J.: Watermill Press, 1990.
Cinderella-style Native American legend. Includes a section on the Algonquian Indian tribes.

Duvall, Jill. *The Penabscot* (A New True Book). Chicago: Childrens Press, 1993.
A story of one Indian nation and their life on the Penabscot River in Maine.

Hausman, Gerald. *Turtle Island ABC*. New York: HarperCollins, 1994.
A unique ABC book of symbols and objects and their meanings to the Native American people.

Hull, Robert. *Native North American Stories*. New York: Thomson Learning, 1993.
A collection of eight Native American legends.

Jeffers, Susan. *Brother Eagle, Sister Sky*. New York: Scholastic, 1992.
A message from Chief Seattle about the great importance of respecting our environment.

Krensky, Stephen. *Children of the Earth and Sky*. New York: Scholastic, 1991.
A collection of five stories about Native American children.

Peters, Russell M. *Clambake*. Minneapolis, Minn.: Lerner Publications, 1992.
Depicts modern Wampanoag Indians from Mashpee, Massachusetts, and their traditional ceremony called Appanaug or Clambake.

Sneve, Virginia Driving Hawk. *Dancing Teepees*. New York: Holiday House, 1989.
A collection of poems of American Indian youth.

Speare, Elizabeth George. *The Sign of the Beaver.* New York: Dell Publishing, 1983.
An Indian boy and a white boy become close friends and teach each other many things.

Steptoe, John. *The Story of Jumping Mouse.* New York: Scholastic, 1993.
A retelling of a Native American legend.

Wolfson, Evelyn. *The Iroquois.* Brookfield, Conn.: Millbrook Press, 1992.
An in-depth look at a large group of northeastern Indians then and now.

Caves and Caverns

Gail Gibbons

New York: Harcourt Brace, 1993

About the Book

Caves and Caverns provides the reader with interesting and easy-to-read scientific information about different types of caves, their magnificent features, and the creatures who dwell inside them. It may serve to pique interests in certain areas as it touches on hobbies and careers in speleology and geology. It also addresses the importance of appropriate equipment, guidance, and safety in the exploration of Earth's mysterious underground places.

Investigations

Investigative Themes

Speleology
Geology
Underground/Inside the Earth
Bats and Other Nocturnal Animals
Safety and Responsibility

Investigative Skills

listening/speaking
reasoning
comparing/contrasting
experimenting
working cooperatively
researching
observing
recording
sequencing
making decisions

writing letters
reading for information
writing creatively
following directions
estimating
predicting
using maps
using numbers
planning

Investigative Materials

1 copy of *Caves and Caverns* for every three or four students
5 to 6 copies of *Looking Inside Caves and Caverns* by Ron Schultz
supporting library books

large chart paper
white, black, brown construction paper
poster board/tagboard
3 x 5 index cards and brown bulletin board paper
flashlights (one for every two students)
spelunking equipment (see back page of book)
a variety of boxes and first-aid supplies
alum, thread, tablespoons, pencils, glass jars, pie tins, and boxes for display
rocks, eyedroppers, vinegar, bricks, coins, nails, and magnifying glasses
large U.S. wall map
U.S. atlas
tracing paper
guide to national parks
sugar cubes, glue, baking pan, small pitchers, food coloring, eye droppers, or spoons
pocket mirrors, blindfolds
poster paper, envelopes, and postage stamps
"nature paints" (dandelions, berries, mud, leaves, etc.)
markers, crayons, paints, etc.

New Words for *Caves and Caverns*

artifacts—things found from long ago that help us learn about ancient people
column—a stalactite and stalagmite connected together
constant temperature zone—an area in a cave that is pitch black and the temperature always remains the same
geologist—a scientist who studies rocks, minerals, and the Earth's features
glacier—a huge piece of snow and ice that travels slowly down a mountainside
karst—cave country
limestone—a type of rock formed long ago by layers of skeletons and shells of tiny ancient creatures
passage—a connection between two caves or two rooms in a cave
solution—a mixture of substances; water and carbon dioxide make a carbonic acid solution
speleothems—formations within a cave
spelunker—a cave explorer
stalactites—iciclelike cave formation built from the ceiling down
stalagmites—cone-shaped cave formation built from the ground up
troglobites—animals that live only in darkness
trogloxenes—animals that live above ground but use caves for sleeping, hibernating, or raising young
twilight zone—area from the mouth of the cave to as far as daylight can be seen

Investigations for Before Reading

Generate Questions to Investigate

In small groups, invite students to share questions that they might have about caves with each other. Ask for each group to share one of the questions they discussed and write them on chart paper to refer to throughout the unit and/or toward the end. You could invite "guesses" as to the answers to these questions as a way to encourage their motivation for listening for the right answers during reading.

Equipment Investigation

Before journeying into the depths of the Earth, one must have the proper equipment. Therefore, before investigating caves via *Caves and Caverns,* students should become familiar with caving equipment. First, ask students to make a list on their own of the things that a spelunker might need. Second, provide students with several different books on caves that also address spelunking equipment. For example: *Looking Inside Caves and Caverns* by Ron Schultz, *Caves* by Ronal C. Kerbo, and, of course, *Caves and Caverns* by Gail Gibbons. Students can then adjust their lists of equipment and discuss why each tool would be necessary. They may also discuss why some of the books mention slightly different tools. If possible, provide as many actual pieces of equipment as you can gather for students to pass around. Next, groups could design posters exhibiting tools for spelunking, including a sidebar or bottom section that tells why each piece is important for the health and safety of the spelunker. They can create a unique title for their poster and display it when complete.

As an additional activity to clarify what exactly is inside a first-aid kit (a required piece of spelunking equipment), you could display several boxes with a red cross on them. Some should be inappropriately large and some inappropriately small. Inside the boxes, place collections of things that one would actually find in a first-aid kit and some that one would

not. Through observation and discussion challenge students to pick out the most appropriate first-aid kit according to size and contents. You may also want to provide a good one that can be purchased at a store.

Rules and Responsibilities

Discuss the "Cave Rules" at the back of *Caves and Caverns* and why they are important rules to follow when spelunking. Students may want to compare this list of rules with rules stated in other sources.

Cave Simulation

To simulate a cave experience, find a small room without windows or emergency lights that will be completely dark when the lights are turned off. You can create damp and cooler air (somewhat) by leaving coolers of ice open around the room. Provide flashlights for each pair of students, but instruct them to keep them off until you give the word. Slowly guide students into the dark room and allow their eyes to adjust to the darkness. Ask them to comment on what they can see or not see. Note that in a real cave, without a light source, you cannot see anything, even your own hands in front of your face. Ask students to turn on flashlights one at a time to see how much light a spelunker might have compared to several spelunkers together.

New Words Investigation

On a large blank wall or bulletin board, design a cave entrance with paper. (See illustration on page 42.) Write new word definitions on small index cards and tack or tape them inside the cave. Write each of the sixteen words on black or brown bats (see pattern in unit appendix). Attach the bats to inconspicuous yet accessible places around the classroom. Make the room as dark as possible and provide pairs of students with flashlights. Invite them to search the classroom with their flashlights for bats. If you have a large class it may be necessary to have them take turns searching. When a pair has located a bat they should carefully remove the bat from the wall and take it with them as they return to their seats and turn their flashlight off. When all sixteen bats have been found turn on the lights and begin reading aloud *Caves and Caverns* to continue the New Words Investigation.

Investigations for During Reading

Suggestions for Reading Caves and Caverns

I recommend reading the book in its entirety out loud to the class as they follow along in their own books or join you in an informal reading circle. After this initial reading I recommend that students read in small groups and/or with partners.

New Words Investigation Continued

During the initial whole class reading, student pairs holding the new word bats should be listening and/or looking for the meaning of their word as it is mentioned during the reading. A few words will not be found in *Caves and Caverns*. You can challenge students to find the resources that would define these remaining words. As the reading mentions each new word, the pair of students holding that word should raise their bat in the air. The reading should pause for a moment as the pair goes to the cave, finds the definition card, reads it aloud, and places the bat above it with a tack or "sticky stuff." Reading should commence when the students have returned to their spots. This activity will provide many breaks in the reading for discussion and encourage close attention to the text.

Once all of the new words are discussed and the bats are displayed in the cave, you may want to remove them and place them in a bag or pocket at the front of the cave to make an interactive display. Later, students can challenge

themselves by matching bats with definitions individually or in pairs. Be sure to include an answer key in the bag for self-checking.

Inside the Earth

Before students read in small groups, show the Reading Rainbow video, *The Magic Schoolbus Inside the Earth*. This will further expose them to cave terminology, build upon their knowledge and curiosity about caves, as well as answer some of their questions previously generated.

Erosion Investigation

Begin by reading more together about the birth of caves from sink holes and erosion of rock in a book such as *Cave* by Lionel Bender. Then in groups, have students make small mountains or plateaus with glue and sugar cubes. Place each sugar hill inside a baking pan and provide each group with a pitcher of warm, colored water and spoons or eyedroppers. Invite students to slowly drip droplets of water with a spoon or eyedropper onto the top of their sugar hills. They should observe the colored water as it seeps through the cracks and crevices, much like carbonic acid seeps through layers of rock in the earth. Then invite students to pour the water from the pitcher over one small spot at the top of their sugar hills. They should observe a wearing away of that spot, similar to how a flowing river can cause erosion and create a sinkhole.

Four Types of Caves

As students read together in small groups, ask them to make a list of the four main types of caves—limestone, ice, underwater/sea, and lava. After reading, instruct students to fold a large sheet of white construction paper in half and then in half again to make a chart with four boxes. They should label each box with one type of cave. Then they should cooperatively record the facts that they have found about each type within the boxes. Students then need to consult additional sources for more information about each type of cave. The book *Looking Inside Caves and Caverns* by Ron Schultz offers sections on each type of cave. Encyclopedias would also be good sources.

Investigations for After Reading

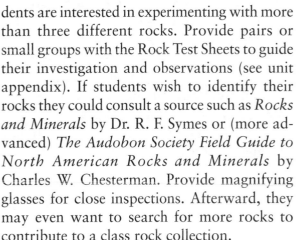

Crystal Investigation

Observe how crystals are formed. In groups, students should dissolve alum (available at drugstores) in about 3 tablespoons of water in a small pie tin. Let the solution sit for several days until crystals have formed. Take the best crystal in the tin and tie a thread around it. Tie the other end of the thread to a pencil. Place the pencil on top of a glass jar so that the thread and the crystal hang down into the jar. Fill the jar with more of the alum and water solution for about ten more days and watch the crystal grow larger and more intricate each day. Students should record what they see in an Observations Booklet (see unit appendix). When the crystals are complete students can display them in dioramas of caves or just inside a box with a dark background.

Rock Investigation—Looking for Limestone

Rocks should be provided by you so that each group has the same rock specimens. Look for rocks at a garden center in the landscaping department. Consult a source such as *Geology* by Graham Peacock and Jill Jesson or *Rocks, Gems and Minerals* by Lisa Sita for information on the three classifications of rocks: igneous, sedimentary, and metamorphic. You may want to include chalk as one "rock" to investigate as it is a form of limestone. Each rock should be clean and numbered for easy reference and recording observations. This investigation can be done in rotating stations so that all of the students can experiment with different rocks and different tests. This investigation can also be done several times with different sets of rocks if students are interested in experimenting with more than three different rocks. Provide pairs or small groups with the Rock Test Sheets to guide their investigation and observations (see unit appendix). If students wish to identify their rocks they could consult a source such as *Rocks and Minerals* by Dr. R. F. Symes or (more advanced) *The Audobon Society Field Guide to North American Rocks and Minerals* by Charles W. Chesterman. Provide magnifying glasses for close inspections. Afterward, they may even want to search for more rocks to contribute to a class rock collection.

As another extension to this activity, have students investigate the map "Limestone Regions of the World" found on page 14 of *Caves* by Stephen Kramer and answer questions such as "Where is most/least of the karst found?" and "Who made this map and how?" and "How might this map change in another twenty years? One hundred years? Why?"

Bat Facts Investigation

Begin spurring curiosity about bats by sharing one or two fiction stories about bats such as *Stellaluna* by Janell Cannon or *A Promise to the Sun* by Tololwa Mollel. Students could choose to write a book response (see Main Appendix) for one or both of these stories. After sharing, invite students to start thinking about bat facts. Record their facts on a very large bat made of light-colored bulletin board paper or drawn on the chalkboard. Then working in groups with different bat resources (see supporting library), have students locate as many bat facts as they can find. One person from each group should record the facts onto the big bat as they find them. It will be important to ask students to read the facts that are already there so as not to write the same facts several times. Another big bat could be used to record the names of different types of bats.

Group Investigation—Finding Information

These activities can be completed on a rotating basis or on the basis of the groups' choices given the options. You need to decide ahead of time whether you want each group to have every experience or just one or two. These activities are meant to give students experience with locating information using tables of contents, headings, indexes, and so on. Two of the four activities include making a minibook that should have a front/back cover with title and authors clearly written and should be bound in some fashion.

National Parks

Using one or two resources such as *National Parks: The Family Guide* by Dave Robertson or *National Geographic's Guide to the National Parks of the United States* by Gilbert M. Grosvenor and a map of the United States, find the three national parks that are closest to your town. Make a minibook that includes their names, locations, and five things that one might see or do at each park with illustrations.

Night Life

Using sources such as *Life in the Dark* by Joyce Pope, *Vampire Bats and Other Creatures of the Night* by Philip Steele, *Cave Life* by Christiane Gunzi, *Caves* by Stephen Kramer, and others, find and list two creatures that are troglobites, two that are trogloxenes, and two that are troglophiles. Make a minibook that gives the names, drawings, and a sentence that tells about each creature. Be sure to include which category each creature is in, by way of headings or labeled, dividing pages.

Famous Caves

Using *Mammoth Cave National Park* by Ruth Radlauer or *Carlsbad Caverns National Park* by David Peterson, choose the four sections that your group finds most interesting and read them together. Make a big poster from chart paper or poster board that shows ten interesting facts with illustrations about this famous park and the caves in it. Also, include a small map of the United States (could be traced using tracing paper) that shows where this park is. This activity can easily be used with two separate groups by giving one group Mammoth Cave and one group Carlsbad Caverns.

Caves of the United States

Using *Atlas of the Great Caves of the World* by Paul Courbon and others and a large map of the United States and/or a U.S. atlas, complete the U.S. Caves Sheet and Map (see unit appendix) with your group.

People, Caves, and Nature Paints

Share the book *Mik's Mammoth* by Roy Gerrard with the class. Although this is a fiction book, invite students to discuss how people have used caves in ancient history. When the discussion turns to cave painting, ask students to think about the materials that were available to cave men to paint with. Provide or invite students to find things in nature that a cave man could have used to paint with (e.g., mushed berries, dandelions, leaves, grass, charcoal, mud, etc.). Give students a day or two to gather such materials from their backyards or parks. Provide a long piece of crumpled (to simulate bumpy cave walls) brown bulletin board paper hung in the hallway or outside to avoid the mess. It should be long enough so that every student has a small spot to experiment with the paint material that they have brought. You may or may not want to dictate the kinds of things that they can paint. After painting, discuss what things worked the best/worst and comments about the experience.

Glowing Investigation

Use *Creatures That Glow* by Joanne Barkan. Read by flashlight in a very dark room. Begin by reading information on how and why some things glow. Show glow-in-the-dark pictures by turning off the flashlight so that students can get the full effect as you read about a variety of glowing creatures. I suggest reading about those that live on land and possibly in caves (fireflies, phengodes, glowworms, bacteria) and then continue as interest demands.

Discuss the characteristics of animals that live in darkness. Help students become aware that many animals who live in complete darkness have lost the use of their eyes. Provide students with pocket-sized mirrors and flashlights as you lower the classroom lights. Invite them to look at how their eyes change as light changes. Ask them to consider what would happen to the eyes of animals without sight. Encourage students to think about what it would be like to live without sight in total darkness and what other senses would take over to help the animals survive. Students can experiment with this idea by being blindfolded and invited to walk around a dark classroom. Some students may not be comfortable with this exercise. They can observe and comment on what they saw happening as the blindfolded students moved around the room. You could also try an unfamiliar dark room as an additional challenge.

Protecting Caves/Writing for Information

Read aloud sections from support books on the protection of caves. Then ask pairs of students to design a small poster for a specific national park (with caves) to hang in their visitor center. See *Looking Inside Caves and Caverns* by Ron Schultz for a partial list of parks with caves. Also, see the national park guides suggested in the support library for selecting those with caves and locating addresses. The poster should attract attention and tell people how they can protect the caves there and why it is so important. When the poster is complete ask students to write a letter to their chosen park explaining what the poster is for and re-questing information about the entire park. Remind students to include their signature and return address. If funds allow, provide envelopes and postage.

You may also want to offer the address of a national caving club to students who are interested in writing to them for information on caving:

National Speleological Society
(Caving Club)
Cave Avenue
Huntsville, AL 35810

Reading and Writing

Read aloud from one of the chapter books suggested in the supporting library and encourage discussion of events that take place on these cave adventures. As students learn more cave facts they will feel more comfortable in their understanding of these stories as well as be motivated (hopefully) to write their own creative cave story/book.

Stalactite/Stalagmite Investigation

Small groups or pairs of students will need a thick piece of string or yarn about 2 feet long, two glass jars, a small plate, water, and Epsom salts. Provide the following instructions: Fill the jars with water and dissolved salts. Put the plate between the jars. Hang the ends of the strings over the jars and in the water. Let some of the string hang down between the two jars over the plate. Watch what happens and record observations in an Observations Booklet (see unit appendix).

Cave Seminar for Parents

Invite parents to an informal seminar put on by students to give students an opportunity to share what they have learned about caves and caving with their parents. Students can design their own invitations or use the one provided in the Main Appendix. Small groups of students could be responsible for setting up information tables to provide information on all of the areas studied throughout the unit. The displays at the tables could consist of projects that have already been completed. Ideas for information tables:

Table 1: Spelunking equipment, including a complete first-aid kit, proper attire for a caving expedition, and posters showing equipment and purposes. Students at this table would tell what each item is and what it is used for in spelunking.

Table 2: Creative cave stories, written by students in the class. Students manning this table would share their stories out loud and answer questions.

Table 3: Cave life. Students at this table would share their projects on cave life, explaining the differences between trogloxenes, troglobites, and troglophiles. They could also use the cave life books listed in the supporting library for parents to look at.

Table 4: Speleothems. Students at this table would explain the procedures used in their experiments in creating stalactites/stalagmites and crystals and how they are actually formed in a cave. They may want to include pictures of other speleothems from books from the supporting library to share as well.

Table 5: Cave parks. Students at this table would share their minibooks on famous caves or caves near us, explaining important facts about these caves and why people should protect and respect them.

Parents should be instructed to rotate among all of the information tables and to ask questions of the students manning the tables. Parents should be informed that they will be asked to fill out a short evaluation at the end of the seminar (see unit appendix). Students should be instructed to take this job seriously as they are playing the role of park rangers who do interpretive talks at the national parks. It may be fun for students to dress prepared for a caving expedition just to set the mood. Be sure to have all supporting library books out and accessible for parents to look at. You may even want to continually show portions of the Reading Rainbow video, *The Magic Schoolbus Inside the Earth*.

PARENT LETTER

Dear Parents,

Next week we will be going on an exciting adventure under the ground as we read *Caves and Caverns* by Gail Gibbons. This book will help us learn about safe spelunking (exploring caves), how caves are made, and the kinds of mysterious things that can be found within caves of all different kinds. You can join our investigation at home by asking your local librarian to help you and your family find other books about caves, rocks, and minerals.

During our cave explorations and investigations we will be doing several scientific experiments and projects. We will need many materials for these activities that you might have at home. Please see the attached "Wanted" sheet. We will appreciate anything you can lend us.

At the end of our unit we would like to share our newly acquired knowledge with you at our Spelunker Beginners Seminar. The seminar will be held on _____ at _____. We sure hope that you will be able to join us for this special and informative event. You will receive an invitation as a reminder, but mark your calendars now!

Farewell from inside the Earth!

Spelunker Beginners Seminar for Parents Evaluation

1.) What was your overall opinion of the seminar? _____

_____

2.) Which table did you find most informative? _____

_____

_____

3.) What is one new thing that you learned as a result of this seminar? _____

_____

_____

4.) What did you enjoy the most about the seminar? _____

_____

_____

5.) Suggestions for improving the seminar next time: _____

_____

_____

Thank you for coming!

Bat Pattern

Today's Observations

Name: _____

Date: _____

Today I see: _____

_____

_____

_____

It has/has not changed since my last observation. This may be due to: _____

_____

_____

Here is a picture of what I see:

Something I am wondering about: _____

_____

_____

Rock Test Sheets

Names:_____

1.) Put a drop of water on each rock. Wait about thirty minutes. Observe if the water has been absorbed or if it still remains on the top of the rock. Record your results.

Rock #1   Rock #2   Rock #3

2.) Try to make marks with each rock on a brick. Record your results.

Rock #1   Rock #2   Rock #3

3.) Try to scratch your rocks with a coin, then a nail. Record your results.

Rock #1   Rock #2   Rock #3

4.) Put a drop of vinegar on each rock. Observe for signs of dissolving (fizzing). Record your results.

Rock #1   Rock #2   Rock #3

5.) Look at each rock carefully with a magnifying glass. Draw and describe what you see.

Rock #1   Rock #2   Rock #3

Rock Test Sheets

Questions:

Which rock do you think acted most like limestone? Why? _____

_____

Comments: _____

_____

Drawings of rock specimens:

Can you identify any of these rocks?

Rock #1   Rock #2   Rock #3

U.S. Caves

Names:_____

Using *Atlas of the Great Caves of the World* by Paul Courbon and others, answer the following questions.

1.) What page numbers cover caves in the United States?_____ to _____

2.) What is the deepest cave in the United States? _____

    Where is it? _____

    How deep is it? _____

3.) What is the longest cave in the United States? _____

    Where is it? _____

    How long is it? _____

4.) What pages tell about caves in your state?_____ to _____

    How many caves are in your state? _____

    Name one: _____

    Where is it? _____

    How big is it? _____

    What are some other interesting facts about this cave? _____

5.) Trace a map of your state (or the nearest state with caves). Label your town and the caves that can be found throughout the state.

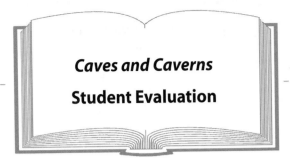

Caves and Caverns
Student Evaluation

Name: _____

1.) During the unit, I worked cooperatively with my groups

      not at all   sometimes   most of the time

2.) During the unit, I tried my best

      not at all   sometimes   most of the time

3.) During the unit, I completed

____ a poster   ____ a chart of cave types   ____ a crystal experiment

____ a letter   ____ observation booklets   ____ a rock investigation

____ a bat facts search   ____ painting with nature   ____ a blindfolded walk

____ a seminar for parents   ____ an atlas investigation ____ a creative cave story

____ a minibook of cave creatures

____ a minibook of national parks

____ a speleothem formation

4.) Something new that I learned about caves is:_____

_____

5.) Something new that I learned about living creatures is:_____

_____

6.) Something new that I learned about rocks and minerals is:_____

_____

7.) One thing that I worked on that I am especially proud of is: _____

_____

8.) My favorite things about this unit were: _____

_____

SUPPORTING LIBRARY

Barkan, Joanne. *Creatures That Glow*. New York: Doubleday, 1991.
A glow-in-the-dark book that tells about living things that glow in the dark.

Bender, Lionel. *Cave* (The Story of the Earth Series). New York: Franklin Watts, 1989.
Explains how limestone caves are formed and how they have been used.

Bendick, Jeanne. *Caves!* (Underground Worlds). New York: Henry Holt, 1995.
Detailed discussion of many aspects of caves, including their beginning, formations, cave life, and exploration. Also includes lists of tools, supplies, and rules for spelunking.

Cannon, Janell. *Stellaluna*. New York: Harcourt Brace, 1993.
A baby bat learns how she is like and unlike baby birds. Includes bat facts at the end of the book.

Chesterman, Charles, W. *The Audobon Society Field Guide to North American Rocks and Minerals*. New York: Alfred A. Knopf, 1978.
An advanced guide to rocks and minerals.

Cole, Joanna. *The Magic Schoolbus Inside the Earth*. New York: Scholastic, 1987.
Ms. Frizzle's class learns about different kinds of rocks and the formation of the Earth.

Courbon, Paul, et al. *Atlas of the Great Caves of the World*. St. Louis, Mo.: Cave Books, 1989.
Lists caves of the world, where they are, and how deep/long they are. Also provides maps and descriptions of many caves.

Earle, Ann. *Zipping, Zapping, Zooming Bats* (Let's-Read-and-Find-Out Science Book). New York: HarperCollins, 1995.
Describes bats and their behaviors, including those beneficial to humans.

Gans, Roma. *Caves* (Let's-Read-and Find-Out Science Book). New York: HarperCollins, 1976.
Describes different kinds of caves and how they are formed.

Gans, Roma. *Rock Collecting* (Let's-Read-and-Find-Out Science Book). New York: Thomas Y. Crowell, 1984.
Explains how to start a rock collection and how to recognize sedimentary, igneous, and metamorphic rocks.

Gerrard, Roy. *Mik's Mammoth*. New York: Farrar, Straus & Giroux, 1990.
A story about a little caveman who makes a big friend.

Gray, Susan Heinrichs. *Bats* (A New True Book). Chicago: Childrens Press, 1994.
Examines different types of bats and their behaviors.

Grosvenor, Gilbert M. *National Geographic's Guide to the National Parks of the United States*. Washington, D.C.: National Geographic Society, 1992.
Describes U.S. national parks by regions. Includes regional maps and color photos.

Gunzi, Christiane. *Cave Life* (A Closer Look Series). New York: Dorling Kindersley, 1993.
Examines the animals and plants that live in and around caves.

Jeunesse, Gallimard, and Pascale deBourgoing. *Under the Ground* (A First Discovery Book). New York: Scholastic, 1990.
Provides a look at all kinds of animals, birds, and insects who live or make nests in the ground or caves. Easy reading.

Julivert, Maria Angels. *Bats* (The Fascinating World of …). New York: Barron's Educational Series, 1994.
Examines the habitats and behaviors of bats.

Kendall, Cindy. *Bats* (Dial Nature Notebook Pop-Up). New York: Dial Books for Young Readers, 1995.
Provides brief descriptions of bats, their behaviors, and notable varieties.

Kerbo, Ronal C. *Caves.* Chicago: Childrens Press, 1981.
Describes caves, animal life, and speleology. Takes the reader on a little cave exploration (good for reading aloud).

Maestro, Betsy. *Bats, Night Fliers.* New York: Scholastic, 1994.
Describes different types of bats and how they live.

Mollel, Tololwa M. *A Promise to the Sun.* Boston: Little, Brown, 1992.
An African legend telling how the bat was a hero among animals but must forever remain hidden during daylight due to a broken promise.

Peacock, Graham, and Jill Jesson. *Geology* (Science Activities Series). New York: Thomson Learning, 1995.
Discusses aspects of being a geologist and what a geologist studies: rocks, minerals, fossils, earth movements, and geologic time.

Peterson, David. *Carlsbad Caverns National Park.* Chicago: Childrens Press, 1994.
Discusses cave formation and special features of Carlsbad Caverns.

Pope, Joyce. *Life in the Dark* (Curious Creatures Series). Austin, Tex.: Steck-Vaughn, 1992.
Describes animals who spend parts or all of their lives in darkness and how they survive.

Radlauer, Ruth. *Carlsbad Caverns National Park.* Chicago: Childrens Press, 1981.
Describes creatures and life in and around the caverns.

Radlauer, Ruth. *Mammoth Cave National Park.* Chicago: Childrens Press, 1978.
An excellent resource for learning facts about one famous cave.

Robertson, Dave. *National Parks: The Family Guide.* Port Roberts, Wash.: On Site Publications, 1991.
Describes all of the national parks, monuments, historic sights, etc. Arranged by state and includes simple state maps.

Russo, Doreen. *AAA Guide to the National Parks.* New York: Collier Books, Macmillan Publishing, 1994.
Covers all of the U.S. National Parks in alphabetical order. Includes a map and a color photo for each park.

Schultz, Ron. *Looking Inside Caves and Caverns* (X-Ray Series). Santa Fe, N. Mex.: John Muir Publications, 1993.
Describes caves and the jobs of cavers/speleologists.

Sita, Lisa. *Rocks, Gems and Minerals* (Exploring Science Series). New York: Thomson Learning, 1995.
Describes different kinds of rocks and minerals including those found in caves. Provides a partial list of
   caves to visit in the United States.

Steele, Philip. *Vampire Bats and Other Creatures of the Night* (Young Observers Series). New York: Kingfisher Books, 1995.
Describes nocturnal animals and how they live. Arranged in three easy-reading chapters with accompanying quiz questions and answers.

Symes, Dr. R. F. *Rocks and Minerals* (Eyewitness Books). New York: Alfred A. Knopf, 1988.
Examines all different types of rocks and minerals, including those found in limestone caves.

Wood, Jenny. *Caves* (Facts, Stories, Projects). New York: Penguin Books, 1990.
Discusses many different aspects of caves as well as provides a story and simple projects.

Read-Aloud Chapter Books

Brenford, Dana. *Danger in the Endless Cave* (A Green Street Mystery). Mankato, Minn.: Crestwood House,
   1988.
Three friends learn about spelunking and unravel a deep underground mystery.

Clyne, Patricia Edwards. *Tunnels of Terror*. New York: Dodd, Mead, 1975.
Five young spelunkers look for cave treasures and find themselves trapped inside by flood waters.

Karr, Kathleen. *The Cave*. New York: Farrar, Straus & Giroux, 1994.
A young girl discovers a cave and makes it her own special place until she finds an incredible secret
   inside.

Stein, Barbara. *Ghost Cave*. New York: Simon & Schuster Pocket Books, 1990.
An adventure of three young boys and their investigation of an unexplored cave.

Video

Reading Rainbow (with Levar Burton). *The Magic Schoolbus Inside the Earth*. Program no. 66.
Provides still-frame views of the story by Joanna Cole. Then Levar takes a trip inside a cave with a guide to
   see and learn about some magnificent cave formations. 28 minutes.

The Magic School Bus: Inside the Human Body

Joanna Cole

NEW YORK: SCHOLASTIC, 1989

ABOUT THE BOOK

The Magic School Bus: Inside the Human Body by Joanna Cole takes Ms. Frizzle's class and the reader on an imaginary trip through Arnold's body when he unknowingly eats the bus. The journey begins with the digestive system and includes stops at the heart, brain, and muscles via the circulatory system. The story concludes when the bus gives Arnold a tickle in his nose and he sneezes it out.

This book not only provides scientific information about our bodies but also entertains the reader with amusing characters, humorous speech bubbles, and easy-to-read student reports. It serves as an exciting and pain-free introduction to the wonders of the human body and its systems, as it piques the interests of all ages.

INVESTIGATIONS

Investigative Themes

Biology
Human Body Systems
Nutrition and Other Healthy Habits

Investigative Skills

making diagrams
categorizing
observing
identifying
gathering data
writing letters
predicting
weighing
following directions

working cooperatively
measuring
recording
alphabetizing
brainstorming
making books
making charts and graphs
listening/speaking
experimenting

comparing/contrasting
defining words
making decisions
planning

using mathematics and calculators
using resources
reading for information

Investigative Materials

1 copy of *The Magic School Bus: Inside the Human Body* for every three students
1 big book of *The Magic School Bus: Inside the Human Body* (optional)
supporting library books

markers, crayons, colored pencils
construction paper: red, pink, yellow, white, black
plastic drinking straws
glue, tape, rubber cement
name tags for guest speakers and students
refreshments for guest speakers
heavy-duty cardboard and clothespins to make clipboards
5 microscopes
eyedroppers, slides, and covers
toothpicks, iodine, onion
small paper cups
sugar, salt, lemon juice, and coffee
cotton swabs
10 to 12 pieces of 8 x 10 (approx.) bubble wrap
3 types of juice
magazines, scissors, large paper plates
blender, a school lunch, heavy-duty 1-gallon freezer bag
pink, red, and blue yarn
measuring utensils: liquid measuring cups, tape measures, rulers, yardsticks, bathroom
    scale
index cards, large or small
ink pad, wide clear tape, powder, hand lotion
5 to 6 magnifying glasses
white bulletin board/butcher paper
calculators, bucket or small basin, red food coloring or Kool-Aid
clock with a second hand

Additional Materials for Health Tables or Centers

tennis ball or rubber ball
bits of clay or Play Dough
X-rays
flashlight
cardboard tubes: paper towel or toilet paper
variety of bones

plastic cups
heavy dark cloth
plastic milk jug bottoms (1 per student)
pipe cleaners (6 per student)
oaktag
doctor's bag of tools

New Words for *The Magic School Bus: Inside the Human Body*

blood vessels—the tubes that carry blood throughout the body: arteries, capillaries, and veins
brain stem—the lowest portion of the brain that controls body functions
cell—the smallest living particle
cerebellum—the small part in the back of the brain that controls coordination and balance
cerebral cortex—the upper, larger part of the brain controlling movement and thought
chamber—enclosed compartment; there are four chambers in the human heart
circulation—moving around and returning to the same place
digestion—changing food into tiny particles that can be absorbed into the blood
esophagus—the tube that connects the throat and stomach; about 9 inches long
germ—tiny bacteria or virus that gets into the body and may cause sickness
intestines—the two tubes that follow the stomach and complete the digestion process
microscope—an instrument that magnifies very tiny objects like cells so that we can examine them
molecule—a tiny piece of matter
nasal cavity—the open part inside the nose
oxygen—the gas we need for life that we get from breathing in
plasma—the colorless liquid that is part of blood
spinal cord—part of the nervous system that sends messages to and from the brain
stomach—an organ in our body that breaks down food into tiny particles

Investigations for Before Reading

Health and Career Investigation

As a kickoff to the unit, invite the school nurse and several local health professionals (physician, dental hygienist, nutritionist, chiropractor, dermatologist, etc.) to visit your classroom on a specified day and time (see Letter of Invite for Professionals in unit appendix). This will obviously need to be done way in advance due to their tight scheduling and time constraints.

One or two days before the visit, place students in small groups and have them brainstorm questions they could ask the visiting health professionals about their jobs, health in general, or about the human body. Each student should have at least one question prepared and written on the My Question Page (see unit appendix). All questions should be screened by you to avoid repetition and inappropriate questions. Supply students with clipboards or make them from sturdy cardboard and clothespins.

Guests should be given name tags and seated in adult-sized chairs in panel fashion without tables. Students should also be given name tags and seated on the floor in front of the guests with their question pages, pencils, and clipboards. Introduce the guests and allow students to ask their prepared questions and write the answers given. Prior to this time you should encourage students to speak quickly yet clearly in order to get to as many questions as possible in thirty-five minutes.

After the panel time, invite guests to partake in some healthy refreshments and informal conversation with students. Encourage students to introduce themselves and shake hands with as many of the guests as they can. This may require a little practice ahead of time so they won't feel so awkward.

After the guests have gone, put all of the question pages together to form a book. Students should decide on a title and design a cover.

Finally, students should form groups to write thank-you letters to each guest. You may need to go over letter-writing format beforehand. You may wish to add your own letter to each guest as well and mail them promptly.

(*Note:* If you are not able to invite health professionals for a question-and-answer panel, perhaps you could visit a local hospital, HMO, or even a museum that offers related exhibits [e.g., "The Hall of Life" in the Natural History Museum in Denver, Colorado] to get your students' "kickoff" questions answered.)

Body Books

Reproduce and assemble "Body Books" from the page provided in the unit appendix. The objective of the "Body Books" is to get students to gather data on themselves to help them discover some existing healthy habits as well as those they need to adopt. The "Body Books" should be started the weekend before the unit begins and continue throughout the unit. You may wish to have students share information from their "Body Books" with their groups daily and/or occasionally with the whole class. The hope is that students will be able to see their data becoming "healthier" as the unit progresses.

New Words Investigation

Using pattern (see unit appendix), trace and cut out school bus shapes from yellow construction paper. Cut white construction paper into halves on the diagonal to make triangle-shaped flags. Provide small groups of students with three to four buses and the same number of straws, flags, and new words (specify which words). Ask them to find out what each word means using all available resources. Then they should write each word with its definition in marker on a white flag and attach a straw to it. Students should design their "magic school buses" with foods that they like to eat like the bus in the story. (See illustration below.) When the buses are complete, one flag should be attached to each bus. Challenge students to put all of the buses in alphabetical order. Display on a wall in the classroom for future reference.

Afterward, you may choose to provide each student with a copy of all eighteen words either with definitions or without so that they can write the definitions in themselves. This would provide all students with exposure to all of the words.

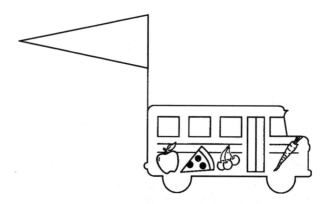

Investigations for During Reading

Suggestions for Reading The Magic Schoolbus: Inside the Human Body

A.) Read aloud straight through to entire class. A big book would be perfect for this!

B.) Students read aloud in small groups. Each student elects to read certain portions of the text. For example, one reads all typed words, one reads speech bubbles, one reads sidebars, labels, and reports. Students could choose to switch parts halfway through the reading.

C.) Reread specific parts/pages out loud in small groups or as a class preceding a related activity. For example, reread the page about the tongue prior to making a model of the tongue and doing taste tests.

Along with daily sharing of the "Body Books," you can begin each day's work with a reading from *Your Amazing Body: From Headaches to Sweaty Feet and Everything in Between* by Jeanne K. Hanson and/or a riddle from *What Can It Be?* by Jacqueline A. Ball and Ann D. Hardy.

Cell Investigation

Share the book *The Microscope* by Maxine Kumin to get students in the mood for science under the microscope.

Provide small groups of students with a microscope, slides (covers are optional), toothpicks, iodine, a cup of water, paper, and an eye dropper. Students can follow the four-step directions in *The Magic School Bus* to examine their own body cells up close. When each student has viewed their own cheek cells ask them to draw what they saw inside the microscope.

Repeat this observation experiment with a very thin layer of onion. Discuss how the cheek cells and the onion cells are similar and different.

Share the book *Cells Are Us* by Dr. Fran Balkwill to learn more about different kinds of cells. Have students make posters that illustrate the different kinds of cells we have in our bodies.

Tasty Investigations

Taste Experiment #1

Provide small groups of students with cotton swabs (four per student) and small amounts of sugar water, salt water, lemon juice, and strong coffee in paper cups. Each student should dip one swab into each solution one time, then touch their tongue with the swab in different areas to see where on their tongue they are able to taste sweet, sour, salty, and bitter. Each student should then make a diagram showing their results (see book for an example).

Make a Tongue

Afterward, provide each group with several small cards, a piece of bubble wrap (approximately 8 x 10), and pink construction paper. They should cut a large tongue shape (see pattern in unit appendix) from the bubble wrap, attach it to the pink paper with rubber cement or clear glue, and trim the paper to match the bubble wrap. Students should then label the small cards with "sweet," "sour," "salty," "bitter," then attach them to the tongue with tape, indicating where the tongue tastes sweet, sour, salty, and bitter.

Just for fun, students can add faces to their tongues by attaching them to a larger piece of white construction paper and drawing the face around it.

Taste Experiment #2

Provide pairs of students with cups of three different kinds of juice. Give them small amounts as they are only supposed to taste, not gulp. Also, give them a full cup of water, and a blindfold (bandannas work great). One student must elect to be the taster and one the experimenter beforehand. The taster should not be allowed to see the juices he or she is tasting. The experimenter should record the taster's responses on the "Which Juice?" taste experiment sheet (see unit appendix). Then, together, they should discuss the answers to the questions. This experiment could be repeated on another day with different juices to give students an opportunity to switch roles.

Nutritious Investigation

Share a book on basic nutrition such as *Health and Food* by Dorothy Baldwin. Then provide small groups of students with magazines, rubber cement, and scissors. Ask them to find pictures of food to represent the four basic food groups. They should look for four or five for each group. Give them two large pieces of construction paper. Model how to divide each paper into two equal halves by folding. Students can trace the folds with a dark-colored marker, then label each half with "Fruits and Vegetables"; "Milk and Dairy"; "Breads, Cereals, and Pasta"; and "Meats, Fish, and Poultry." Ask students to attach their foods on the chart with rubber cement (better than glue for magazine cuttings) under the appropriate labels. Then help students attach the two pieces of paper together with tape on the back to form one large chart.

In addition, you could have students cut out pictures of "junk food" while they are looking for representatives for the four food groups and make a separate class chart for all of these foods as well.

You may also wish to have students look for additional pictures that represent each group that could be put together for an appetizing, balanced meal. Have students attach their pictures onto a large paper plate. Then have them attach the plate to a "placemat" (large piece of construction paper) where they can add utensils, a napkin, and a healthy beverage.

Another book to share that provides another angle on eating healthy food is *Why Do I Eat?* by Rachel Wright. It discusses healthy food in terms of carbohydrates, proteins, and vitamins.

Digestion Investigation

Share the book *What Happens to a Hamburger* by Paul Showers. Purchase a school lunch. Place all food items inside a heavy-duty 1-gallon freezer bag. Then ask two students to be "the teeth." They should use their hands to mash the contents of the bag. Add a little water to represent saliva. Then ask another student to

be the "esophagus" and squeeze the contents into a blender. Ask two more students to be the "stomach" by adding some more water and pressing the buttons on the blender to grind up the food into a liquid form. The students will think this is quite disgusting, but it is a great way to show what happens to the food we eat.

Afterward, because we cannot demonstrate the work of the intestines breaking food into molecules, the students can look at the intestines in a different way. Give small groups of students a skein of pink yarn and a piece of red construction paper, about 6 x 8 inches. Have each group choose a measuring tool and measure out 7.5 meters or 25 feet of the yarn. Have them double-check their measurements before cutting. Once the yarn is cut, they should stretch it out to observe the length of the adult intestines. Then to illustrate how they might look on our insides, have students glue the yarn to the piece of red construction paper in long squiggles going back and forth across the paper. Also, using white paper arrows, students could label where the food comes from before reaching the intestines (stomach) at one end of the yarn and where it goes after (waste) at the other end of the yarn.

Germ Investigation

Share the book *Germs Make Me Sick* by Melvin Berger and/or *Cell Wars* by Dr. Fran Balkwill to discover more specifics about germs and how our bodies deal with them.

Next, make flip-action booklets. Give each student a piece of light oaktag or two large index cards. They need to cut eight small, matching rectangles from their material. Then they should line up their cards on a desk or table and illustrate each card showing a white blood cell slowly moving in on and consuming a few germs. Each picture needs to be drawn approximately the same size, shape, and color. Each successive picture should show a slight difference in the attack process. When all eight pages are complete, students should put them together in order and staple at one end. The object is to use their thumb to quickly flip through the pages to imitate the movement of the white blood cell attacking a germ.

Discuss the rules for good health at the end of the book. Brainstorm rules that could be added and write them on the chalkboard. Have pairs of students choose one rule to design a poster for on large, white construction paper. Each poster should include the rule clearly written and an illustration showing that rule in action.

Afterward, watch the Reading Rainbow video entitled *Germs Make Me Sick*, which will present the story again but also share additional information about germs, white blood cells, antibodies, and other tiny invisible microbes.

"Muscle of the Day" Investigation

Consult a resource, such as *The Children's Atlas of the Human Body* by Richard Walker (page 16 and life-sized poster) or an encyclopedia, to help you identify names and locations of muscles in our bodies. To kick off this activity, read the section entitled "Muscles Help You Move" from Joanna Cole's book *Your Insides*. Pick one muscle per day to focus on and invite students to locate that muscle on their own bodies. Offer sample exercises that they could do to make that muscle stronger. Some students may even be able to make up their own exercises once they have become accustomed to the sensation of their muscles contracting. Examples of exercises you could share with your students:

For quadriceps—lean against a wall with feet shoulder-width apart; keeping your back flat against the wall, slide your body down the wall until your upper legs are parallel to the floor; your feet should be perpendicular to the floor so that you appear to be sitting in an invisible chair.

For hamstrings—get on your hands and knees; lift one leg in the air parallel to the floor; flex your foot and bend and straighten your lifted leg.

For biceps—stand straight with feet shoulder-width apart; raise both arms straight out to your sides; curl both arms in toward your head with clenched fists, keeping your elbows even with your shoulders.

For triceps—stand straight with feet shoulder-width apart; clasp your hands together and raise them above your head with your elbows next to your ears; keeping your elbows in position, raise your hands above your head, then lower them behind your head; try holding a weight of some sort in your hands for this exercise.

For abdominals—lay on the floor with your knees bent; fold your arms across your chest; pull your upper body upward in a crunch toward your bended knees.

For the heart—run, jump rope, walk very fast, skip, or gallop for about ten minutes.

For the gluteus maximus—Place your hands on your hips or out to your sides; stand with toes pointing out and feet a little more than shoulder-width apart; keep your upper torso straight and bend your knees slowly, then straighten; if you lean forward you will feel this exercise more in the quadriceps; if you lean backward with your buttocks tucked under you will feel it in the gluteus maximus.

Remind students to record these exercises in their "Body Books."

Investigations for After Reading

The "Inside Story"

Provide small groups with white bulletin board paper. Each group needs to elect one student to lie on the paper while another student traces around the outside of their body. Then have students illustrate what is on the inside of our bodies. They should consult resources from the supporting library to help them make their illustrations accurate. In order to see things clearly and not overlap, I suggest that they draw the muscles in one leg, the bones in the other; the nerves in one arm, the blood vessels in the other (students could use different color yarn pieces for nerves and blood vessels); the brain and the internal organs should be drawn in their approximate places.

Another option to this activity is to have students focus only on the skeletal system. Share the book *The Skeleton Inside You* by Philip Balestrino and draw only the skeleton inside the traced body. Then challenge them to label each bone and/or choose different colors for bones that support and bones that protect.

The "Outside Story"

Share the books *Why Does That Man Have Such a Big Nose?* by Mary Beth Quinsey, *Two Eyes, a Nose and a Mouth* by Roberta Grobel Intrater, *People* by Caroline Grimshaw, and *People* by Peter Spier. These books address how people are different on the outside and discuss the different ways that people think. Invite students to write their own versions of these books that tell how people are different.

Make graphs to show how people can be different within your classroom. For example, measure the arm length or height of each student and create a bar graph. Students can make separate graphs for girls and boys and to see if there are any noticeable differences based on gender. They could also graph eye color or hair color.

Fingerprint Investigation

Share the first part of the video *Bill Nye the Science Guy: The Human Body—The Inside Scoop*. It talks not only about the uniqueness of human fingerprints but every aspect of the largest human organ: the skin.

Invite students to make a set of their own fingerprints using an ink pad and an index card. They should press their fingers onto the pad, then firmly onto the card, then label the print with left/right hand (they should press in the order of thumb, index, middle, ring, pinky). Provide students with magnifying glasses so

that they may examine their prints. See *My First Body Book* by Lara Tankel Holtz and/or *The Bones and Skeleton Gamebook* by Karen C. Anderson and Stephen Cumbaa to note the characteristics of human fingerprints (arch, whorl, loop) and challenge students to categorize their prints.

Invite students to become detectives. Provide small groups with a clear glass, powder, hand lotion, wide clear tape, and dark-colored paper. Each group chooses one person to be the detective. All detectives leave the room for a moment as the other group members put on some hand lotion (to make the prints show up better). Then one student acts as the culprit and lifts the glass. The detective then returns to the room and searches the glass for fingerprints. To dust for prints and make them show up better, he or she should shake some powder over the prints found on the glass and blow off the excess. To lift a print from the glass, the detective presses a piece of wide clear tape onto the print, then carefully transfers the tape to a dark-colored piece of paper. The real challenge is to match the print with a print from the print cards from the previous activity to find out who was the culprit who touched the glass. This activity can be repeated many times to allow different students to become the detective.

Blood Investigation

Provide small groups of students with calculators, liquid measuring cups, a water faucet, and a bucket or small basin, and have a scale on hand for determining each student's weight. Invite each student to figure out how many quarts of blood they have circulating throughout their bodies by using this number sentence equation:

your weight _____ ÷ 25 = _____ quarts of blood

To figure out how many cups that would be, use this number sentence:

# of quarts _____ ÷ 4 = _____ cups of blood

To get an idea of what that amount really is, have each student measure their cups of blood.

They should use a measuring cup to measure out cups of water into a bucket or small basin. Color could be added by way of red food coloring or a pinch of red Kool-Aid.

For more information on our blood and the circulatory system, view the second part of *Bill Nye the Science Guy: The Human Body—The Inside Scoop*.

"What's in It?" Investigation (Fat Testing and Nutrition Labels)

One way for students to find out what is in the foods they eat is to read nutrition labels. To begin this activity, share the book *Why Do I Eat?* by Rachel Wright and provide each student with a copy of a nutrition label to examine as a whole class. Provide small groups with packages from two different brands of similar foods with the same serving sizes. For example, different brands of candy bars, cereals, yogurts, crackers, breads, margarines, and frozen dinners could be compared, but they must have the same serving size. Then using the What's in It? sheet (see unit appendix), have students record the data from the packages and try to determine the brand that is the most nutritious.

Another way to determine what is in our food is by looking at the napkin or plate that it has been sitting on. Provide small groups of students with a variety of foods to test (tomato, cheese, chocolate, potato chips, grapes, bread, a stick of butter) for fat content, along with several brown school-type paper towels (these will work the best, but cheap paper napkins or plates will work also). They should rub each food onto a napkin and write the name of the food on the napkin. Students can predict what they think will happen to each napkin, then wait several hours for any moisture to evaporate. Each napkin should be examined for remaining grease stains. The biggest stains were caused by the foods highest in fat content. Have students put them in order from the least fatty to the most fatty. Then offer them a few new foods (green pepper, mayonnaise, bagel) and ask them to predict their fat content. They can predict whether they think each food will be high or low in fat or

how each food may be similar to ones already tested. Then students should test their predictions and perhaps come up with two generalizations about foods and fat contents.

How Hard Are You Working?

Help each student find their pulse in their necks just below their jawbone. Once everyone has found their own pulse ask them to sit quietly for one minute then count the beats in their pulse for one minute. You should use a clock or watch with a second hand for this. Students should also count the number of times they breathe in and out in a minute of resting. Students should record all information on the How Hard Are You Working? sheet (see unit appendix).

ABC's of the Human Body

Challenge each student to write about and illustrate one thing about the human body that corresponds to a given letter of the alphabet. For example, "B" is for blood that is made of red blood cells, white blood cells, and plasma; "I" is for our intestines that are part of the digestive system; "N" is for nutrition—the healthy food that our bodies need at each meal. Provide each student with a large piece of white construction paper. Encourage them to write clearly and use the whole paper for their illustrations. Ask each student to let you know what they are working on so that there are no repeats. Assemble all pages together to make a class big book entitled "The ABC's of the Human Body."

My Favorite Body Part Project

Invite each student to choose one body part (inside or outside) as their favorite. They may want to consult some of the books from the support library for ideas. Once they have decided, they need to gather a little bit of information, write a minireport (see unit appendix) and design a model out of clay or some other materials, or a poster depicting the body part. The minireport and model/poster should be shared in small groups or with the whole class.

One idea for sharing the information is to invite small groups of students to interview the body parts researched in the minireports. The student who did the research will speak for the body part while the interviewers ask questions such as: Where are you located in the body? What is your function?, etc.

It's My Body Fair

Choose a date and time in advance in order to invite a kindergarten/first-grade class in your school. The object of this fair should be for students to share their newly acquired body knowledge with an interested audience. They can do this by displaying their finished projects, posters, models, and books, and by offering some simple activities at health tables. Each health table or project table should be manned by at least one student who can direct the kindergarten children in the activities and answer questions and/or tell about their projects. The following suggestions might be used to create health tables and/or could be used during the unit as center activities:

A.) How hard is your heart working? Try squeezing a rubber ball or a tennis ball 90 to 100 times in one minute. That is the average number of times your heart pumps just when you are doing nothing!

B.) Can you see your pulse? Put a piece of clay on the inside of your wrist. Stick one end of a straw into the clay, then wait a minute or two. Watch the other end of the straw as it starts to slightly move. Count the number of times it twitches in one minute. Now you have seen your pulse!

C.) What do bones really look like? Examine the insides and the outsides of different animal bones (cut and uncut) from a butcher's shop and/or last week's dinner. Can you guess the animal the bone belongs to? Include a magnifying glass at this table.

D.) How do doctors see our bones? Examine real X rays of different bones in the human body. Include a good light source at this table. Contact your local hospitals for donations.

E.) Can you hear your friend's heartbeat? Because stethoscopes are too expensive and sensitive for untrained people to use, try using a cardboard tube to find your friend's heartbeat within his/her chest. Count how many times it beats in one minute. Then have your friend do twenty jumping jacks and listen and count again. What happened?

F.) Can you hear your blood moving in your body? Place a plastic cup over your ear. The rushing sound you hear is your blood moving through your inner ear.

G.) What's inside your hand? Stand in a dark room or place a heavy, dark cloth over your head and hands. Hold up your hand and shine a flashlight behind it. What do you see inside your hand?

H.) Can you find your friend's knee reflexes? Ask your friend to sit on the table with their legs dangling over the side. Touch their knee with your hand and try to find the soft spot between the bones. Gently hit that spot with the straight side of your hand. If you have found the right spot, their leg should gently kick out as an involuntary reflex. In other words, they are not trying to kick their leg, it just happens.

I.) What's in the bag, Doc? Investigate the instruments that a doctor uses in his/her office. Try to guess what each instrument is used for. (You may be able to borrow from a school nurse or a local doctor. Better yet, get them to come with their instruments to share them with the children. If you can't get your hands on the real things, improvise with play doctor's bags.)

Other Things to Do for the Fair

- Make a cozy reading area with books about the human body
- Wear "lab coats." Adult button-down dress shirts work great for this. Lab coats could be worn by participants and/or the students putting it on.

- Carry clipboards. Make them with heavy-duty cardboard and clothespins.
- Offer healthy snacks at the end such as carrot sticks, celery sticks with peanut butter, or watermelon.
- Make brain caps for participants to wear. Each student needs the bottom of a plastic milk jug, six pipe cleaners, tape, glue, and a piece of oaktag. Students need to research what part of the brain controls balance, movement, hearing, seeing, touching, and speech. Design a simple picture on oaktag to represent each of these. For example, a hand may indicate touch, a mouth may indicate speech, and so on. Then pretending that the plastic is a model brain, poke holes in the plastic in the places where they are controlled. Feed a pipe cleaner almost all the way through each hole. Bend the end inside the cap and tape it in place. Attach the oaktag pictures to the ends of the pipe cleaners outside the cap. Add strings on the sides to tie under the chin if the cap won't stay on. Wear proudly on head during the fair to illustrate what is going on all the time inside the different parts of our brains.

PARENT LETTER

Dear Parents,

Our next adventure in learning will be a ride on The Magic Schoolbus with Ms. Frizzle's class on a fascinating trip inside the human body. Our trip takes place in the pages of *The Magic School Bus: Inside the Human Body* by Joanna Cole.

Through many different projects and experiments, we will be exploring our bodies' various systems and how they work together. Please see the attached "Wanted" sheet for any items that you might be able to send from home to help us with these activities.

We will be paying special attention to keeping our bodies healthy and strong. Today your child is bringing home a "Body Book" to gather information in. He or she should bring this book to and from school every day throughout this unit. Offer assistance in recording information only if requested by your child.

At the end of the unit we will be sharing our knowledge and enthusiasm with a class of younger students in our It's My Body Fair. You are welcome to join us.

Also, if you or a relative are in a health-related profession and would be willing to come in and share your expertise with us, please let us know as soon as possible.

Remember to visit your local library with your child to learn more about the wonders of our bodies!

Here's to your health!

My Body Book

Name: _____   Page: _____

Today's date: _____

What did I eat for …

Breakfast? _____   Lunch? _____

_____   _____

Dinner? _____   Snacks? _____

_____   _____

What did I do for my …

Body? _____

_____

Brain? _____

_____

Soul? _____

_____

What are some feelings I had today? _____

_____

What time did I go to bed? _____

What time did I get up the next morning? _____

How many hours of sleep did I get altogether? _____

Schoolbus Pattern

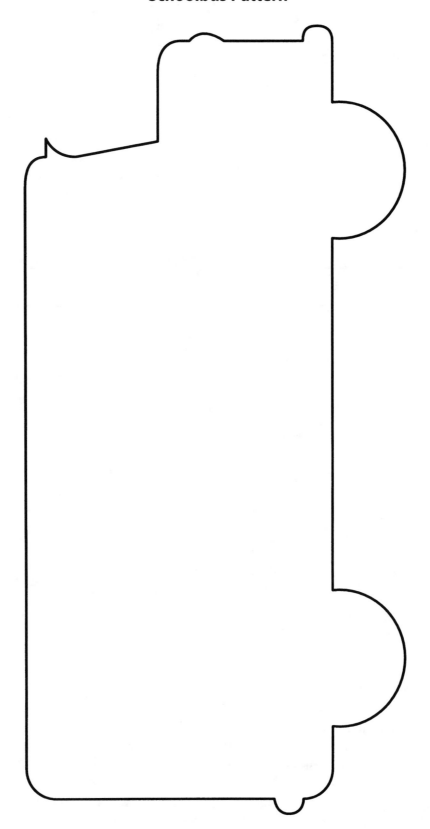

Letter of Invite for Professionals

Dear _____,

    Our class will soon begin learning more about the wonders of the human body. We are hoping to gather new knowledge from many different sources, including professionals who know lots about how our bodies work. We would like to invite you to our classroom for a short question-and-answer panel with other professionals like yourself. This will take place on _____, beginning at _____ and ending at _____. We are aware that your time is very valuable and will stick to the following schedule if you should choose to join us:

        5-minute introduction of panel members
        35 minutes of questions prepared and posed by students, with answers from various professionals
        20 minutes of informal visiting with refreshments

    We would greatly appreciate your attendance on our panel of professionals and providing us with this rich opportunity. Please R.S.V.P. by calling our school office at _____ by _____. Thank you.

Sincerely,

My Question Page

Name:_____

My question:_____

_____

I addressed my question to:

(name)_____

(profession)_____

The answer I received was:_____

_____

_____

_____

Other questions I would like to ask this professional:_____

_____

_____

Which Juice?

Name of taster:_____

Name of experimenter:_____

Directions: Blindfold the taster. Get 3 cups of different juices and a cup of water. Ask taster to keep their nose plugged and taste each juice, rinsing with water in between tastes. Do not tell the taster what the juices are yet!

Record a "+" sign if they guess the type of juice correctly. Record a "–" sign if they guess incorrectly.

With blindfold and nose plugged:

Juice #1   Juice #2   Juice #3

Now have the taster unplug their nose but keep the blindfold on and repeat the tasting, but give them the juices in a different order. Record results below.

With blindfold only:

Juice #1   Juice #2   Juice #3

Look at your results. What can you conclude about how we taste things?_____

_____

What does this tell you about how we taste things when we have a cold?_____

_____

In what way do you think our tongue helps protect us? _____

_____

Tongue Pattern

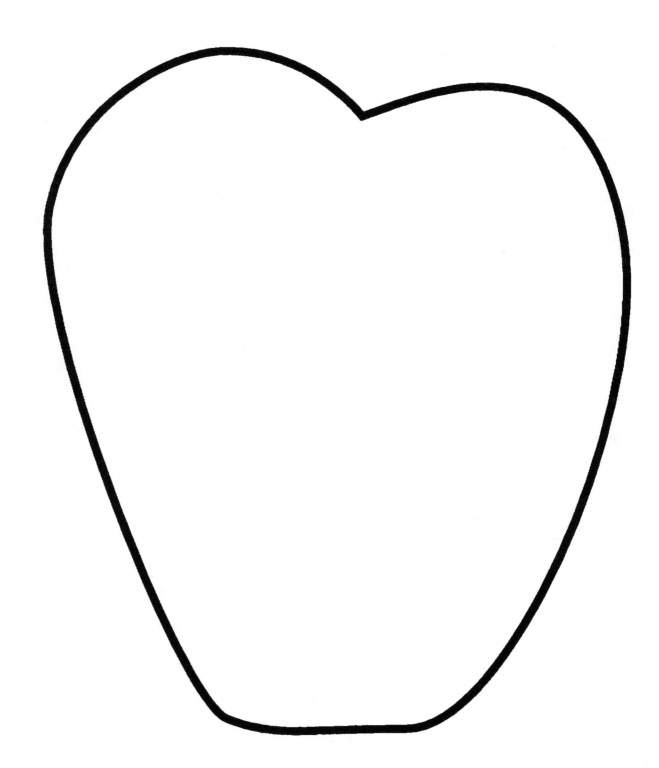

What's in It?

Examination of Food Nutrition Labels

Names:_____

Food type:_____

	Brand #1	Brand #2
	_____	_____
	(name of product)	(name of product)
Calories	_____	_____
Fat	_____	_____
Carbohydrates	_____	_____
Protein	_____	_____
Salt (sodium)	_____	_____
Vitamin C	_____	_____
Vitamin B	_____	_____
Vitamin D	_____	_____
Calcium	_____	_____
Cholesterol	_____	_____

Main ingredients (first two listed under ingredients):_____

_____

According to the information you have gathered here, which brand do you think would be a healthier choice for you? Why? _____

_____

How Hard Are You Working?

Name:_____

Using your first two fingers, find your pulse in your neck just below your jaw. Be still and rest as you feel your pulse beating for at least one minute. Then, using a clock with a second hand, count how many beats you feel in one minute. This is your resting heart rate. Record below.

Resting heart rate _____

Try the following activities. But first predict your heart rate and record. Then count and record the actual rate.

	Prediction	**Actual**
Stand up and sit down 10 times	_____	_____
5 jumping jacks	_____	_____
Run in place for 3 minutes	_____	_____

What do these results tell you about your heart and exercise? _____

_____

What do you think would happen if you ran in place for an hour? _____

_____

What happens to your breathing as your heart works harder? _____

_____

Do you think breathing and heartbeats are related? How? _____

_____

My Favorite Body Part Minireport

Name:_____

What is its name? _____

What does it look like? _____

_____

Where is it in the body? _____

_____

What is its function? _____

_____

Why it's my favorite part: _____

_____

The Magic School Bus:
Inside The Human Body
Student Evaluation

Name:_____

1.) During the unit, I worked cooperatively with my groups

      Not at all   sometimes   most of the time

2.) During the unit, I tried my best

      not at all   sometimes   most of the time

3.) During the unit, I completed

____ a "Body Book"   ____ a flip-action booklet

____ a drawing of cells   ____ exercises for my muscles

____ a model of a tongue   ____ a graph of differences

____ a balanced meal plate   ____ a card of my fingerprint

____ a food groups chart   ____ lifting fingerprints

____ fat content testing   ____ a "What's in It?" chart

____ my favorite body part report/project ____ an "It's My Body Fair" table

____ a page for the "ABC's of the Human Body" ____ a life-sized diagram

____ a question/answer for a health professional

4.) One thing that I learned about my blood is:_____

5.) One thing that I learned about digestion is:_____

6.) One thing that I learned about muscles is:_____

7.) Some healthy habits I have now are:_____

_____

And some that I need to work on are:_____

_____

8.) My favorite things about this unit were:_____

_____

Supporting Library*

Anderson, Karen C., and Stephen Cumbaa. *The Bones and Skeleton Gamebook*. New York: Workman Publishing, 1993.
A collection of more than sixty games, puzzles, and activities.

Baldwin, Dorothy. *Health and Food*. Vero Beach, Fla.: Rourke Enterprises, 1987.
Discusses basic aspects of nutrition and foods in the four food groups.

Balestrino, Philip. *The Skeleton Inside You* (Let's-Read-and-Find-Out Science Book). New York: Thomas Y. Crowell, 1989.
Explains the functions of the skeletal system. Easy reading.

Balkwill, Dr. Fran. *Cell Wars*. Minneapolis, Minn.: Carolrhoda Books, 1993.
Tells about the defenders inside our bodies and how they help our body fight viruses and bacteria. Written in comic book style.

Balkwill, Dr. Fran. *Cells Are Us*. Minneapolis, Minn.: Carolrhoda Books, 1993.
Describes what our cells can do and the different types of cells within our bodies. Written in comic book style.

Ball, Jacqueline A., and Ann D. Hardy. *What Can It Be? Riddles About Our Bodies*. Englewood Cliffs, N.J.: Prentice-Hall, 1989.
Riddles about fifteen different body parts.

Berger, Melvin. *Germs Make Me Sick* (Let's-Read-and-Find-Out Science Book). New York: HarperCollins, 1995.
Describes germs and how our bodies handle them. Easy reading.

Carola, Robert. *How Do I Grow?* Lake Forest, Ill.: Forest House, 1990.
Simple answers to more than forty questions about the human body.

Catherall, Ed. *Exploring the Human Body* (Exploring Science Series). Austin, Tex.: Steck-Vaughn, 1992.
Describes many aspects of the human body. Includes activities and questions.

Cole, Joanna. *Your Insides*. New York: Putnam & Grosset, 1992.
Provides a simple look at what's inside our bodies with four see-through, labeled diagrams.

Grimshaw, Caroline. *People* (Connections! Series). New York: Thomson Learning, 1995.
Includes fifty questions and answers about human beings, what makes us tick, and how we get along.

Hanson, Jeanne K. *Your Amazing Body: From Headaches to Sweaty Feet and Everything in Between*. New York: Freeman, 1994.
Gives short explanations of body phenomena such as hiccups, blushing, daydreaming, yawning, goose bumps, and much more.

Haslam, Andrew. *Make It Work! BODY*. New York: Thomson Learning, 1994.
Provides information along with numerous challenging projects.

Holtz, Lara Tankel, ed. *My First Body Book*. New York: Dorling Kindersley, 1995.
Provides easy-to-read information about our bodies. Includes see-through pages to see inside the human body.

Intrater, Roberta Grobel. *Two Eyes, a Nose and a Mouth.* New York: Scholastic, 1995.
A celebration of the different facial features people have. Very easy reading.

Kumin, Maxine. *The Microscope.* New York: Harper & Row, 1984.
The rhyming story of a Dutch scientist who loved to look at things under the microscope.

Miller, Jonathan, and David Pelham. *The Classic Three-Dimensional Book: The Human Body.* New York: Viking Penguin, 1983.
A pop-up book that discusses body parts in general with large print and specifics in small print.

Myers, Jack Ph.D., *How Do We Dream?* Honesdale, Pa.: Bell Books, Highlights, 1992.
Questions about our bodies from children all over the country are answered by Highlights science editor.

Parker, Steve. *Human Body* (Eyewitness Explorers). New York: Dorling Kindersley, 1994.
Provides a variety of interesting facts about the human body.

Peacock, Graham, and Terry Hudson. *The Super Science Book of Our Bodies.* New York: Thomson Learning, 1993.
Describes many things about the human body including the brain, body cells, the senses, and staying healthy.

Quinsey, Mary Beth. *Why Does That Man Have Such a Big Nose?* Seattle, Wash.: Parenting Press, 1986.
Provides questions and answers about the differences in people's outsides.

Richardson, James. *The Science Dictionary of the Human Body.* Mahwah, N.J.: Troll Associates, 1992.
An easy-to-read dictionary of body terms from the abdomen to the wrist.

Rojany, Lisa. *Exploring the Human Body.* New York: Barron's Educational Series, 1992.
Includes pull tabs, flaps, a magic viewer, and thirty-four activities to teach children about the human body.

Rowan, Dr. Pete. *Some Body!* New York: Alfred A. Knopf, 1994.
A detailed book offering information on more than fifteen body parts and functions, including the blood, brain, cells, and nose.

Royston, Angela. *My Body: What's Inside.* New York: Dorling Kindersley, 1991.
A simple look at the insides of various body parts.

Saunderson, Jane. *Muscles and Bones* (You and Your Body Series). Also available: *Brain, Ears, Eyes, Heart, and Lungs.* Mahwah, N.J.: Troll Associates, 1992.
Describes a variety of bones and muscles and their functions.

Showers, Paul. *A Drop of Blood.* New York: HarperCollins, 1989.
A simple introduction to blood and all of its functions.

Showers, Paul. *What Happens to a Hamburger* (Let's-Read-and-Find-Out Science Book). New York: Thomas Y. Crowell, 1985.
Explains what happens to food in the digestive system.

Spier, Peter. *People.* New York: Bantam, Doubleday, Dell, 1980.
Discusses the many differences in people throughout the world.

Vaszily, Diane A., and Peggy K. Perdue. *Bones, Bodies and Bellies.* Glenview, Ill.: Goodyear Books, Scott Foresman, 1994.
Provides hands-on activities and experiments in anatomy, physiology, and nutrition. Designed for grades 3–6.

Walker, Richard. *The Children's Atlas of the Human Body.* Brookfield, Conn.: Millbrook Press, 1994.
Describes the human body with actual-size illustrations and a life-sized human anatomy chart.

Wright, Rachel. *Why Do I Eat?* (Aladdin Basics). New York: Aladdin Books, Macmillan Publishing, 1992.
Discusses why we need food, what kinds of food we should eat, and what happens once we've eaten it.

Videos

Disney Home Video. *Bill Nye the Science Guy: The Human Body—The Inside Scoop!*
Provides facts, experiments, and humor to make learning about our skin and the circulatory system very entertaining. Approximately 49 minutes. Each program about 22 minutes.

Reading Rainbow. *Germs Make Me Sick* by Melvin Berger. Lincoln, Nebr.: GPN/WNED TV (800-228-4630), 1986.
Host LeVar Burton learns about germs and other living microbes. Approximately 30 minutes.

*Note: Although there are many other excellent resources on the human body, I have purposefully not listed any titles that included pictures and extensive discussion on the reproductive system, as it may not yet be appropriate for your students.

Color

Ruth Heller

New York: Putnam & Grosset, 1995

About the Book

Written with rhyme and humor, *Color* by Ruth Heller gives the reader a unique look at colors and how they can be applied, changed, and used to magically create moods and drama by artists and printers. By overlapping pictures and pages, one can see how primary colors can be combined to make secondary hues and then blended again to make many more color variations.

Investigations

Investigative Themes

Colors and Light
Painting
Famous Artists
Experimentation and Creativity
Camouflage and Color in Our Environment

Investigative Skills

experimenting
creative expression
observing
predicting
evaluating
artistic techniques
graphing

writing
speaking
comparing/contrasting
planning
designing
recording
classifying

Investigative Materials

1 copy of *Color* for every three to four students
supporting library books

7 rulers	coffee filters
5 to 6 large shoe boxes	vegetable oil
paper plates for each student	5 to 6 pocket mirrors
10 to 20 plastic eyedroppers	paint color strips (from a paint store)
5 to 6 ice cube trays	corrugated and heavy cardboard
food coloring	milk (about a quart)
5 to 6 flashlights	5 to 6 glass jars
paper towels	colored plastic wrap
wipes (Wet Ones or baby wipes)	cardboard tubes
5 to 6 baking pans	dye for tie-dyeing
large chart paper	small notebooks
rubber bands	refreshments and paper goods
index cards (7 per group) for art exhibit	

Art Supplies

acrylic paints	colored chalk
oil paints	oil pastels
watercolor paints	crayons
finger paints	fat-tipped markers
brushes	colored pencils
white bulletin board paper	poster board
scissors	lots of paper of varying weights
glue	art smocks (old shirts)
tempera/poster paint	
newspapers	

other application tools (sponges, rollers, sticks, straws, palette knives, vegetables, pieces of wood, etc.)

New Words for *Color*

achromatic—free from color
=another word for an acrobat[*]

advance—to come forward
=to place an advertisement

camouflage—a color or pattern of something that matches its background
=the scientific name for a camel's hump

complimentary—colors opposite each other on the color wheel
=put together in a nice fashion

cyan—a greenish blue color
   =a type of pepper

hue—having color
   =to feel relief

magenta—dark pink color
   =a scarf used in advanced magic tricks

medium—material from which one can create art
   =a type of airplane used for skywriting

minuscule—very tiny
   =a type of paintbrush

primary color—the three basic paint colors: red, blue, and yellow
   =the first color in a row of colors

recede—to fall into the background
   =to look at something again

secondary color—colors made by mixing primary colors (e.g., orange, purple, green)
   =all of the dark colors of the rainbow

shade—color mixed with black or gray
   =a small flat shovel

tint—color mixed with white
   =a shelter made of colorful fabric

*Note: "=" means nonsense definitions to be used in New Words Investigation.

Investigations for Before Reading

Investigating New Words

Prepare ahead of time: 7 long pieces of white bulletin board paper, 7 different mediums (tempera paint, watercolors, acrylic paint, finger paint, crayons, oil pastels, and colored chalk), brushes for the painting tables, 7 bottles of glue, 7 pairs of scissors, 7 black markers, 7 rulers, 7 pencils, and 14 word cards (these should be made table tent style with the word printed clearly on the front and the two definitions to choose from written on the inside, the correct definition written on a piece of tape or a card taped to the underside of a desk or chair so that groups can self-check after reaching consensus and before writing the definition). Also, provide wet wipes and have art smocks on hand for each student. Arrange desks table-style (two or four desks together) with newspapers over them.

Put students into seven groups. Then give each group about eight sheets of white paper (8½ x 11). Ask students to glue their papers together lengthwise so that they have one long strip.

Place one medium and one word card at each table and instruct students to write their word cooperatively onto the white paper with the given medium. Students can take turns writing letters so that each student can get a chance to use each medium. Students will also cooperatively decide which definition is correct on the inside of the word card, then check under their table or chairs to see if they have chosen correctly and print the definition under the new word in black marker. Encourage the students to write large to fill up the paper. When the definition is written, ask students to draw a straight line using a pencil and a ruler. Then go over the pencil with the given medium to divide the spaces between words. (See illustration below.)

Groups should rotate to the different tables at the sound of a bell or some other signal so that they all change at once. Due to there being fourteen new words all together, I recommend taking two days to complete this activity, doing seven words one day and seven the next. Each medium will be used twice.

> new word
> (in acrylics)
>
> new word
> (in crayon)
>
> new word
> (in oil pastels)
>
> new word
> (in colored chalk)

When groups have completed all fourteen words, hang their work from the ceiling to the floor for reference throughout the unit.

Investigate Favorite Colors

Ask students to name colors and list them on the chalkboard. From the list of colors, ask each student to vote on their favorite color. Keep tally marks next to each color as you count votes. Transfer this information onto graph paper to show which colors are the most popular. This can be done using a simple bar graph with color names on the bottom and numbers of students choosing the colors on the left side. The bars can be drawn with the matching color. Graph paper will help keep lines and bars neat and even. If students are not familiar with this type of graphing I suggest guiding them through it on an overhead projector.

A "Color a Day"

On the first or second day of the unit, share the story *Red Day, Green Day* by Edith Kunhardt and begin a "color a day" focus. Choose one color to start with (perhaps the most popular color on the graph from the previous activity) and ask students to look for this color wherever they go. They should keep a small notebook with them at all times to record everything that they see in that color. You may wish to award a small prize (a pack of crayons, markers, or paints) to the student who comes up with the most recorded items.

Also, ask students to bring one thing to school the following day that represents the color to share with the class. Spend a few minutes the next day to have a quick show-and-tell of these items. As a class or in groups, students can classify these items according to specified attributes or they can arrange them in order according to the shade or tint of their color (dark to light, light to dark).

Share one or two stories during the day that involve the day's color such as *The Purple Coat* by Amy Hest, *Harold and the Purple Crayon* by Crockett Johnson, and/or color poetry such as *Hailstones and Halibut Bones* by Mary LeDuc O'Neill. Then invite students to write creative stories with illustrations about the day's color. Ideas for story starters could be:

What if the whole world were purple?
What if purple disappeared?
Purple is best because …
I dreamed I had a magic purple pebble …
The day the purple monster came to town …
What purple means to me …

Ask volunteers to provide simple snacks to represent the color of the day. Also, invite students to wear clothing in the day's color.

Play "I Spy" with the color throughout the day to improve students' observation skills in the classroom.

Working Colors/Colors in Our Environment

Share Tana Hoban's book *Colors Everywhere* to get students thinking about colors in our environment. Tape several large chart papers to a bulletin board or wall and place a large circle of one color (red, green, yellow, orange, blue, etc.) in the middle of each. Ask students to brainstorm what each color means in our environment. For example, yellow indicates warning, blue is for disabled signs, red means stop, and so on. Write their thoughts on the chart paper around the circle of color. Throughout the unit, students can add things to these charts when they learn how colors can be cool or warm or create moods and perhaps how these colors got their names. Students can also add things that are usually a certain color. For example, grass is usually green, the sun is considered yellow, water blue, and so on.

As an extension to this activity, students can investigate colors in the night environment. Provide medium- to large-sized shoe boxes for each group of students. Ask them to cut a small hole in one end of the box for looking through.

Give them several balls of different-colored paper (wadded up sheets of paper). Ask them to predict which colors will show up the best inside the dark shoe box and rank order them. Then instruct them to place each paper ball inside the box one at a time and look inside with the cover on. They should observe and record in rank order which colors actually did show up the best inside of the dark box.

Color Investigation

Put students in small groups. I recommend using smocks and newspapers for this activity. Provide each group with plastic eyedroppers and an ice cube tray filled halfway with water. Add food coloring to three of the cubes—red, blue, yellow. Invite students to experiment with these primary colors and keep a log of the colors they mix and what new colors are made. They can do this by writing the names of the colors used to create the combination on a piece of white construction paper and dropping a spot of the new color next to the words. Allow them to dump their trays and start with new primary colors and begin experimenting again when all of the cubes have color in them.

See-Through Color Investigation

Share the book *Color Dance* by Ann Jonas. Provide groups of students with cardboard tubes, small squares of different-colored plastic wrap, and rubber bands. Ask students to make colored telescopes and look through them and discuss with their group what they see. Have them experiment by putting two or three different colors on the same telescope. Have a whole class discussion about looking through the colored lenses.

You can add to this experience by giving each group a flashlight and turning off the lights. They can experiment by putting the colored plastic over the flashlights with the rubber bands and shining the light on different things.

Investigations for During Reading

Suggestions for Reading Color

I recommend that you read aloud straight through, simply to enjoy the author's rhyme, rhythm, and humor. After this initial reading, choose one of the investigations for during reading to do with the class. On the following day, I would suggest another shared reading perhaps with students taking turns reading while looking/listening for things like mediums, primary colors, secondary colors, printer colors, tools, and so on. This information could be recorded on the chalkboard or chart paper and discussed either during or after the shared reading. Afterward, choose another investigation for during reading. A third reading should take place in the form of partners or small groups reading aloud and really getting a chance to manipulate the see-through pages. This, again, can be followed by an investigation for during reading.

Shades and Tints Investigation

Provide groups of students with several paint color strips (available at your local paint store). They should observe the many slight variations of the same color. Ask them to cut the colors apart and try to put them back together in order from light to dark or dark to light. Students can discuss the significance of the shade names as well, in that some names just sound or mean something slightly lighter or darker.

Provide students with newspaper to protect their work area, smocks, mixing trays (Styrofoam egg cartons would work), one color of paint, white and dark gray paint, brushes and about seven index cards. Students should paint one index card with the unmixed color and paint the others with the shades and tints of that color. Shades and tints will be made by mixing white and gray with the original color. They should create at least three of each. While the paint is drying students should give a name to each color/tint/shade. When the paint is com-

pletely dry, students can glue their index cards to a larger piece of oaktag to create a big paint color strip to be displayed in honor of shading and tinting.

Color Wheel Investigation

Provide each student with a lightweight white paper plate, ruler, pencil, and crayons. Invite them to create a color wheel that shows the primary, secondary, and intermediate colors. See *A Color Sampler* by Kathleen Westray for an example. Students who need a little extra challenge could also include complimentary colors on their color wheel as seen in *Color* by Ruth Heller. Many students may need guidance in how to divide the plate evenly. I recommend a minilesson on fractions either before or as part of this activity. Students will gain experience with halves, quarters, and thirds by folding their paper plates and drawing the dividing lines before they fill in the colors. Students should label their colors by name and type in black marker before they color with crayon.

Water Prism Investigation

Provide each group of students with a pan filled with water, a flashlight, a mirror (a perfect size is 5 x 7 inches), and a white piece of heavy construction paper or oaktag. One student holds the mirror in the water tilted upward. Another student shines the flashlight onto the mirror and holds the white paper up to catch the mirror's reflection. Students should observe the colors they see and re-create their rainbow on separate pieces of paper with markers or oil pastels. (They could use the paper they used for the reflection.) If necessary, consult sources from the support library, such as *The Science Book of Color* by Neil Ardley or *Colorful Light* by Julian Rowe, or *Color and Light* by Barbara Taylor, for illustrations of this experiment.

When discussing why the rainbow appears, students may wish to investigate further on their own, or a simple explanation that white light is actually made up of the colors of the rainbow may suffice. Students can have another chance at observing a rainbow simply by combining oil and water in a shallow pan out in the sunshine.

Make a "Color Top"

Provide pairs of students with a circle of heavy white tagboard, a sharp pencil, and the six main colors of the rainbow—red, orange, yellow, green, blue, and violet. Ask students to divide their circles into six equal parts and color each part with the colors above and in the same order. Then they should poke the pencil through the middle of the circle, make some predictions about what they think they will see, and then spin it like a top. Students will see that a fast-spinning color top will become a blur of yellowish white in our eyes. If time or supplies allow, students can experiment with color tops of different combinations.

Chromatography Investigation

Provide each group of students with a baking pan filled with water, three or four different colored markers, and coffee filters. Instruct students to cut filters into strips and color one small circle of each marker color onto each strip about halfway up. Students should hold the strips so that they dangle in the water. (They should predict what they think will happen before they place it in the water.) As the water is absorbed, students will see that some colors separate and some do not.

Students could further investigate colors with coffee filters and water by folding them up and dipping corners in different colors of food coloring and water. When they unfold their filter they will see how the colors blended together and bled throughout the filter in a tie-dye fashion.

Investigations for After Reading

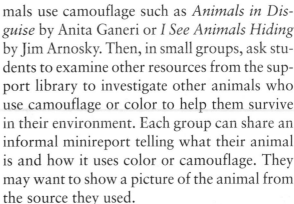

Paint and Tool Investigation

Read aloud *A Painter* by Douglas Florian to introduce the work and tools of a painter.

Provide small groups of students with several different tubes of acrylic paint colors and newspapers to protect their work areas. Give each group a variety of tools with which to apply paint, such as sticks, straws, sponges, old playing cards, rollers, cardboard tubes, blocks, a variety of brushes, and so on. Give each student in each group their own large, sturdy piece of paper to experiment on. Students should be allowed to rotate among the colors and tools freely to create their own abstract art. Smocks should be worn for this activity and rules should be stressed ahead of time, including proper treatment of paint and other materials. To encourage free creativity, it is important to remind students that they are all there simply to experiment with tools and colors, and that they are not to evaluate or judge one another's work.

The "Art" of Camouflage

Begin by sharing the poem "Camouflaged Amphibian" on page 35 of *A Tree Place* by

Constance Levy. Follow with one or more books about how animals use camouflage such as *Animals in Disguise* by Anita Ganeri or *I See Animals Hiding* by Jim Arnosky. Then, in small groups, ask students to examine other resources from the support library to investigate other animals who use camouflage or color to help them survive in their environment. Each group can share an informal minireport telling what their animal is and how it uses color or camouflage. They may want to show a picture of the animal from the source they used.

Students could take this a step further by illustrating or locating a picture of their chosen animal. Then using a variety of art supplies they could create a background of their environment and place the animal picture in it to show how the animal blends in.

To gain firsthand experience in camouflage have students try to camouflage themselves. First, they have to create their environment on a large piece of bulletin board paper using any design they desire. Then they need to camouflage themselves (with clothing, costume pieces, odds and ends, face paints, etc.) so that when they stand or sit in front of their background they blend in with their own design. Students need to keep in mind that they are not trying to be animals. Their background and camouflage should be abstract, using color in unique ways. This will require a great deal of thought and planning (several days) as to what clothing they might have or available art supplies—one day to plan, one day to create the background, and one day to bring in materials to camouflage themselves with their background.

Famous Painter Investigation

In partners or small groups, have students select one painter from a list (on which you can provide resources—see support library). When they have chosen an artist, they should read one main source and consult another such as the encyclopedia. As they read and acquire information about their artist, they should complete an Artist Question/Source Chart (see unit appendix). They should then organize their information in paragraph form and write a short report. Each group should share their reports with another group. While the groups are presenting, each member of the listening group should use the Presentation Checklist (see Main Appendix) to evaluate the presenting group. When the report is complete, the two groups should discuss the report checklist. It is important that students see the checklist before and throughout their writing, so that they are aware of what the other group is listening for, as well as what they will need to listen for when they are the audience.

Colors and Moods Investigation

Read aloud *Colors* by Philip Yenawine as a minilesson on the value of colors with respect to expressing moods and feelings.

Invite students to experiment with different mediums and colors to express particular moods. When they have finished a piece they can ask others to try to guess what mood they have tried to portray. Save for display at the art exhibit.

Book Project

Using all available resources, each student should independently create an illustrated book on one of the following topics:

A.) A color book for a preschool age child—see *One Yellow Lion* by Matthew Van Fleet or *My First Look at Colors* by Tori Rann for appropriate examples.
B.) A book of sayings that use colors and what they mean—examples would be "once in a blue moon" or "beet red" or "white as a ghost."
C.) A book of mediums or artists tools and how they can be used.
D.) A color book patterned after one of Gabrielle Woolfitt's books: *Red* or *Yellow* or *Blue*.
E.) A creative story book patterned after *The Orange Book* by Richard McGuire.
F.) A book of color in your environment with photographs or illustrations of colorful things you see each day in your neighborhood.

Home Project

After consulting the available resources on paint and painting, students should choose one paint project to complete at home. Their project should consist of three or more colors and at least two different tools. On the day the projects are due, each student should be prepared to share their project procedures and materials with the class.

These projects should be included in the art exhibit and therefore should be framed properly for hanging. Interesting frames can be constructed out of painted corrugated cardboard or decorated heavy cardboard. Buttons, grass, sand, paper clips, glitter, pieces of pasta, or fabric could be used to decorate the frame. Other projects previously completed can also be framed at this point.

Group Project

Small groups or pairs of students can choose from the following list of projects to complete for display at the art exhibit.

A.) Sidewalk art—using sidewalk chalk or washable paint, design a mural on a sidewalk outside your school.

B.) Color creature—using paint or oil pastels on bulletin board paper, design a creature that is at least twelve different colors.

C.) Window painting—using thick washable poster paint in many colors, design a mural for the inside of your classroom windows.

D.) Vegetable prints—make a mural showing the different textures that can be achieved by using vegetables to apply paint; use different colors and label the vegetables that were used.

E.) Marbling—make marbled paper; fill a baking pan with water and a few drops of vinegar, then add drops of oil-based paint (or tempera with vegetable oil added). Swirl the paint drops. Carefully place plain white paper on the surface of the water, then gently lift off and place on newspaper to dry.

F.) Tie-dyeing—bring in a white T-shirt, rubber bands, and some small rocks. Tie the rocks into the shirt with tightly wrapped rubber bands. Dip the shirt into a tub of dye solution. Let the shirt dry, then take out the rubber bands to find that no dye has reached the areas that were tied tightly together.

G.) Color from plants—gather colorful foods. Try spinach, strawberries, blueberries, onion skins, tea, turmeric powder, avocado, or beets. Mash and add a little water to make a dye solution. (And possibly heat to bring out the colors.) Soak white fabric or paper in your mashed food dye. Dry flat on newspaper.

Art Exhibit

This is a culminating activity to proudly display projects, books, and learnings from the color unit. You and your students decide who you would like to share this with. It could be parents, other classes, teachers, administrators, community members, office staff, or a combination of all of them. Students can create and send special invitations to those they decide to invite. Or if they would prefer a more open invitation, they can design advertising posters to invite all who wish to attend.

Depending upon the type of affair you plan with your students, you may want to offer some refreshments (including napkins and cups) such as at a real art exhibit opening. For smaller groups you could offer sparkling grape juice with cheese and crackers. For larger groups you may consider Kool-Aid and saltines. Students may also wish to have music playing during their art exhibit to help create atmosphere.

Art Museum/Gallery Field Trip

Take your students and several parents on a trip to your local art museum for a guided tour. Keep in mind that this age group may not be able to appreciate fully all that a large museum may have to offer, so the tour should be kept brief and age-appropriate. You may want to request that your students look for and/or evaluate specific things such as a certain piece, a certain artist, or a certain artistic style, which may require you to visit the museum ahead of time to see what they are showing at the time.

If you feel that the whole museum would be too overwhelming for your students, consider taking them to a small local gallery. You may even be lucky enough to meet one of the artists who has their work displayed there.

PARENT LETTER

Dear Parents,

Next week we will begin an adventure into the wonderful world of color with the book *Color* by Ruth Heller. We will be exploring primary and secondary colors; how printers make colors; camouflage and color in our environment; mixing colors; famous artists; paint and painting; color and light; and creative expression. Your child will be given the opportunity to experiment with many different materials as they learn and create.

Several of our hands-on projects will require materials that you may be able to provide from home. Please see the attached "Wanted" sheet to see if there is anything that you could contribute. We will greatly appreciate your assistance!

As part of our learning experiences your child will be responsible for choosing and completing a home project with paints. Be looking for more information coming your way soon.

At the end of our unit we will hold an art exhibit in our classroom. It is scheduled for _____ from _____ to _____. We hope that you will be able to join us for a treat for your eyes and refreshments as well.

Also, we will be taking a field trip to _____ on _____. Please be looking for further information and a permission slip coming your way soon. We invite you to join us for this special opportunity.

During the next few weeks, try to remember to take a moment to appreciate the beauty and color that surrounds you!

Au revoir!

Artist Question/Source Chart

Artist:_____

	Source #1	Source #2
1.) When did this artist live?		
2.) Where did this artist live?		
3.) What was this artist's childhood like?		
4.) Who/what encouraged or inspired this artist?		
5.) What mediums and tools does this artist use?		
6.) What is this artist's style?		

7.) What is one famous work by this artist? Describe it. _____

_____

_____

_____

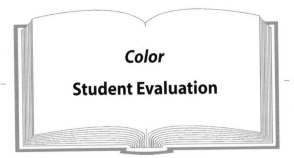

Color

Student Evaluation

Name:_____

1.) During the unit, I worked cooperatively with my groups

      not at all   sometimes   most of the time

2.) During the unit, I tried my best

      not at all   sometimes   most of the time

3.) During the unit, I completed

____a color wheel   ____a color story/book   ____a color top

____color experiments   ____a tool investigation   ____a favorite color graph

____shading and tinting   ____a water prism   ____chromatography

____a camouflage project   ____a mood expression   ____a book project

____a home project   ____a group project

____a famous artist chart and report

4.) Something new that I learned about color is: _____

_____

5.) Something new that I learned about artists is: _____

_____

6.) Something new that I learned about paint/painting is: _____

_____

7.) One thing that I worked on that I am especially proud of is: _____

_____

8.) My favorite things about this unit were: _____

_____

9.) If I were an artist what three things would be essential to me? _____

_____

SUPPORTING LIBRARY

Ardley, Neil. *The Science Book of Color.* New York: Harcourt Brace Jovanovich, 1991.
Provides twelve experiments/projects with color.

Baker, Alan. *White Rabbit's Color Book.* New York: Scholastic, 1994.
Provides an introduction to mixing the three primary colors as a little rabbit dips into paint pots.

Bragg, Ruth Gembicki. *Colors of the Day.* Saxonville, Mass.: Picture Book Studio, 1992.
Author/illustrator associates colors with times of the day.

Dewey, Ariane. *Naming Colors.* New York: HarperCollins, 1995.
Describes how many colors got their names. Provides an index for easy reference in looking up a particular color name.

Ehlert, Lois. *Color Zoo.* New York: J. B. Lippincott, 1989.
Introduces colors and shapes by forming zoo animals with cutouts.

Gaudrat, Marie-Agnes, and Thierry Courtin. *Discover Colors.* New York: Barron's Educational Series, 1994.
A big book of colorful animals told in rhyme.

Hamanaka, Sheila. *All the Colors of the Earth.* New York: Morrow Junior Books, 1994.
A poetic description of the special colors of children everywhere.

Hest, Amy. *The Purple Coat.* New York: Four Winds Press, 1986.
Gabby wants a purple coat. Mother thinks it should be navy. Grandfather has a solution.

Hoban, Tana. *Colors Everywhere.* New York: Greenwillow Books, 1995.
Wordless book filled with photographs depicting the many colors in our environment.

Jackson, Ellen. *Brown Cow Green Grass Yellow Mellow Sun.* New York: Hyperion Books for Children, 1995.
A colorful cycle from the yellow sun to butter.

Jenkins, Jessica. *Thinking About Colors.* New York: Dutton Children's Books, 1992.
Looks at colors and their different shades and some of the meanings associated with them.

Jeunesse, Gallimard, and Pascale de Bourgoing. *Colors* (A First Discovery Book). New York: Scholastic, 1989.
Introduces the mixing of primary colors to get secondary colors using see-through pages.

Johnson, Crockett. *Harold and the Purple Crayon.* New York: Harper, 1955.
A youngster draws what he imagines with his purple crayon.

Jonas, Ann. *Color Dance.* New York: Greenwillow Books, 1989.
Children dance with scarves to show blending of primary colors (and white and black) to create new colors.

Kunhardt, Edith. *Red Day, Green Day.* New York: Greenwillow Books, 1992.
Andrew and his kindergarten class celebrate color days.

McGuire, Richard. *The Orange Book*. New York: Children's Universe, 1992.
The story of where fourteen oranges end up after being picked from a tree. Illustrations are colorless except for the oranges.

O'Neill, Mary LeDuc. *Hailstones and Halibut Bones*. New York: Doubleday, 1989.
A book of poems about twelve different colors.

Parton, Dolly. *Coat of Many Colors*. New York: HarperCollins, 1994.
A young girl proudly wears her coat of many colors sewn with rags and love despite the teasing of other children.

Rann, Toni (art editor). *Colors (My First Look At)*. New York: Random House, 1990.
Provides photographs of objects to represent nine colors.

Rowe, Julian. *Colorful Light* (First Science). Chicago: Childrens Press, 1993.
Introduces color and light concepts through simple experiments and projects.

Spinelli, Eileen. *If You Want to Find Golden*. Morton Grove, Ill.: Albert Whitman, 1993.
Describes colors you can find in a city.

Taylor, Barbara. *Color and Light* (Fun with Simple Science). New York: Warwick Press, 1991.
Provides experiments and facts about color.

Taylor, Barbara. *Color and Light* (Science Starters). New York: Franklin Watts, 1990.
Examines how we see and use colors. Includes several projects.

Thomson, Dr. David. *Visual Magic*. New York: Dial Books, 1991.
A collection of optical illusions using color, line, and shape.

Van Fleet, Matthew. *One Yellow Lion*. New York: Dial Books for Young Readers, 1992.
A color book for preschoolers with colorful foldout creatures.

Westray, Kathleen. *A Color Sampler*. New York: Ticknor & Fields, 1993.
Discusses primary, secondary, and intermediate colors as well as tinting, shading, and the tricks that colors can play on our eyes.

Williams, Sue. *I Went Walking*. New York: Harcourt Brace, 1989.
A young child goes on a walk and finds animals of different colors following her. (Also available in Spanish.)

Woolfitt, Gabrielle. *Red. Yellow. Blue*. Minneapolis, Minn.: Carolrhoda Books, 1992.
These are three separate books that describe the many unique and different things that can be of a certain color.

Yenawine, Philip. *Colors*. New York: Delacorte Press, 1991.
Discusses the use of colors to express moods and ideas in works of art. Includes examples of artwork of famous painters.

Camouflage Books

Arnosky, Jim. *I See Animals Hiding*. New York: Scholastic, 1995.
Describes how animals hide, blend in, or change colors to camouflage with their environment.

Ganeri, Anita. *Animals in Disguise*. New York: Simon & Schuster, 1995.
Describes a variety of animals who use their coloring to protect and/or hide themselves in their surroundings.

Levy, Constance. *A Tree Place*. New York: Margaret K. McElderry Books, Macmillan Publishing, 1994.
A book of poetry in nature. See "Camouflaged Amphibian" on page 35.

Pope, Joyce. *Mistaken Identity* (Curious Creatures). Austin, Tex.: Steck-Vaughn, 1992.
Provides information on how some animals use camouflage and coloring to protect themselves.

Powzyk, Joyce. *Animal Camouflage* (A Closer Look). New York: Bradbury Press, 1990.
Discusses fifteen-plus animals who use one of six different types of camouflage.

Ryder, Joanne. *Lizard in the Sun* (A Just for a Day Book). New York: Morrow Junior Books, 1990.
A child becomes a chameleon for a day.

Sowler, Sandie. *Amazing Animal Disguises* (Eyewitness Juniors). New York: Alfred A. Knopf, 1992.
Discusses the many ways in which various animals can disguise themselves.

Taylor, Kim. *Too Clever to See* (Secret Worlds). New York: Delacorte Press, 1989.
Introduces several creatures who use forms of camouflage.

Wilson, April. *Look Again*. New York: Dial Books for Young Readers, 1992.
Challenges young eyes to look for changes in two nearly identical pictures as animals use camouflage for
survival. Also see *Look* by April Wilson.

Wright, Rachel. *Look at Color and Camouflage*. New York: Franklin Watts, 1989.
Describes how many different animals use their coloring to their advantage.

Paint/Painting/Painters

Florian, Douglas. *A Painter* (How We Work Series). New York: Greenwillow Books, 1993.
Very simple text describes how a painter works and what he paints.

Hodge, Anthony. *Painting* (Hands-on Arts and Crafts). New York: Gloucester Press, 1991.
Introduces types of painting and expression through the use of different materials and techniques.

Lepscky, Ibi. *Leonardo da Vinci*. New York: Barron's Educational Series, 1984.
Describes the childhood of the famous artist.

Lepscky, Ibi. *Pablo Picasso*. New York: Barron's Educational Series, 1984.
Describes the childhood of the famous artist.

Pluckrose, Henry Arthur. *Paints* (Fresh Start). New York: Franklin Watts, 1987.
Provides directions for paint projects using a variety of tools.

Sirett, Dawn. *My First Paint Book*. New York: Dorling Kindersley, 1994.
Provides directions for many unique and colorful projects using paints and other materials.

Tofts, Hannah. *The Paint Book*. New York: Simon & Schuster, 1989.
Describes a variety of paint projects using different tools and materials.

Venezia, Mike. *Getting to Know the World's Greatest Artists Series.* Chicago: Childrens Press, 1994.
Sixteen different books about famous artists. Easy-reading biographies.

Waters, Elizabeth, and Annie Harris. *Painting: A Young Artist's Guide* (Royal Academy of Arts). New York:
    Dorling Kindersley, 1993.
A complete look at the skills and tools of painting.

Siggy's Spaghetti Works

Peggy Thomson

NEW YORK: TAMBOURINE BOOKS, 1993

ABOUT THE BOOK

In *Siggy's Spaghetti Works* by Peggy Thomson, Siggy leads a group of children and the reader on a fascinating tour of his pasta factory. He describes the importance of the wheat farmers, the trucking industry, and the railroad. He shows the children how to make pasta by hand and machine. Siggy also offers tips for safety and fun inside the pasta factory as he discusses the history of pasta, how different colors and shapes are made, and the origins of some of the pasta names.

INVESTIGATIONS

Investigative Themes

Factory Production
Career Choices
Creating and Preparing Pasta

Investigative Skills

observing
graphing
categorizing
researching
patterning
measuring
using maps
estimating
writing
using numbers
following directions

predicting
thinking critically
comparing/contrasting
solving problems
sequencing
making decisions
working cooperatively
reading for information
listening/speaking
planning

Investigative Materials

1 copy of *Siggy's Spaghetti Works* for every three or four students
5 copies of *Pots and Pans* by Anne Rockwell
supporting library books

rolling pins
cookie cutters
cookie sheets
measuring cups
measuring spoons
colanders
whisks
pasta maker
large pots
butter knives
other chef's tools
pasta—2 examples of each variety
    (tubes, strings, ribbons, rods, shapes),
    some different colors, different brands

tape measures or rulers
small scales for weighing
glue
permanent markers
large U.S. wall map
tagboard, cardboard
Ziploc baggies (two for each student)
white construction paper
white tissue paper
disposable forks, spoons, bowls, napkins

eggs
flour (regular)
semolina flour
spices (for sauce)
fresh tomatoes
heavy cardboard pieces
empty and full boxes of pasta
(of different shapes and sizes)
Parmesan cheese
butter/margarine
12 pieces of lasagna pasta for new words

New Words for *Siggy's Spaghetti Works*

al dente—cooked but still chewy
chute—something like a slide that transports a product to the next level
conveyor belt—a machine-operated belt that moves a product from one place to another in the factory
cookbook—a book with many different recipes (instructions) for making meals, snacks, desserts, and more
dies—round disks used for pressing and cutting different shapes of pasta
durum wheat—a hard-grained type of wheat that is grown specifically for making semolina flour
factory—a place where a product is mass-produced
macaroni—another name for pasta (In Italian, macaroni means "Ah my dearest darlings!")
pasta—food made from flour, water, and sometimes eggs (In Italian, it means "paste.")
pasteurization—steam heating food (at 200°F) to kill any bacteria
semolina—rough-textured flour made from ground durum wheat
vegetarians—people who do not eat meat

Investigations for Before Reading

What Is It?

Provide small groups with the "What Is It?" questionnaire to guide group work (see unit appendix) and a variety of shapes, colors, and sizes of dried pasta for investigation, comparison, measuring, and sorting. Save all empty boxes and bags for package investigation.

Investigating New Words

Using a permanent marker write each new word on a piece of uncooked lasagna. Give one word to each small group of students. Their job is to cooperatively find the definitions from any possible source (Siggy, dictionary, empty pasta boxes, cookbooks, supporting library books, etc.). When the group has located and agreed on the correct definition, one person should write the definition on the back of the lasagna and put into a large, empty cooking pot. When all twelve pieces of lasagna have been placed into the pot, invite each group to present their word to the class. Keep the pot accessible to students for future reference in the classroom throughout the week.

Package Investigation

Provide small groups with the "Read the Label!" sheet (see unit appendix) and several empty packages of different brands of pasta to investigate.

Investigate Tools for a Chef

After discussing what a chef does and reading *A Chef* by Douglas Florian, provide groups of children with different kinds of tools and utensils that a chef may use in food preparation. Students should try to name as many as they can and try to guess what they are each used for. Rotate items or students until everyone has had a chance to see and touch each tool. Give groups a copy of *Pots and Pans* by Anne Rockwell to help them identify unfamiliar tools. Afterward, talk about the ideas they had for uses of each tool.

For further extension, invite a local chef to come and speak to the class about the tools and utensils that he or she uses in their kitchen.

Investigations for During Reading

Suggestions for Reading
Siggy's Spaghetti Works

I recommend beginning with reading the story aloud straight through, pausing for questions and taking time to look closely at the illustrations and diagrams. Then guide students in a second reading, followed by students reading aloud together in small groups. Students can take turns reading each smaller section, sidebars, and speech bubbles.

Recipe Investigation

Throughout the unit invite students to explore kids' cookbooks for recipes using pasta. Also, via the parent letter, ask parents to contribute some of their favorite recipes for pasta dishes.

At the end of the unit, compile all of the recipes into one "Pasta Only" cookbook for the class and parents.

How Is It Made?

Ask students to recall the recipe that Siggy gives in the book for making pasta. Then share *Pasta* by Kate Haycock. Ask students to listen for another pasta recipe. Ask them how the two recipes might turn out differently. Then divide the class in half and provide small groups in one half with Siggy's ingredients and the other half with the ingredients from *Pasta*. Discuss differences throughout the mixing. Then roll out the dough and cut it into strips like fettuccine. Compare while rolling, cutting, and after the strips have dried. Put pasta samples in separate Ziploc baggies for each student and refrigerate until the end of the day. Then send the pasta home to be cooked and tasted. Students can report their comparison findings at school the following day. When all data is in, invite students to conclude if one recipe is better than the other.

Wheat to Flour

Provide groups with small amounts of different kinds of flour: regular (bleached), semolina (made from durum wheat), and whole wheat or unbleached. Students should be encouraged to examine each type of flour by sight, touch, smell, taste, and adding water. Ask students to record the things that were the same and the things that were different. Discuss findings with the class.

Afterward, provide each student with a U.S. map and ask them to locate, label, and color some of the durum wheat-farming states in the United States (North Dakota, South Dakota, Minnesota) from page 3. Invite them to do further research to find other wheat-growing states using an encyclopedia and color them a different color on the map.

For further extension, plant and compare different types of wheat. Ask students to save their milk cartons. Provide pairs of students with potting soil and two different kinds of wheat seeds to plant separately. After planting, it should be the students' responsibility to care for the seeds. Each pair should make a little notebook (five to ten sheets of approximately 5-x-7-inch white paper stapled together) to record their observations. Each observation should compare the two seeds/sprouts and include the date and a drawing.

Siggy's Pasta Quiz

Provide small groups with a mixed variety of uncooked pasta from a previous activity. Invite them to sort the pasta according to Siggy's Pasta Quiz (strings, rods, tubes, ribbons, and shapes). After groups have finished sorting,

check to see that all groups agree on the placement of each type of pasta into the different categories.

Afterward, students can create a pasta poster by gluing examples of pasta onto a large piece of tagboard or cardboard. Each piece of pasta should be labeled with its own name and its type (string pasta, rod pasta, etc.). The leftover pasta can be used to create pasta mosaics (see unit appendix).

A Factory Checklist

Invite small groups to look through *Siggy's Spaghetti Works* for things that would be necessary in running a pasta factory. Also, share *Pasta Factory* by Hana Machotka. Make a list on the chalkboard. Share books on different kinds of factories, such as *Cookies* by William Jaspersohn and *Bike Factory* by Harold Roth, and make lists for these types of factories. Then invite students to compare the separate lists and find similarities in each list. Circle everything that was listed for all of the factories. Erase things that were only listed once. Invite small groups or pairs to make a minibook with illustrations about the things that a factory needs to operate.

Siggy's Employee Handbook

In small groups, ask students to look for tips that Siggy offers throughout the book, such as "no gobbling on the job," doing the "spaghetti-legs-rag" to shake off the flour, what to do with leftover U's, walking carefully, and so on, and make a list of these. Students can add their own ideas such as wearing hats and aprons and working hard. There should be a logical accompanying reason for each item on the list. Each group can then turn the list into a book titled "Siggy's Employee Handbook," with tips, suggestions, rules and reasons, and illustrations. To personalize the books, after Siggy's name students could add their own names. For example, "Siggy's and Sara's and Tom's and Susan's Employee Handbook."

Investigations for After Reading

A Package for Siggy

Invite individuals or pairs of students to design a package for any type of Siggy's pasta. Students can use packages from the previous activity for ideas, then cover the boxes with white paper and make a colorfully designed package that would attract customers to buy Siggy's brand. Packages should include some of the information normally found on other brands of pasta.

When the package is complete, ask students to write Siggy a letter explaining why their new package idea would help sell more pasta. Also in the letter, they should inquire about taking a field trip to his factory, saying why our class would like to have a tour, what they would especially like to see, and suggestions for homework.

Plan a Dinner Party

Share *Wednesday Is Spaghetti Day* by Maryann Cocoa-Leffler. In small groups, invite students to imagine that they are to host a dinner for teachers in the school. They need to plan the dinner party, including who will be invited, the number of guests, drinks, food to be served, dessert, serving, and cleaning up. All details of the party should be written in a dinner plan. A sample invitation should accompany the plan with all necessary information, including what is happening, where and when it is happening, and an R.S.V.P.

Rotating Group Investigations

Divide the class into five groups to work on the following. Groups can rotate through the activities. It would be helpful to have adults to work with each group.

Group One

1.) Adult reads *Gino Bandino* by Diana Engel aloud to the group.
2.) Comments and discussion.
3.) Students choose activities.
(These activities could be completed in pairs or independently.)

a. Design a magazine ad or billboard to promote the Bandinos' new pasta.
b. What else could Gino make to "spice up" the boxes of pasta? Draw it or make it with clay.
c. Help Gino's grandmother come up with some ideas for new colors or flavors for their pasta. Write her a letter to tell her your ideas.

Group Two

1.) Adult reads *Strega Nona* by Tomie dePaola to the group.
2.) Students view the nine-minute video of *Strega Nona*.
3.) In pairs or independently, students can compare and contrast the book and the video using a Venn diagram form (poster size for whole group) or some other chart form to illustrate similarities and differences.
4.) Write a letter to Big Anthony with some advice that you would give him.

Group Three

1.) Brainstorm "products" that the group could make in their own factory. Choose one to design in an imaginary factory. An example could be a (paper) car factory where separate workers are responsible for special jobs on an assembly line: body, lights, windows, doors, paint, decals, tires, etc.
2.) Decide on the things and attitudes needed to make the factory run. Use factory books for ideas.
3.) After gathering materials and assigning jobs (each person in the group needs a special job in the assembly line), try operating your factory. Encourage problem solving as problems occur. If no problems occur, adult can create a problem by timing the workers for faster production to meet a deadline.
4.) Each student should write a short summary (a couple sentences) about their group's experience.

Group Four

1.) Read "pasta poetry" (see supporting library).
2.) Use "Recipe for a Hippopotamus Sandwich" from *A Light in the Attic* by Shel Silverstein as a pattern for your own poem such as "Recipe for the Perfect Meatball" or "Recipe for the Biggest Spaghetti Dinner Ever," or write your own creative pasta poem and illustrate it.
3.) Read and compare several recipes (several interesting ones need to be chosen and copied ahead of time for students to examine and compare).
4.) Talk about which ones sound yummy with your group. Make a class graph. Each person votes for their favorite one by placing a sticky note with their name on it next to their choice on a piece of large chart paper.

Group Five

Write and illustrate your own book using one of the following ideas:

1.) Read *Wednesday Is Spaghetti Day* by Maryann Cocoa-Leffler, and use it as a pattern for writing your own story.
2.) Read *From Cotton to Pants* by Ali Mitgutsch, and write a story in a similar style that shows how pasta begins and ends.

Chefs for a Day

Begin by reviewing the job of a chef. Show the pasta preparation portions of the video *Pasta*. Students will be able to see a real chef in action—mixing the ingredients, making the dough and kneading it, flattening it, and cutting it to the desired shape. I do not recommend showing the entire thirty minutes of the video.

Guide each student in making a chef hat for him or herself. Give each student a strip of white construction paper (4 x 18 inches) to measure around their head. Staple twice when it fits and cut off any excess. Then give each student a piece of large white tissue paper. They need to glue the ends of the tissue inside their white strip leaving the middle to puff out like a chef's hat. You may need to model this first.

Once each student has their official chef-for-a-day hat, the cooking area(s) should be cleaned and prepared.

Provide groups with materials: ingredients, measuring cups, rolling pins, cookie cutters, blunt butter knives, cookie sheets for drying, and (hopefully) a manual pasta maker like the one shown on the video. Be sure to have all ingredients and utensils divided and ready to go for each group ahead of time.

Allow students to measure, mix, kneed, and create their own pasta according to one of the previously researched recipes. You might want to allow students to experiment with adding tomatoes, spinach, or lemon for color and taste variety. Cook the chefs' creations and simply serve with butter to taste.

Create a simple sauce recipe. Using a large Crock-Pot, have the children help measure, add ingredients, and taste (with disposable spoons). Let it simmer while you enjoy the aroma.

A Spaghetti Lunch

Give parents plenty of notice and invite them to join you for lunch. Ask for an R.S.V.P. so that you know how many guests will be attending. Make sure you have adequate food and paper goods on hand according to the R.S.V.P.s received. Serve spaghetti with sauce and Parmesan cheese. Heat sauce in one or two Crock-Pots in the classroom so that you can enjoy the aroma as it cooks. Several students could be elected to wear their chef hats and dish the pasta, sauce, and cheese into bowls while the other students act as waiters/waitresses and serve the bowls of spaghetti with napkins and forks. They can wear aprons (white T-shirts tied around their waists) to serve as makeshift uniforms.

Students may wish to provide some entertainment during lunch in the form of silly pasta poems (see supporting library) and/or the song "On Top of Spaghetti" (see unit appendix). Students may also wish to read aloud books written during the unit as a special "author's chair." Be sure to have all student projects on display for parents to enjoy before or after lunch.

Investigate a Pasta Restaurant

Take the class on a delicious field trip to a local restaurant, such as The Olive Garden, where a large variety of pasta is served and where children are welcome. Students will get a chance to read menus, give their orders to a waitress, and pay their own bill. They should also have the opportunity to meet the chef, to see a restaurant pasta maker, and sample various shapes, colors, and sauces for pasta for their lunch. Parents are invited to attend via the parent letter and should be informed at a later date as to how much money to send with their child on the day of the trip.

During the field trip take pictures and develop the film at a one-hour photo lab. Invite students to write text for a class book about the trip.

Other Challenging Ideas to Consider

1.) *Italian Pasta Shop*—Using dried pasta (more durable than fresh) set up a small shop by arranging pasta in baskets or trays. Decide how much to charge for the pasta, considering the money spent on ingredients and the time spent making it. Additional planning questions: How will the shopkeeper wrap the pasta for the customers? Who will be the customers/workers? What else could the shop offer its customers?

2.) *Food! Food! Food!*—Using the timeline book called *FOOD* by Richard Tames, write minireports on the origins of food. Consult other sources for more information. Or find a food that is new and interesting to you in the book, describe it in writing, and illustrate it to display on an "Interesting Foods" bulletin board.

PARENT LETTER

Dear Parents,

Beginning next week, your child will be involved in a deliciously exciting learning adventure using the book *Siggy's Spaghetti Factory* by Peggy Thomson. We will learn about many different varieties of pasta and as "chefs" we will make our own pasta. We will also investigate running a factory and visit a restaurant, as well as plan our own spaghetti lunch where you will be our guests. Keep your eye out for the invitation coming soon but mark you calendars now for our special luncheon on _____ at _____.

Please take a look at the attached "Wanted" sheet to see if you might be able to send any of the supplies we will need for our projects and investigations during the unit.

Also, if you have any delicious pasta recipes that you make for your family and would like to add them to our "Pasta Only" class cookbook, please send us a copy during the next week.

Lastly, we will be taking a field trip to _____ on _____ for lunch. Please sign and return the attached permission slip as soon as possible. We hope you can join us!

Bon appétit!

Mosaic Instructions

Materials
glue
markers
pencils
different sizes and shapes and colors of pasta
sturdy piece of cardboard

1.) Students should think of what they would like to have as a finished product.
2.) Using a pencil, students should draw or sketch their design onto the cardboard if they have a good idea of what they want it to look like.
3.) Students should use a variety of pasta to glue onto their pencil drawing. They can use markers to create new colors to suit their design.
4.) Students should attempt to cover the entire piece of cardboard whether it is an abstract or concrete design.

On Top of Spaghetti

(Sung to the tune of "On Top of Old Smokey")

On top of spaghetti, all covered with cheese,
I lost my poor meatball when somebody sneezed.
It rolled off the table and onto the floor,
And then my poor meatball rolled out of the door.
It rolled in the garden and under a bush,
And then my poor meatball was nothing but mush.
That mush was so tasty, as tasty could be.
Early that summer, it grew into a tree.
The tree was all covered with such lovely moss.
It grew lots of meatballs and tomato sauce.
So if you eat spaghetti all covered with cheese,
Hold onto your meatball and don't ever sneeze.

What Is It?
(Group Questionnaire)

Names:_____

1.) How does it smell? taste? look? feel? _____

_____

2.) What shapes are there? Why are there different colors? _____

_____

3.) Sort them into groups. How many different groups can you make? _____

_____

4.) Measure it with rulers. Sequence the shapes from shortest to longest, widest to skinniest, and so on. _____

_____

5.) Weigh different kinds with a scale. Which types are heaviest? lightest? _____

_____

6.) What kinds do your family eat? Do you know their special names? _____

_____

7.) How do you think the different shapes and colors are made? _____

_____

8.) How do you think it is cooked? Why do you think so?_____

_____

9.) What do you think would happen if you put it in water? Try it. _____

_____

Read the Label!

Names:_____

1.) What are the names of the factories that make the pasta? _____

_____

2.) Where are they? Locate them on the map. How far does pasta travel to our grocery store? (Use the distance scale.) _____

_____

_____

3.) What are the ingredients? Are they all the same? _____

_____

_____

4.) What other information does each box/bag give? _____

_____

5.) Do all of the brands have the same nutritional value? If not, which one seems to be the best?

_____

_____

6.) Which package would you buy? Why? _____

_____

_____

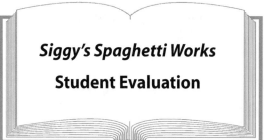

Siggy's Spaghetti Works
Student Evaluation

Name:_____

1.) During the unit, I worked cooperatively with my groups

      not at all   sometimes   most of the time

2.) During the unit, I tried my best

      not at all   sometimes   most of the time

3.) During the unit, I completed

____ a story	____ a letter	____ a new package
____ a poem	____ a labeled map	____ homemade pasta
____ a pasta poster	____ a factory mini book	____ an employee handbook
____ a dinner party plan	____ a factory job	____ a chef's/waiter's job
____ a pasta investigation	____ a package investigation	

4.) Something new that I learned about pasta is:_____

_____

5.) Something new that I learned about preparing food (cooking) is:_____

_____

6.) Something new that I learned about factories is:_____

_____

7.) Something that I worked on that I am especially proud of is:_____

_____

8.) My favorite things about this unit were:_____

_____

SUPPORTING LIBRARY

Bastin, Marjolein. *Vera in the Kitchen*. New York: Barron's Educational Series, 1987.
A little mouse reads cookbooks, makes treats, and eats!

Cocoa-Leffler, Maryann. *Wednesday Is Spaghetti Day*. New York: Scholastic, 1990.
This is the story of Catrina the cat who hosts a spaghetti dinner for all the neighborhood cats while her owners are away.

dePaola, Tomie. *Strega Nona*. New York: Simon & Schuster, 1975.
Strega Nona's helper, Big Anthony, gets into a heap of trouble (of spaghetti, that is) when he uses her magic pot without permission.

Engel, Diana. *Gino Badino*. New York: Morrow Junior Books, 1991.
The littlest member of the family saves the day and his family's pasta factory by creating something out of the ordinary.

Florian, Douglas. *A Chef*. New York: Greenwillow Books, 1992.
The reader spends a day in the life of a chef.

Gelman, Rita. *More Spaghetti I Say*. New York: Scholastic, 1977.
A monkey is too busy to play with her friend because she is doing something very important … eating spaghetti in many unusual ways.

Haycock, Kate. *Pasta*. Minneapolis, Minn.: Carolrhoda Books, 1991.
Describes history, preparations, and recipes for pasta.

Krahn, Fernando. *A Flying Saucer Full of Spaghetti*. New York: E. P. Dutton, 1970.
This is a wordless book that tells the story of how seven little gnomes take a plate of spaghetti from a rich little girl who found spaghetti distasteful and delivered it to a very hungry and appreciative little girl.

Rockwell, Anne. *Pots and Pans*. New York: Macmillan Publishing, 1993.
Two young children show the reader all the pots, pans, and utensils in their kitchen.

Tames, Richard. *FOOD: Feasts, Cooks and Kitchens* (Timelines). New York: Franklin Watts, 1994.
Describes the timeline and evolution of different foods from many different places.

Books About Factories

Jaspersohn, William. *Cookies*. New York: Macmillan Publishing, 1993.
This book takes the reader to a factory in Georgia where Famous Amos chocolate chip cookies are made.

Machotka, Hana. *Pasta Factory*. Boston: Houghton Mifflin, 1992.
Children take a trip to the Tutta Pasta factory in New York City.

Mitgutsch, Ali. *From Cotton to Pants*. Minneapolis, Minn.: Carolrhoda Books, 1977.
One of the books in the series that take the reader from beginning to end in the making of a product.

Roth, Harold. *Bike Factory*. New York: Pantheon Books, 1985.
This book takes the reader to a factory in Massachusetts where Columbia bicycles are made.

Cookbooks for Kids

Ault, Roz. *Kids Are Natural Cooks.* Boston: Houghton Mifflin, 1972.

Lansky, Vicki. *Microwave Cooking for Kids.* New York: Scholastic, 1991.

Moore, Carolyn, Mimi Kerr, and Robert Shulman. *Young Chef's Nutrition Guide and Cookbook.* New York: Barron's Educational Series, 1990.

Poetry

Silverstein, Shel. *A Light in the Attic.* New York: Harper & Row, 1974.
  "Recipe for a Hippopotamus Sandwich" (page 115)
  "Spaghetti" (page 100)

Westcott, Nadine Burnard. *Never Take a Pig to Lunch.* New York: Orchard Books, 1994.
  "How to Eat like a Child" (pages 54 and 55)
  "Lasagna" (page 23)
  "Oodles of Noodles" (page 25)
  "Spaghetti! Spaghetti!" (page 22)

Videos

Pasta (Cooking at the Academy). San Francisco, Calif.: Culinary Academy, 1991.
A chef demonstrates how to make several pasta dishes. 30 minutes.

Strega Nona. Weston, Conn.: Weston Woods, 1978.
The story of *Strega Nona* by Tomie dePaola. 9 minutes.

Stepping Through History: The Mail

Peggy Burns

NEW YORK: THOMSON LEARNING, 1995

ABOUT THE BOOK

Stepping Through History: The Mail by Peggy Burns provides the reader with views into ancient messenger services, the Pony Express and other unusual delivery methods, along with today's multifaceted postal system. The author discusses how stamps and mailboxes came to be, and how they are used today, as well as postal careers of yesterday and today. The book offers an abundance of interesting photographs, drawings, and maps with captions, and concludes with a timeline of postal history.

INVESTIGATIONS

Investigative Themes

World and U.S. History
U.S. Mail Delivery
Postal Careers
Stamps and Collecting (Philately)
Letter Writing

Investigative Skills

writing letters
sorting
using maps
examining
categorizing
making charts
solving problems
acting out
reading for information
working cooperatively

communicating
researching
collecting
comparing/contrasting
listening/speaking
sequencing
defining words
recording
using numbers
making books

Investigative Materials

1 copy of *Stepping Through History: The Mail* for every three students
supporting library books

1 large class mailbox, real or homemade
1-cent stamps, 12 for each group (optional)
cardstock or oaktag to run off postcards
ink pad and and assortment of rubber stamps, 1 for each group
12 paper lunch bags labeled with new words
art scraps (wallpaper, brown paper grocery bags, construction paper, fabric, ribbons, yarn, glitter, wrapping paper, etc.)
glue, rubber cement, tape
index cards
lots of envelopes
a variety of different papers for letter writing
crayons, markers, colored pencils, etc.
visors and mailbags for postal carriers of the day
clay
white construction paper
white bulletin board paper
candles, old crayons, matches
carrots, 1 for every 2 students
large paper clips
several small tubs or trays for soaking envelopes
plain white paper towels
a 3-ring binder for stamp collection
graph paper
assorted mail collected before the unit begins
clean, half-gallon milk cartons
stamps catalog and "Introduction to Stamp Collecting" booklet (both available from the U.S. Post Office)

Note: This unit is well suited for February around Valentine's Day when everyone is thinking about sending and receiving valentines in the mail.

When you are ready to begin the unit, you can help set the mood by hanging all different kinds of things that come in the mail from the ceiling of your classroom. Save your own mail, and ask friends, neighbors, or relatives to save their junk mail too. Use a letter opener to open your mail so that you don't destroy the envelopes. You should also alert your school office to save any interesting packages, stamps, and envelopes for you. Save some of the mail that you collect for an activity later in the unit.

Bring in or make a large mailbox to use as the class mailbox throughout the unit. Visors or homemade hats and "mail delivery" bags for the day's postal carriers would be great too. Also, make sure that you have a copy of all student addresses on hand.

New Words for *Stepping Through History: The Mail*

abroad—overseas; foreign countries
convenient—easy, handy; without much trouble

destination—the ending point of a journey
forge—to make an illegal copy of something
highwayman—a robber on a public road
papyrus—an early kind of paper made from papyrus reeds
perforations—a series of tiny holes made for easy tearing
philately—stamp collecting
postmark—a mark to cancel a stamp and give the place and date of mailing
remote—far back; not near
route—course of travel
valuables—items of value or worth

Investigations for Before Reading

New Words Investigation

Read aloud *The Long, Long Letter* by Elizabeth Spurr and *The Jolly Postman or Other People's Letters* by Janet Ahlberg and Allan Ahlberg for a "jolly" way to get started. Afterward, discuss what makes up addresses, where stamps are placed, and examine postmarks. Divide students into small groups and give them six copies of the "Dear Jolly Postman" reproducible on card stock or oaktag (see unit appendix), scissors, and a list of the twelve new words. Ask them to cut the postcards apart and find definitions for each word using all available resources. Students should "address" the postcards by writing an imaginary address for the Jolly Postman on the lines provided, or the class can create one together. Once all group members agree on each definition, one person can write it on the postcard. Then all group members sign the postcard. When all of the postcards are written, students can design the opposite side. They can also design the stamps, or you may want to provide them with 1-cent stamps for this activity. When complete they should be "mailed" in the class mailbox.

Select several students to be postal workers and sort the "mail" by placing the postcards (according to the word defined on them) in paper lunch bags labeled with the twelve different words. While postal workers are sorting, read *Dear Peter Rabbit* by Alma Flor Ada, and ask students to compare it to *The Jolly Postman*. When the sorting is complete, ask students to rejoin their groups and give each group three or four of the mailbags. Provide them with a copy of the new words with the correct definitions, an ink pad, and a rubber stamp. (The stamp does not need to be "postal related"—a bear, a balloon, or something else will work fine.) As postal workers, their job now is to read the definitions written on each postcard and compare them with the correct definitions. If the group decides that the definitions match, they put a "cancellation stamp" with the rubber stamp over the postage stamp. If the group decides that the definitions do not match, they write "return to sender" on the postcard in pencil and place it back into the class mailbox. Act as postmaster to deliver any returned postcards so that the students in that group can rethink and rewrite their definition. As postmaster, you should oversee the canceled postcards to be sure everyone is doing their job. Once you have checked the postcards, one person in each group could act as the postman to deliver canceled postcards back to their original groups.

Make Your Own Mailbox

Provide or ask each student to bring in an empty, clean, half-gallon milk carton. Invite each student to design the outside of his or her own mailbox using anything they wish: old scraps of fabric, wrapping paper, wallpaper, construction paper, magazine pictures, yarn, glitter, and so on. Once the outside is complete, give each student a half of a 3 x 5 index card. Each student needs to clearly print their name and address on the card. Then with the milk carton standing on its end, glue the address card to the outside. Place all mailboxes along a wall, on a shelf, or on the floor, with address labels showing for easy access.

Write I—Writing a Request

Share the book *Where Does the Mail Go?* by Melvin Berger and Gilda Berger. Review parts of a letter with your students by sharing the book *Messages in the Mailbox* by Loreen Leedy. As a class, design a simple letter to the U.S. Postal Service to ask for the "Introduction to Stamp Collecting" booklet. Each student can copy the letter and include his/her own name and address in order to receive their own copy of the booklet during the unit. Use a stamp from those collected from home via the parent letter. Provide each student with an envelope and the address to print clearly on the front:

U.S. Postal Service
Stamp Services
475 L Enfant Plaza SW
Washington, DC 20260-2439

If there is a convenient corner mailbox in which students can drop their letters, take a little walk to mail the letters. If not, simply take them yourself to the school office or, better yet, to the post office to be sure they are quickly on their way.

Write II—Writing Friendly Letters

Share *Dear Annie* by Judith Caseley and *Dear Fred* by Susanna Rodell. These will give students examples of what to write about in friendly letters. Afterward, discuss other topics that would be good to write about in such a letter. If needed, refer again to *Messages in the Mailbox* by Loreen Leedy. Next, invite students to write a friendly letter to a classmate. Each student should write to the person whose mailbox is to the right of theirs in the row of per-

sonal mailboxes. Provide plenty of different kinds of paper on which to write the letters and provide the envelopes to put the letters in. Pictures and designs can be optional if time permits. The envelopes should have complete mailing addresses and postage stamps. Stamps can be hand drawn or cut out from the stamps catalog from the post office. All letters should be mailed in the class mailbox to be postmarked and mailed by that day's postal carriers. I suggest that each day throughout the unit, every student writes to another (different) student. To ensure that each student receives at least one letter per day, continue using the names in the row of milk carton mailboxes. For example, on the second day, each student writes to the name two boxes to the right of theirs, on the third day, each student writes to the name three boxes to the right, and so on. If time allows, encourage students to write additional letters to classmates of their choosing after they have written to their assigned name.

Write III—More Friendly Letters

To provide students with more modeling of correct format and examples of adequate friendly letters, ask adults in your school to participate in a weekly letter-writing exchange. You may find willing adults in parents, previous teachers, office or kitchen staff, or custodians. You can use the Letter of Inquiry to invite them to participate (see unit appendix). Provide plenty of different kinds of paper for writing and envelopes for addressing and mailing. Letters received should be dropped off in the classroom mailbox and then delivered in personal mailboxes by the postal carriers of the day or week.

If you are unable to enlist willing adults, choose another class in your school with the same number of students to exchange letters with. Students can choose or be assigned a pen pal.

If you and the students wish, these activities could continue beyond the mail unit for as long as interest and participation remains strong. You may also want to plan a special event for the pen pals to get together to either kick off or conclude this activity.

Investigations for During Reading

Suggestions for Reading
Stepping Through History: The Mail

I recommend that the reading be done out loud, alternating between you reading aloud to the whole class and your students reading with others in their groups. Within each section, group members can take turns reading the beginning bold-type text, the main text, and the captions. They can switch parts before beginning the next group-read section.

I also recommend a second reading after the entire book has been read. For this reading students can choose their group members and the sections that they wish to reread. I suggest that they choose at least six sections to read with their group on the basis of interest and/or further understanding.

Unique Mailbox Show-and-Tell

After reading "Goodbye Forever" and looking at the assortment of mailboxes in the photograph on page 5, invite students to search their homes for something that could be used for a mailbox. Brainstorm the characteristics or attributes that make up a mailbox. Make an attribute chart, copy it, and send it home with students. Within those guidelines anything goes. Ask students to present their unique mailbox to the class, explaining how and where it could be placed for easy access by their postal carrier. They should also explain how the postal carrier would know that it was their mailbox and why they believe it would make a good mailbox.

The Message Game

To illustrate pre–letter-writing times and how messages by word-of-mouth sometimes got mixed up, play the classic message game. Students should sit in a circle. Make up a message and whisper it into the ear of one student. Once a message is spoken, it cannot be repeated for the listener. The listener must pass on what they heard by whispering it to the person next to

them. I suggest playing this game with some background noise such as a noisy playground or a radio playing so that they cannot eavesdrop.

Creating Clay Letters

After reading "How the Mails Began," invite students to experiment with writing their own clay letters. Provide each student with soft clay to form a letter and an envelope for the letter to go inside. Challenge students to find utensils in the classroom that could be used for writing in the clay. Then have each student choose a partner, write a note to them in the clay, and deliver the letter to them. Afterward, discuss the drawbacks to this letter-writing and delivery system.

Benjamin Franklin Investigation

After reading the "Royal Mail" section, share chapter 2 of Mail Call! by Nancy O'Keefe Bolick, entitled "Benjamin Franklin: Father of the U.S. Postal Service" to learn more about Ben Franklin and the U.S. Post Office. While you are reading aloud ask students to listen carefully and write down the things that Ben Franklin did to improve postal services and the positions that he held. Afterward, ask students to share what they have written and record it on the chalkboard. Turn these facts into a class book entitled "I'll Bet You Didn't Know That About Ben Franklin." To make it a predictable book add the title sentence after each fact written on each page.

Moving the Mail

After reading the sections "Mail on the Move" and "International Mail" ask small groups of students to design arrow charts that illustrate the increasing speed with which mail has moved from ancient history to the present day. Students will draw pictures on the arrow itself. They should begin by drawing and cutting a large and long arrow shape from white bulletin board paper. Then, starting from the blunt end of the arrow, they should show mail being carried on foot, followed by a single rider on horseback, a mail coach, a mail train, a sailing ship, a steamship, and, lastly, an airplane. (See illustration below.) Remind students to draw in pencil first to make sure they will have enough room to put the airplane in the point of the arrow. All illustrations should be labeled with smaller arrows separating each one. Color should be optional.

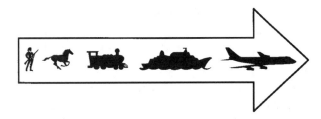

Extend this activity by sharing the book *Hail to Mail* by Samuel Marshak. This book illustrates that mail is still moved by some of the methods in their arrow charts depending upon where it is traveling. After reading this book aloud, attach pieces of yarn with sticky stuff to a large world map to show the path that John Peck's letter took as it followed him around the world. Later, invite students to attach little pictures over the yarn to show how the letter traveled (by train, by ship, by plane, etc.).

Design Your Own Postage Stamp

Share sections of *Stamps! A Young Collector's Guide* by Brenda Ralph Lewis entitled "What Stamps Tell You" (page 24), "Why Stamps Are Issued" (page 35), "Stamps with Messages" (page 64), and "Parts of a Stamp" (page 92). Provide each student with a piece of white construction paper (8 x 12 inches) and challenge them to design an oversized stamp (using the whole piece of paper) that tells about something important to them and that could be used in our country. Each stamp must include the parts mentioned in "Parts of a Stamp." Model how to cut scalloped edges to resemble the perforated edges of a real stamp. Hang them

proudly for display when completed. At the completion of the unit you may wish to send one or two with parent permission to the U.S. Postal Service, Stamp Services, 475 L Enfant Plaza SW, Washington, DC 20260-2439. Who knows, one of your students may have designed the next U.S. postage stamp!

Investigate Envelope Information

Provide small groups of students with several pieces of mail (collected prior to the unit's beginning) and the investigation sheet "Where Is It Going? Where Has It Been?" (see unit appendix). Invite students to examine closely the different pieces of mail and record the information for each piece.

Old-Fashioned Seals Investigation

As per the picture caption on page 18, before there were envelopes, wax was used to seal a letter before mailing it. Students can try this with one of the letters they send to a classmate. This can be done in pairs or groups of three with close supervision. I suggest inviting parents or other adults to help supervise. After the letters are written and ready to send, fold the letter business-style so that the wax can be dripped onto the open flap. Before melting the wax, give each student half of a carrot and a paper clip. Ask students to use the paper clip to carve their initial (reversed so that the letter will appear correctly when printed) into the flat end of the carrot. This will form a stamp to be pressed into the hot wax to identify the sender of the letter. (In olden days, monogram stamps were made of metal.) Provide each group with a candle, several old crayons, and matches. Then, using lighted candles, melt the crayons so that they drip a blob of colored wax onto the paper. Wait about thirty seconds for the wax to set, then press the monogrammed carrot firmly into the wax. The seal is made when the wax cools and hardens.

This activity can be further extended by providing old-fashioned quill pens and ink (calligraphy pens will work) to do the writing of the letter to be sealed.

Apply to Ride for the Pony Express

After reading the "Pony Express" section, share *Special Delivery* by Betty Brandt, particularly pages 13–16 about the pony express.

Also share *The Pony Express* by Steven Kroll. Then provide each student with an application for the job of pony express rider (see unit appendix).

Investigations for After Reading

A Visit with a Postal Carrier

Invite the postal carrier who brings the mail to your school to speak to the students about his or her job, using the Letter of Invite in the unit appendix. Before his or her arrival, share the book *Red-Letter Day* by Patricia Lakin to learn more about the duties of a postal carrier and to generate possible questions for your guest. Make sure to follow up with a class thank-you note afterward.

Postman Appreciation Day

Share the books *Grace and Joe* by Maribeth Boelts, *Good-bye, Curtis* by Kevin Henkes, *Katie Morag Delivers the Mail* by Mairi Hedderwick, and *No Mail For Mitchell* by Catherine Siracusa about special mail carriers. Ask students to write appreciation notes to the person who delivers the mail to their house. If they do not know the name of their mail carrier, they can call their local post office and ask.

What If Your Mail Could Talk?

Share the poem "Summer Mail" from the book *The Country Mail Is Coming* by Max Fatchen. Invite students to create their own stories or poems with letters as main characters.

Field Trip to the Post Office

Plan a trip to the nearest major post office (with machines that postmark and sort) to see mail in motion. Before the visit, share several books that tell about what students might see there such as *Postal Workers A to Z* by Jean Johnson, *A Visit to the Post Office* by Sandra Ziegler, *Here Comes the Mail* by Gloria Skurzynski, *Where Does the Mail Go?* by Melvin Berger and Gilda Berger, *The Post Office Book* by Gail Gibbons, and *What's It Like to Be a ... Postal Worker?* by Morgan Matthews. Because these books contain similar information, students could read different books aloud in small groups and then return to the large group to share something new that they learned from the book that they read. Also, challenge students to count how many times the mail is sorted by person or machine in their book.

Following the field trip, invite students to choose between the following activities:

A.) Create minibooks of postal workers, showing the different jobs that can be done in the postal service.

B.) Create a flowchart showing an example of how a letter is moved and sorted in the U.S. postal system.

Write IV

Invite students to write to a celebrity, athlete, or government official from *The Kid's Address Book* by Michael Levine. Be sure to share the "Author's Note to Kids" before students begin their writing. Also, see *Free Stuff for Kids* by Bruce Lansky. Provide two envelopes and two stamps (from those donated by each parent via the parent letter) for each student and take a class walk, if you can, to mail the letters.

Collection Investigation

Read "What Shall I Collect?" (page 14), "Mint or Used?" (page 22), and "Famous Collectors" (page 28) from *Stamps! A Young Collector's Guide* by Brenda Ralph Lewis. Begin a class stamp collection, asking each student to bring in a stamped envelope from home. Remove stamps from white- or light-colored envelopes as follows:

1.) Place envelope stamp side down in a tub of warm water.

2.) Wait until the stamp floats by itself.

3.) Carefully remove stamp from water.

4.) Gently hold the stamp under cool running water to remove any excess glue.

5.) Place wet stamps on a piece of white paper to dry for ten to fifteen minutes.

6.) Place stamp between two layers of clean, white paper towels.

7.) Put the paper towels between two heavy books.

As a class, discuss the different stamps that the students have provided. What do they represent? How much are they worth? What message do they send? Which stamps go together and why? Mount the stamps in a collection notebook filled with graph paper to help put the stamps on straight. Serious stamp collectors use hinges to mount stamps, which are available at a hobby store; however, you may elect to use bits of two-sided tape or even rubber cement for this collection. Mount only on the front side of each page to avoid any pages and/or stamps sticking together. Students may wish to print their name under the stamp that they contributed.

For students who are interested in further information they can write (and enclose a self-addressed stamped envelope) to:

Junior Philatelists of America
P.O. Box 850
Boalsburg, PA 16827-0850

Mail Yourself!

Listen to the sound recording of "Mail Myself to You" (written by Woody Guthrie, recorded by John McCutchen). In small groups, students can choose between the following activities:

A.) Make a book by illustrating the lyrics of the song; remind students to make sure that they acknowledge Woody Guthrie as the author and themselves as the illustrator. Also, encourage students to mail the book to a person they don't get to see very often.

B.) Act out the lyrics of the song for the class; use props such as paper, ribbon, glue, large homemade stamps, and so on.

PARENT LETTER

Dear Parents,

We will soon begin an amazing investigation into the postal service of yesterday and today using the book *Stepping Through History: The Mail* by Peggy Burns. We will learn about mail delivery methods of long ago and how mail moves in today's more efficient postal system. Your child will write several letters during this unit that we will actually mail. For this, we are requesting that you send three postage stamps to school to be used for mailing your child's letters.

We will visit the _____ post office on _____ and talk with postal workers about their careers. We would love to have you join us. Look for the permission slip coming your way soon. Please sign and return it as soon as possible.

In the meantime, if it's possible for you to save some of the mail that comes in your mailbox for our inspection during the unit, we will examine the stamps, the postmarks, and the addresses, as well as the size, shape, and type of mail. We are especially interested in any unusual or interesting stamps that come on your envelopes to add to our new stamp collection. We will remove the stamps from the envelopes ourselves. We do not need the contents of any of the mail itself. Send any mail that you can donate to school with your child starting next week. Also, please see the attached "Wanted" sheet for any other items that you might be able to send from home to help with our mail projects.

Lastly, we would greatly appreciate several parents to join us in making old-fashioned letter seals of melted wax on _____at _____ . Please let me know if you can help out. Thanks so much!

Speedy delivery!

Where Is It Going? Where Has It Been?

Names:_____

Directions: Inspect the mail with your group. For each piece, locate the following information and record it on this page.

1.) Where is it going? (mailing address) _____

_____

2.) Who received it? (name on the address) _____

3.) Where did it come from? (return address) _____

_____

4.) Who sent it? (name on return address) _____

5.) Where was it postmarked? _____

6.) When was it postmarked? _____

7.) How much did it cost to mail it? _____

8.) Is there a bar code? If there is, draw it here:

9.) What is special or unusual about this piece of mail? _____

_____

_____

Letter of Inquiry

Date _____

Dear _____,

    Our class is beginning to learn about postal history, mail delivery, and letter writing. We will be writing many letters to all kinds of different people and places. I was wondering if you might be willing to participate in a weekly letter exchange with me during this unit. We would write approximately three letters to one another. Please mark yes or no on the bottom of this letter. If your answer is yes, I will write a letter to you first, then you can write a letter back to me within a few days. Please deliver letters to me to our classroom mailbox. If your answer is no, I will understand. Thanks!

Sincerely,

(name of student) _____

(room number or class) _____

_____Yes, I will participate

_____ No, I cannot participate

Application for the Pony Express

Name:_____

Address:_____

_____

Previous experience _____

_____

Age (circle one)   Under 18   Over 18

How many miles can you ride? (circle one)

20–30 miles   40–50 miles   75–100 miles

How do you like to ride your horse? (circle one)

slow   fast   very fast

What is your approximate weight? (circle one)

under 120 lbs.   over 120 lbs.

What would you carry the mail in? _____

What would you do if you came across hostile Indians? _____

_____

What would you do if it begins to rain? _____

_____

What would you do if robbers tried to steal the mail? _____

_____

Any other special skills that would make you a good pony express rider:_____

_____

Dear Jolly Postman,

Did you know that
the word _____
means _____
_____
_____
_____

Now you know!

From, _____

To: The Jolly Postman

_____
_____
_____

Dear Jolly Postman,

Did you know that
the word _____
means _____
_____
_____
_____

Now you know!

From, _____

To: The Jolly Postman

_____
_____
_____

Letter of Invite

Date _____

Dear _____,

We will soon be studying the U.S. Postal Service of yesterday and today. We would be honored if you would visit our classroom to briefly speak to the students about your job as mail carrier. We were hoping that you could also bring any equipment that you use each day that would help us understand your job more completely. We understand that you have a busy delivery schedule, so we would like to invite you at your convenience during the week of _____. I will contact you soon and, if you are willing and able to join us, we will discuss the exact time and place. Thank you.

Sincerely,

Stepping Through History:
The Mail
Student Evaluation

Name: _____

1.) During the unit, I worked cooperatively with my groups

      not at all   sometimes   most of the time

2.) During the unit, I tried my best

      not at all   sometimes   most of the time

3.) During the unit, I completed

____ a mail investigation   ____ a postcard   ____ a letter of request

____ a mailbox   ____ two friendly letters ____ a clay letter

____ an arrow chart   ____ a book   ____ a poem or story

____ a thank-you note   ____ a seal

____ a pony express application

____ a Ben Franklin class book

____ a contribution to the class stamp collection

4.) Something new that I learned about mail is: _____

_____

5.) Something new that I learned about postal workers is: _____

_____

6.) Something new that I learned about stamps is: _____

_____

7.) Something that I worked on that I am especially proud of is: _____

_____

8.) My favorite things about this unit were: _____

_____

SUPPORTING LIBRARY

Ada, Alma Flor. *Dear Peter Rabbit*. New York: Atheneum, 1994.
A story of friendly letters written to several make-believe characters including Peter Rabbit, Goldilocks, and the Three Pigs.

Ahlberg, Janet, and Allan Ahlberg. *The Jolly Pocket Postman*. Boston: Little, Brown, 1995.
A sequel to *The Jolly Postman or Other People's Letters*.

Ahlberg, Janet, and Allan Ahlberg. *The Jolly Postman or Other People's Letters*. Boston: Little, Brown, 1986.
A collection of a postman's deliveries to make-believe characters, with pullout letters, postcards, and so on.

Baker, Keith. *The Dove's Letter*. New York: Harcourt Brace, 1988.
A dove delivers a special letter to many people she meets along her way.

Berger, Melvin, and Gilda Berger. *Where Does the Mail Go?* (Discovery Readers). Nashville, Tenn.: Ideals Children's Books, 1994.
Follows a letter to the U.S. Postal Service stamp collection department.

Boelts, Maribeth. *Grace and Joe*. Morton Grove, Ill.: Albert Whitman, 1994.
A preschooler finds a friend in her neighborhood mail carrier.

Bolick, Nancy O'Keefe. *Mail Call!* New York: Franklin Watts, 1994.
An in-depth look at the history of the U.S. Postal Service.

Brandt, Betty. *Special Delivery*. Minneapolis, Minn.: Carolrhoda Books, 1988.
Describes the history of the U.S. Postal Service.

Briggs, Michael. *Stamps* (Hobby Handbooks). New York: Random House, 1993.
An in-depth look at collecting stamps as a hobby.

Caseley, Judith. *Dear Annie*. New York: Greenwillow Books, 1991.
A story about the letter exchange between Annie and her grandfather.

Fatchen, Max. *The Country Mail Is Coming*. Boston: Little, Brown, 1987.
Poems from "down under," including "Summer Mail" about letters who talk to each other.

Gibbons, Gail. *The Post Office Book: Mail and How It Moves*. New York: Thomas Y. Crowell, 1982.
Describes how mail reaches its destinations. Easy reading.

Granger, Neill. *Stamp Collecting*. Brookfield, Conn.: Millbrook Press, 1994.
Provides information about the history of stamps, what to look for as a collector, and how to get started.

Hedderwick, Mairi. *Katie Morag Delivers the Mail*. Boston: Little, Brown, 1984.
The story of a young girl who gets the royal mail a bit mixed up.

Henkes, Kevin. *Good-bye, Curtis*. New York: Greenwillow Books, 1995.
Everyone in the neighborhood says good-bye to their beloved mail carrier who is retiring.

Henri, Adrian. *The Postman's Palace.* New York: Atheneum, 1990.
Based on the real story of a postman who single-handedly built a palace in France.

Jacobsen, Karen. *Stamps* (A New True Book). Chicago: Childrens Press, 1983.
An easy-to-read beginner's guide to collecting stamps.

Johnson, Jean. *Postal Workers A to Z.* New York: Walker, 1987.
An alphabet book of terms, tools, and jobs within the postal system.

Kroll, Steven. *The Pony Express.* New York: Scholastic, 1996.
Discusses the eighteen-month history of the pony express.

Lakin, Patricia. *Red-Letter Day* (My Community Series). Austin, Tex.: Raintree/Steck-Vaughn, 1995.
A mail carrier shows the reader the different parts and jobs of the post as she delivers the mail.

Lansky, Bruce. *Free Stuff for Kids.* New York: Meadowbrook Press, 1996.
Lists a variety of things that kids can send away for, for free or up to $1.00. Also provides a section on how to write requests. Updated yearly.

Leedy, Loreen. *Messages in the Mailbox.* New York: Holiday House, 1991.
Mrs. Gator explains how to write, address, and send all kinds of correspondence.

Levine, Michael. *The Kid's Address Book.* New York: A Perigee Book, Berkley Publishing Group, 1994.
Provides more than 2,000 addresses for athletes, celebrities, TV shows, clubs, and government officials.

Levinson, Nancy Smiler. *Snowshoe Thompson.* New York: HarperCollins, 1992.
A brave man on skis delivers mail across the Sierra Nevadas.

Lewis, Brenda Ralph. *Stamps! A Young Collector's Guide.* New York: Lodestar Books, 1990.
Provides information on stamps, what they mean, how they're used, how to collect them, and more.

Marshak, Samuel. *Hail to Mail.* New York: Henry Holt, 1990.
A certified letter follows John Peck all over the world and back.

Matthews, Morgan. *What's It Like to Be a … Postal Worker?* Mahwah, N.J.: Troll Associates, 1990.
Describes the different jobs that are part of the postal system as a letter makes its way to a pen pal.

McCutchen, John. *Mail Myself to You.* Cambridge, Mass.: Rounder Records, 1988.
Sound recording (CD) of twelve songs for children, including "I'm Gonna Mail Myself to You" by Woody Guthrie.

Rodell, Susanna. *Dear Fred.* New York: Ticknor & Fields Books for Young Readers, 1995.
A young mouse writes a letter to her half brother in Australia.

Rylant, Cynthia. *Mr. Griggs' Work.* New York: Orchard Books, 1988.
Mr. Griggs the postman loves his work and thinks about it all the time.

Siracusa, Catherine. *No Mail for Mitchell.* New York: Random House, 1990.
A very easy-to-read book about a mailman who wants to receive some mail for a change.

Skurzynski, Gloria. *Here Comes the Mail.* New York: Bradbury Press, 1992.
The reader follows the route a letter takes in the postal system when Stephanie sends a picture to her cousin.

Spurr, Elizabeth . *The Long, Long Letter.* New York: Hyperion Books for Children, 1996.
Aunt Hetta finally gets the long letter she is waiting for.

Ziegler, Sandra. *A Visit to the Post Office.* Chicago: Childrens Press, 1989.
A class takes a trip to the post office to mail their valentines and finds out what goes on inside.

Pioneers
A Library of Congress Book
Martin W. Sandler
NEW YORK: HARPERCOLLINS, 1994

ABOUT THE BOOK

Pioneers is rich with the history of some of the bravest and strongest people who ever lived in America. It illustrates what it was like for a pioneer family to journey westward, the challenges and hardships they faced, and the new lives they built together. It speaks of the events and the people, including Native Americans, lumberjacks, miners, farmers, cowboys, legendary heroes, and others who have shaped our country's history. *Pioneers* tells the story of adventure, sacrifice, and reward in making dreams into reality.

INVESTIGATIONS

Investigative Themes

Pioneer Life
Cowboys
Native Americans
Tall Tales and Heroes
The Gold Rush
Frontier Women
Farming

Investigative Skills

writing creatively
reading for information
comparing/contrasting
working cooperatively
making books
making lists
writing letters

thinking critically
using maps
problem solving
speaking
planning
creating charts and diagrams
making decisions

sequencing
brainstorming
following directions
using weights

following a recipe
using numbers
measuring

Investigative Materials

1 copy of *Pioneers* for every three students
supporting library books

glue, markers, crayons
butcher/chart paper
U.S. maps (see Main Appendix) with transparency of same
overhead projector
large wall map of the United States
laundry baskets, gallon jugs, shoe boxes, crates, blankets, tape/string for packing the
    wagon in section 3
thread, needles, fabric scraps, scissors, batting, back fabric, and sewing machine for quilting
    bee
Recipe ingredients, cooking utensils, and oven for cooking in section 6
old-fashioned pitcher and bowl with towels for washing up
gold spray paint, pebbles, rocks, sand, water, large tub, metal pie dishes, scale with weights,
    plastic drop cloth, and towels for panning for gold in section 2
gardening tools (shovel, rake, watering can, hoe, etc.), pencils or sticks, small tagboard
    squares, small freezer bags, seeds, planters or a planting area for the planting season
foods with seeds for dissecting—pumpkins, squash, peas, etc. in section 6
necessary supplies, materials, and refreshments for the fair activities planned, including
    tables and display boards for children's work
small sturdy boards, chalkboard paint or slick board Contac paper, chalk or erasable mark-
    ers, old (clean) socks for erasing
candle-making supplies—paraffin (1 pound will make 3 or 4 candles), 12-inch
    wicking for each student, old crayons, 2 to 4 burners, 2 to 4 large coffee cans, hot
    pads/oven mitts, clothesline, and clothespins

New Words for *Pioneers*

agriculture—the production of crops, livestock, or poultry
Conestoga—the name for the covered wagons used in the early westward migration
contradiction—opposite thoughts or words
crops—produce grown from the ground
essential—absolutely necessary and important
frontier—the farthest limit of a country's settled regions
independence—the freedom to explore new opportunities
inspiration—an encouraging influence
legendary—famous by the telling of unprovable and often exaggerated stories
lumberjack—one who cuts and splits timber for market

missionary—one who is sent to preach religion
pioneer—one who first enters or settles a region
prairie—large grassy rolling land
sacrifice—giving up something of value for the sake of something else
territories—large pieces of land
wilderness—uninhabited, untamed regions; in a natural state

Investigations for Before Reading

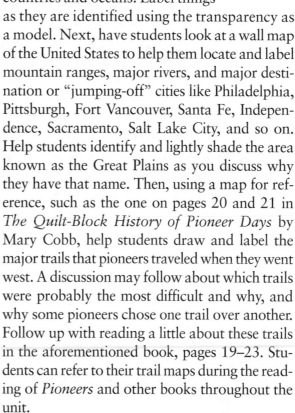

Investigating New Words

Provide groups of students with sixteen copies of the Conestoga wagons and ask them to print one word on each wagon. Then give each group the page of definitions on wagon wheels (see page 144). By using all available resources students should cooperatively decide which wheels should be glued onto which wagons. When all groups have finished, discuss words as a whole class and collect one wagon for each of the sixteen words to hitch together and display in a visible place in the classroom. You could also ask each group to cooperatively create sentences for the words as each one is discussed. Coloring could be an option for groups who finish early.

Hero Investigation

After reading Martin Sandler's introduction in *Pioneers,* invite the whole class to brainstorm characteristics of heroes or heroines. Write these words on chart paper to create a "hero web" that can be added to throughout the unit.

Map Investigation

Provide each student with a copy of a U.S. map (see Main Appendix). Using a transparency of the same map on an overhead projector, invite students to identify bordering countries and oceans. Label things as they are identified using the transparency as a model. Next, have students look at a wall map of the United States to help them locate and label mountain ranges, major rivers, and major destination or "jumping-off" cities like Philadelphia, Pittsburgh, Fort Vancouver, Santa Fe, Independence, Sacramento, Salt Lake City, and so on. Help students identify and lightly shade the area known as the Great Plains as you discuss why they have that name. Then, using a map for reference, such as the one on pages 20 and 21 in *The Quilt-Block History of Pioneer Days* by Mary Cobb, help students draw and label the major trails that pioneers traveled when they went west. A discussion may follow about which trails were probably the most difficult and why, and why some pioneers chose one trail over another. Follow up with reading a little about these trails in the aforementioned book, pages 19–23. Students can refer to their trail maps during the reading of *Pioneers* and other books throughout the unit.

For further extension of this activity, challenge students to create a distance scale for their map.

Investigations for During Reading

Suggestions for Reading Pioneers

I recommend using a variety of strategies while reading *Pioneers* due primarily to the length of the text. I would begin reading the first section "Westward Ho!" together to maximize opportunities for discussion and set the tone for the rest of the book. Then, depending on the skill level of your students and the time you wish to devote to each section, you could rotate between having students read aloud in small groups, with a partner, or with you in small groups. You may also choose to continue with guided reading aloud throughout the book or just for the longer sections.

I also suggest reading from *The Way West* by Amelia Stewart Knight at the beginning of each day of the unit. This book has forty-eight entries that tell the story of one pioneer family's journey west. You can break up the readings according to the time you want to spend on the unit.

As an ongoing project during reading, have students look for and complete pages for a "Pioneer People Book" using the pattern found in the unit appendix. Students should include people such as lumberjacks, hunters, trappers, missionaries, trailblazers, trail guides, cowboys, miners, pony express riders, farmers, and so on.

In addition, students can work on the Pioneer Math sheet (see unit appendix) throughout their reading.

Section 1 … Westward Ho! (pages 6–19)

Read together or read aloud to students as an introduction, inviting their comments and questions. After a general discussion, this is the perfect time to introduce the concept of tall tales, stories that often became exaggerated as they were passed on by word-of-mouth. I have suggested several collections of tall tales along with specific tall-tale books and videos (see supporting library). These resources can be used in a variety of ways.

A.) They can be used to exemplify the literary style of tall tales with the idea that students will write their own original tall tales.
B.) They can be used to compare and contrast between two different book versions. See the Compare/Contrast Report in Main Appendix.
C.) They can be used to compare and contrast between book versions and video versions.
D.) They can be used for simple enjoyment as examples of the "bigger-than-life" kinds of stories that were told in the wagon circles and beyond.

Create a large Venn diagram (see Main Appendix) on the chalkboard showing the simi-larities and differences between the pioneers and the pilgrims.

Section 2 … Off to the Far West (pages 20–25)

After reading this section share a story about the gold rush such as *Treasure in the Stream* by Dorothy Hoobler or *The Bite of the Gold Bug* by Barthe DeClements.

Set up a "panning claim" in the classroom for students to test their gold-finding skills. Using tiny gold spray-painted pebbles and spray-painted nuts, bolts, and washers mixed with sand, rocks, and water in a large tub, let students use metal pie plates to pan for the gold pebbles. Use a plastic drop cloth underneath the tub, and provide towels for drying hands. Also, provide a clear plastic container for students to collect their "nuggets" in and a scale with weights to weigh their findings. Students should return the gold pebbles to the tub when they are through panning so that the next student can strike it rich.

This would be an appropriate time to examine the Plains Indians of yesterday and today, including their history with white people, by sharing books such as *Indians of the Great Plains* by Karen Harvey and *Plains Indians* by Kate Petty. I have also suggested a video collection (see supporting library) for older students that adequately addresses the lives of Native Americans today. As the discussions about the white man's injustices to the Native Americans may bring about strong emotions in children, it may be important to provide an outlet for these emotions. This could be done by having them write a short essay that simply tells how they feel. Or it could take the form of a letter to one of the great Indian chiefs mentioned in the books or videos.

Section 3 … Leaving for a New Land (pages 26–35)

After reading this section students can discuss with a partner the things that they would choose to bring along on a move to the West. Then, using string or tape, section off the amount of space that would be available to them in a typical covered wagon. Students can experience how much space would be available to them considering the wagon would be carrying a family of five or six people, possibly a family pet, and supplies for the journey. Use students themselves to take up body space. Give them laundry baskets to take up space for food and plastic gallon containers to take up space for water and blankets that would be used for sleeping. Ask students if they can think of other essential items that a family of five or six might need on the journey (first aid? extra clothes? food for pets and livestock? tools for cooking? tools for wagon maintenance? firearms? etc.). For each item, include a crate or shoe boxes to take up space. After most of the space is filled up ask students to reevaluate the treasured items they thought they might bring. Ask each student to think of one thing that they absolutely could not do without that would fit in the remaining space in the wagon. The following day, they can share either orally or "show-and-tell" style, describing the item and why it would be essential to them.

Follow this activity by sharing the story *Wagon Train* by Courtni C. Wright or *Dandelions* by Eve Bunting.

Section 4 ... By Stagecoach, Boat, and Train (pages 36–43)

After reading this section and discussing the advantages of utilizing new inventions students can design advertisements for one of the three modes of transportation discussed. In pairs or small groups, students should think of at least one reason why one mode might be more ap-

pealing than another. They should name their transportation company, state the advantage of traveling with them, state the price, the number of days in a journey, and where the journey would end. They should try to make their advertisement as appealing and "eye-catching" as possible. Some ideas might be to create the shape of the chosen mode, use fancy print, or use beautiful colors.

Section 5 ... The American Cowboy (pages 44–49)

After reading this section share a couple books specifically about cowboys such as *Cowboy Country* by Ann Herbert Scott and *Jack Creek Cowboy* by Neil Johnson. Follow these books by providing each student with a Cowpuncher Application (see unit appendix).

Section 6 ... The Frontier Family (pages 50–59)

After reading this section share a story of a pioneer farm family such as *My Prairie Year* by Brett Harvey. Then ask students in small groups to discuss and make a chart of the endless jobs and the hardships that a pioneer family must endure in order to survive on the plains (see example below). Also, write on the chart how the jobs or hardships would be different for today's plains farmers.

Students can then take pieces of this information and, with a partner or independently, create a book depicting all of the hardships that a pioneer family might have had to endure to find a home and farm the land. They could come up with creative titles such as "Nature's

	For yesterday's pioneers	For today's farmers
jobs/chores		
hardships		

Setbacks" or "Pioneer Challenges" or "What Else Could Go Wrong." Their book may (or may not) include a final page or two that would describe if and how these hardships exist for today's plains farmers.

On the following day, or perhaps the same day if time allows, read aloud a few sections of *A Child's Day* by Bobbie Kalman to help children try to imagine what it was like to grow up in a pioneer family. Then invite students to make their own picture book that shows what pioneer children did with their time, including chores, school, and recreation.

Another activity to add to the farming flavor is to provide students with foods that were important to pioneers such as corn, squash, pumpkins, and peas. In groups, have students "dissect" each food and find the seeds. The seeds should then be laid out to dry for "planting season" later in the unit.

This would also be an excellent time to do a little cooking with the children. With parent helpers and several batches of materials, students can work in groups and be more participatory. A recipe for corn bread muffins, commonly served at pioneer meals, can be found in the unit appendix. Or you could use the recipe for fried apples and onions on page 11 in *A Child's Day* by Bobbie Kalman or the recipe for Succotash on page 49 in *The Quilt-Block History of Pioneer Days* by Mary Cobb. As an added pioneer attraction provide several bowls and pitchers with small towels for students to use to "wash up" before eating.

Section 7 ... Women on the Frontier (pages 60–63)

After reading this section share a couple more books about women on the frontier such as *Warm as Wool* by Scott Russell Sanders. Ask students to think about the women they know and consider the courage and strength that it took to be a pioneer woman. Provide each student with a copy of the "Pioneer Courage Ribbon" (see unit appendix) to cut out, color, and present to a woman in their life that they think would have made a good pioneer woman.

Because sewing was primarily woman's work, this would be a great opportunity to introduce quilting using the book *The Quilt-Block History of Pioneer Days* by Mary Cobb. You may choose to read sections of this book aloud, particularly the "Quilts and History" section, to provide students with general background, or you may choose to read the entire book as it has a great deal to offer on the subject of pioneer life. You could then select one or several of the reproducible quilting activities to offer to students.

As a class, brainstorm and make a list of all of the jobs that women were responsible for on the prairie farm. Students could use *Pioneers* to refer to or one of the books on frontier women such as *Buffalo Gals* by Brandon Marie Miller for further ideas. Each student could then select a job and illustrate it on a square piece of paper. For larger classes, some students will have to select the same jobs. Then the squares can be assembled quilt-style onto a large piece of colored bulletin board paper. Students may want to add blank squares of color, a title for the quilt, a date, or other decorations. The quilt should be proudly displayed for all to admire.

Also, if you have not yet spent time on tall tales, this would be a good time to read about legendary heroines in books such as *The Story of Stagecoach Mary Fields* by Robert H. Miller and *Sally Ann Thunder Ann Whirlwind Crockett* by Steven Kellogg.

Section 8 ... Miracle of Machinery (pages 64–67)

After reading this section share a book of modern-day farms and machinery such as *Portrait of a Farm Family* by Raymond Bial, *Farm Machinery* by R. J. Stephen, or *Farming the Land* by Jerry Bushey. Discuss the jobs that machines do for farmers today and how these same jobs were probably done before the invention of machinery.

As another connection to the development of farm machinery, look at the history of haystacks by reading the book *Haystack* by Bonnie

Geisart and Arthur Geisart. It tells how haystacks used to be made and how they were used. Students could design flowcharts, perhaps in a circular shape, to show this information.

Section 9 ... Fun on the Frontier (pages 68–75)

After reading this section students should begin planning a day of old-fashioned pioneer fun—a FAIR! This is a day for whole families to participate in, so it needs to be planned for a Saturday morning or afternoon. Teachers should select the date and times ahead of time to give parents advance notice via the parent letter. Students can select the activities such as sack races, bicycle races, square dancing (perhaps with the help of the P.E. teacher), corn-husking races, pea-shucking races, stilt-making races, homemade pie or cookie competitions, arts and crafts (making cornhusk dolls or fishing poles), checkers tournaments, a baseball game, and more. During the activities, refreshments, such as popcorn and lemonade, could be served. Another nice touch is to have a live fiddler playing music. The day's activities could end with a "bring your own" picnic. Families should be encouraged to wear pioneer clothing. After students select the activities it is essential to start inviting, informing, and enlisting the help of the parents. Students should fill out and send their own invitations accompanied by "Wanted" sheets (see Main Appendix).

Section 10 ... Schools and Towns (pages 76–81)

After reading this section students in small groups can complete a Venn diagram (see Main Appendix) or a simple list that compares yesterday's schools with today's schools. Help children add to their lists by getting them to think about things such as clothing, food, transportation, sports, scouts, chores, teachers, time, recess, video/TV, homework, books, and so on.

Students can create a fictional pioneer character and write a story or a book about their school day. It may be helpful to refer again to *A Child's Day* by Bobbie Kalman. Students can then write a parallel story using themselves as the character, telling about a typical school day that they would have.

Provide students with small chalkboards or slick boards that can be made with paint or Contac paper. Give them chalk or erasable markers and small rags for erasing (old socks work well). Students can experiment with these writing tools for one day, then discuss advantages, disadvantages, and their feelings about using these instruments. With a limited supply you could rotate the materials to different students throughout the day so that each student has a chance to use them.

Section 11 ... America's Breadbasket (pages 82–87)

After reading this section invite students to make a class book of letters to the pioneer farmer. Each student is responsible for writing a letter to a pioneer farmer thanking him or her for enduring the hardships to head west, for making the Great Plains into America's breadbasket, and for providing food for all of us. Once compiled, this book can be dedicated to and sent to the nearest farmers' association as a real token of our appreciation for their difficult and often thankless job.

Investigations for After Reading

Quilting Bee

Plan an optional quilting bee for children and parents after school. Provide scissors, thread, needles, and scraps of fabric. The fabric can be donated from friends or parents or perhaps a local fabric store. Another option is to visit a thrift store and buy old curtains and use the fabric. Each parent and child team cuts squares of fabric using a pattern so that they are all the same size. Then, using small hand stitches, they should sew the squares together. When all the squares are sewn together and the desired size has been reached, you or a volunteer can sew on the back (with a thin layer of batting in between) using a sewing machine. The finished quilt could be displayed and/or raffled off to one of the quilting bee parent/ child teams.

Dangers vs. Opportunities Debate

Some of the children in your class will be open and willing to debate in groups and some will not. After informing students what a debate is and what this debate will be about, ask for volunteers to be on the Pioneers team or the City Slickers team. The debate should consist of arguments for and against leaving the city life and moving west. This should not be a formal debate, but the groups should have time to brainstorm (about ten to twenty minutes) what points will be said and who will say them. Each group should be given the same amount of time to present (about five minutes), then they should brainstorm again (ten minutes), and present again (five minutes). Students who are in the audience should be keeping track of the points being made by each team in the form of tally marks. The audience will determine the winner of the debate after counting tally marks and discussion.

Pioneer People

Each student should assemble the pages that they have completed throughout the reading of *Pioneers*. After designing covers, these shape books will then be ready to take home and share with parents. You could include a tear-out page at the end of the book for the parents to sign and return, indicating that they have read the "Pioneer People" book with their child.

Planting Season

As a class, discuss the basic steps of planting and what makes plants grow. Share *Growing Food* by Claire Llewellyn. After gaining permission to use a small sunny area for farming outside on school grounds, students can take turns using shovels, rakes, and hoes in preparing an area for planting. Students can then observe the changes in the seeds that have been drying since reading section 6. They can also investigate additional seeds that you provide such as beans, barley, oats, wheat, and herbs/ spices such as dill weed or basil. Students should make markers for each seed that is planted using tagboard attached to the end of a stick or a pencil and covered with a small freezer bag. Students will then take turns being responsible for caring for the new plants in whatever manner that works for you. Students can keep growing journals in which they record comments and drawings of the growth.

Of course, if it is not possible to do the planting outside, use milk or egg cartons with potting soil and a sunny windowsill.

Read, Compare, Share

Share additional pioneer stories with students to illustrate different kinds of pioneers such as *Wagon Train* by Courtni C. Wright, *Sarah, Plain and Tall,* or *Little House on the Prairie.* The latter two are both available in book and video versions. Another video I recommend is *Home at Last* to explore yet another type of young pioneer. Students can compare versions of stories versus video or they could look for similarities among all the different types of pioneers. See Compare/Contrast Report in Main Appendix.

Just for Fun

Using the book *Settler Sayings* by Bobbie Kalman, test kids on their word savvy by asking them to guess the meanings of pioneer sayings. You could try this as a game with students in teams or just informally during transition times. Also, invite students to share some of today's sayings and/or sayings that their parents used and their meanings. This information could be turned into a big "Interesting Sayings" chart headed "from 100 years ago," "from 20 years ago," and "from today." This information could also be turned into book form with illustrations.

Candle-Making Project

Melt paraffin in several large coffee cans. Add colors by melting old crayons with the wax. Give each student a straight piece of 12-inch wicking. Instruct students to dip the wick into the hot wax and hold it above the can for a moment to catch any drips. After each student dips, they should let the wax dry by walking carefully around the classroom. When dry and cool, the wick is ready for the next dip. When the candle is partially done, it should be hung to cool completely by a clothespin on a line. Dipping can resume the following day to finish the candle. Students can choose to stick with one color or combine them. They can also choose the height of their candle and cut the wick to size. As the widths of their candles may vary and conventional candleholders may not be suitable, ask students to think of what the pioneers might have used as a candleholder. Display candles and holders at the Pioneer Fair. (*Note:* This project should be closely supervised by several adults to prevent serious accidents.)

Pioneer Fair Day

Planning for this day should have taken place after reading section 9 and should serve as a culminating activity. Projects completed during the unit should be on display for children to share with their families on this day.

PARENT LETTER

Howdy Partners!

During the next several weeks we will be embarking on an incredible journey west as pioneers. The book we will be using is *Pioneers* by Martin W. Sandler. It will guide us in learning more about the kinds of heroic people who dared to make a new life in the "Wild West." I encourage you to hit the trail to your local library to check out some Wild West books to share with your whole family. Along with sharing a wide variety of pioneer stories we will also be investigating tall tales spurred by the westward movement, so pick up a few of those at your library as well and have fun with them.

In addition to discovering great books we will be participating in several projects and activities, some of which we would love your participation at as well! These include baking (and eating!) cornbread and perhaps other pioneer treats, candle making, a quilting bee, and a Pioneer Family Fair. The fair is planned for _____ at _____, so mark your calendars for some old-fashioned fun for the whole family.

Please check the attached "Wanted" sheet for supplies and/or volunteer time that we are in need of. If you can help out in any way during our pioneer unit, we would greatly appreciate it.

Happy trails!

Pioneer People Pattern

Pioneer Person: _____

_____

Jobs: _____

_____

_____

Tools: _____

_____

_____

Today: _____

_____

Wagon Wheels Patterns with Definitions

the production of crops, livestock, or poultry

the name for the covered wagons used in the early westward migration

famous by the telling of unprovable and often exaggerated stories

one who cuts and splits timber for market

opposite thoughts or words

produce grown from the ground

one who is sent to preach religion

one who first enters or settles a region

absolutely necessary and important

the farthest limit of a country's settled regions

large grassy rolling land

giving up something of value for the sake of something else

the freedom to explore new opportunities

an encouraging influence

large pieces of land

uninhabited, untamed regions; in a natural state

Conestoga Wagon Pattern

Pioneer Courage Ribbon Pattern

PIONEER COURAGE

Cowpuncher Application

Name:_____

Address:_____

_____

Phone number:_____

List your job experiences and cowhand skills:_____

_____

_____

List the pieces of equipment that you would need for the job and why you need each piece:

Equipment	Reason
_____	_____
_____	_____
_____	_____
_____	_____

Why do you think that you would make a good cowpuncher? _____

_____

List two references

Name:_____   Name:_____

Address:_____   Address:_____

_____   _____

_____   _____

Phone number:_____   Phone number:_____

Pioneer Math

Name:_____

Figure the problems using *Pioneers* as a reference.

1.) How many years was it between the settling of the original colonies and the settling of most of the western frontier? (Hint: see page 16)

2.) About how many hours did some city children work in factories per day? (Hint: see page 27)

3.) How many weeks were the typical wagons on the trail? How many months? (Hint: see page 30)

4.) If there were four people in a family and each person required at least 2 quarts of water each day to drink, how many quarts would that family need for an entire trip? How many gallons is that? (Hint: use information from #3)

5.) How many hours altogether might a cowboy spend in a saddle during a five-month cattle drive? (Hint: see page 47)

6.) How many more acres could a farmer in the 1800s plant due to the invention of machinery? (Hint: see page 65)

7.) How many people moved to and settled in Mason City, Iowa, between 1870 and 1890? How many years is that? (Hint: see page 80)

8.) Think about it …
How many trees did it take to build a log cabin? How many chunks of sod did it take to build a soddie? Which one do you think was easier to make?

Answers to Pioneer Math

1.)
```
    1860        1890
   -1790       -1790
     70          100        A. 70–100 years
```

2.) Dawn to Dusk   A. About 12 hours

3.) 150 days 150/7 = 21   150/30 = 5   A. 21 weeks; 5 months

4.) 4 people x 2 quarts = 8 per day
150 days x 8 quarts per day = 1,200 quarts
1,200/4 = 300 gallons
A. 1,200 quarts; 300 gallons

5.) 18 hours per day x 30 days in a month = 540 hours
540 hours per month x 5 months = 2,700 hours
A. 2,700 hours

6.)
```
     135
   -   7
     128        A. 128 more acres
```

7.)
```
   10,000
   -  700
    9,300       A. about 9,300 acres
```
```
    1890
   -1870
      20        A. 20 years
```

Corn Bread Muffins Recipe

Ingredients

    1 cup flour
    1 cup yellow cornmeal
    $1/4$ cup sugar
    4 tsp. baking powder
    $3/4$ tsp. salt
    2 eggs
    1 cup milk
    $1/4$ cup oil

Directions

Beat ingredients until somewhat smooth. Place paper baking cups into muffin tin. Spoon batter into cups, about $1/2$ full. Bake at 425°F. for 15 to 20 minutes. Makes 8 to 10 muffins.

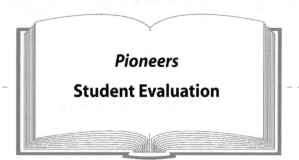

Pioneers
Student Evaluation

Name:_____

1.) During the unit, I worked cooperatively in my groups

     not at all   sometimes   most of the time

2.) During the unit, I tried my best

     not at all   sometimes   most of the time

3.) During the unit, I completed

____ a tall tale	____ a reading response
____ an invitation	____ a letter
____ a compare/contrast report	____ a chart
____ a wagon trail map	____ a list
____ a group book	____ pioneer math problems
____ a shape book	____ a job application
____ a courage ribbon	____ a pioneer project

4.) Something new that I learned about pioneers is:_____

_____

5.) Something new that I learned about Native Americans is:_____

_____

6.) Something new that I learned about the West is:_____

_____

7.) One thing that I worked on that I am especially proud of is: _____

_____

8.) My favorite things about this unit were:_____

_____

9.) I think that I would/would not have made a good pioneer because:_____

_____

SUPPORTING LIBRARY

Native Americans

Freedman, Russell. *Buffalo Hunt.* New York: Holiday House, 1988.
Examines the great importance of the buffalo to the Plains Indians.

Harvey, Karen. *Indians of the Great Plains.* Philadelphia: Running Press, 1993.
A miniature book loaded with information on the Plains Indians of yesterday and today.

MacDonald, Fiona. *Plains Indians* (Insights Series). New York: Barron's Educational Series, 1993.
A complete look at who the Plains Indians were, how they lived, and the changes forced upon them due to the arrival of the settlers.

Petty, Kate. *Plains Indians* (Small World Books). New York: Gloucester Press, 1988.
An easy-reader on the lives and customs of the Plains Indians until their defeat by the U.S. cavalry.

Taylor, Dr. Colin. *What Do We Know About the Plains Indians?* New York: Peter Bedrick Books, 1993.
Examines all aspects of the lives of the Plains Indians, including small sections on the changes that took place and how they live today.

The Gold Rush

DeClements, Barthe. *The Bite of the Gold Bug.* New York: Puffin Books, 1992.
Beginner chapter book. A story of a twelve-year-old boy and his father and their Alaska gold rush adventure.

Hoobler, Dorothy. *Treasure in the Stream.* Morristown, N.J.: Silver Burdett Press, 1991.
Beginning chapter book. A story of a ten-year-old girl and her family and how the gold rush changed their lives.

Stein, Conrad R. *The California Gold Rush* (Cornerstones of Freedom). Chicago: Childrens Press, 1995.
Describes the massive movement of people in search of their fortunes in gold, the resulting boomtowns, and the mining life that followed.

Van Steenwyk, Elizabeth. *The California Gold Rush: West with the Forty-Niners.* New York: Franklin Watts, 1991.
Describes the 1849 gold rush and life for the miners during and after the rush.

Cowboys

Johnson, Neil. *Jack Creek Cowboy.* New York: Dial Books for Young Readers, 1993.
Depicts a ten-year-old boy's modern-day cowboy summer on his family's ranch in Wyoming.

Landau, Elaine. *Cowboys.* New York: Franklin Watts, 1990.
Depicts how cowboys of the Old West raised cattle and spent their days.

Murdoch, David. *Cowboy* (Eyewitness Books). New York: Dorling Kindersley, 1993.
Describes a cowboy's job, dress, equipment, and lifestyle.

Sandler, Martin. *Cowboys* (A Library of Congress Book). New York: HarperCollins, 1994.
A complete look at the life and times of the American hero, the cowboy.

Scott, Ann Herbert. *Cowboy Country.* New York: Clarion Books, 1993.
An "old buckaroo" tells about cowboy life of past and present.

Frontier Women

Alter, Judith. *Women of the Old West*. New York: Franklin Watts, 1989.
Looks at the various roles women had in the Old West.

Fox, Virginia. *The Story of Women Who Shaped the West* (Cornerstones of Freedom). Chicago: Childrens Press, 1991.
Provides a look at the women who made history as they lived and worked in the western frontier.

Miller, Brandon Marie. *Buffalo Gals*. Minneapolis, Minn.: Lerner Publications, 1995.
Advanced reading about frontier women including many vintage photographs.

Sanders, Scott Russell. *Warm as Wool*. New York: Bradbury Press, 1992.
A story based on an actual pioneer woman who raised a flock of sheep to provide wool for warm clothing for her children.

Tall Tales and Pioneer People

Bird, E. J. *Ten Tall Tales*. Minneapolis, Minn.: Carolrhoda Books, 1984.
A collection of short original tall tales. Great for exemplifying tall-tale writing style.

Dewey, Ariane. *The Narrow Escapes of Davy Crockett*. New York: Greenwillow Books, 1990.
Exaggerated stories intermingled with facts about the American hero, Davy Crockett.

Fleischman, Sid. *McBroom's Wonderful One-Acre Farm*. New York: Greenwillow Books, 1992.
A collection of three original tall tales. Great for a humorous read aloud.

Gleeson, Brian. *Pecos Bill*. Saxonville, Mass.: Rabbit Ears Books, 1988.
The tall tales of the legendary Pecos Bill.

Greene, Carol. *Daniel Boone: Man of the Forests* (A Rookie Biography). Chicago: Childrens Press, 1990.
A realistic account of the life and times of Daniel Boone. Easy reading.

Kellogg, Steven. *Mike Fink*. New York: Morrow Junior Books, 1992.
A tall tale of the "keelboat king."

Kellogg, Steven. *Pecos Bill*. New York: Morrow Junior Books, 1986.
The tall tales of the legendary Pecos Bill.

Kellogg, Steven. *Sally Ann Thunder Ann Whirlwind Crockett*. New York: Morrow Junior Books, 1995.
A tall tale of the legendary Sally Ann, wife of Davy Crockett.

Levinson, Nancy Smiler. *Snowshoe Thompson*. New York: HarperCollins, 1992.
Based on a true story, tells the story of a man who delivers the mail over the mountain pass on skis.

Miller, Robert H. *The Story of Stagecoach Mary Fields*. Morristown, N.J.: Silver Burdett Press, 1995.
The tale of the first American woman to deliver the U.S. mail.

Osborne, Mary Pope. *American Tall Tales*. New York: Scholastic, 1991.
A collection of nine tall tales.

Robison, Nancy. *Buffalo Bill* (A First Book). New York: Franklin Watts, 1991.
Tells the complete story of the life and times of William F. Cody as hunter, author, showman, guide, and pony express rider.

San Souci, Robert. *Larger than Life.* New York: Doubleday, 1991.
A collection of five tall tales of American legendary heroes.

Shepard, Aaron. *The Legend of Lightning Larry.* New York: Charles Scribner's Sons, 1993.
A humorous tale of an original western hero.

Small, Terry. *The Legend of Pecos Bill.* New York: Bantam Little Rooster, 1992.
The tall tales of the legendary Pecos Bill in rhyme.

Walker, Paul Robert. *Big Men, Big Country.* New York: Harcourt Brace Jovanovich, 1993.
A collection of nine American tall tales.

General

Anderson, Joan. *Joshua's Westward Journal.* New York: William Morrow, 1987.
An historical photo essay written in journal style. Tells the story of one family's move west. (*Note:* Story deals with the death of a family member along the way.)

Armstrong, Jennifer. *Black Eyed Susan.* New York: Crown Publishers, 1995.
A beginner's novel about a ten-year-old girl and her family in the South Dakota prairie.

Beekman, Dan. *Forest, Village, Town, City.* New York: Thomas Y. Crowell, 1982.
Depicts the evolution of settlements to large cities.

Bial, Raymond. *Portrait of a Farm Family.* Boston: Houghton Mifflin, 1995.
Depicts the daily operations of a farm and how each member of the family helps out. Photographs included.

Bouchard, David. *If You're Not from the Prairie.* New York: Atheneum, 1995.
In verse; tells of the special things in nature that make prairie life unique and wonderful.

Bunting, Eve. *Dandelions.* New York: Harcourt Brace, 1995.
A pioneer family finds strength in each other as they make a new home for themselves in Nebraska.

Bushey, Jerry. *Farming the Land.* Minneapolis, Minn.: Carolrhoda Books, 1987.
Looks at the machines that help perform various farming operations. Easy reading.

Cobb, Mary. *The Quilt-Block History of Pioneer Days.* Brookfield, Conn.: Millbrook Press, 1995.
Describes how quilt patterns tell stories of pioneer life. Includes many projects using easily obtainable materials and reproducibles.

Courtault, Martine. *Going West, Cowboys and Pioneers.* Ossining, N.Y.: Young Discovery Library, 1986.
Describes the westward movement of all kinds of pioneers.

Fiday, Beverly, and David Fiday. *Time to Go.* New York: Gulliver Books, Harcourt Brace, 1990.
A young child thinks about all the things he will miss as he and his family prepare to leave their farm.

Fradin, Dennis. *Pioneers* (A New True Book). Chicago: Childrens Press, 1984.
Discusses why pioneers went west, the hardships they faced, and the influence they had on history. Easy reading.

Geisart, Bonnie, and Arthur Geisart. *Haystack.* Boston: Houghton Mifflin, 1995.
Tells how huge haystacks were made and used prior to the invention of modern hay-baling machines.

Gibbons, Gail. *Farming.* New York: Holiday House, 1988.
Shows everything that needs to done on a farm during the four seasons.

Harshman, Marc. *Uncle James.* New York: Penguin Books, 1993.
Uncle James realizes that his family needs help with their farm not tall tales from the Wild West. (Could be used as an introduction to tall tales.)

Harvey, Brett. *My Prairie Year.* New York: Holiday House, 1986.
Based on the diary of Elenore Plaisted; tells the story of a year in the lives of a prairie family.

Henry, Joanne Landers. *Log Cabin in the Woods.* New York: Macmillan Publishing, 1988.
A true story from the diary of eleven-year-old Oliver Johnson telling of his pioneer experience.

Kalman, Bobbie. *A Child's Day* (Historic Communities Series). New York: Crabtree Publishing, 1994.
Describes what a child's life was like in the pioneer days.

Kalman, Bobbie. *Settler Sayings* (Historic Communities Series). New York: Crabtree Publishing, 1994.
A collection of sayings and their meanings that came about during the time of pioneers, of which many are still used today.

Knight, Amelia Stewart. *The Way West.* New York: Simon & Schuster Books for Young Readers, 1993.
Adapted from the diary of A. Knight, written in journal form. Tells the story of the Knight family's pioneer journey from Iowa to Oregon in 1853. Forty-eight entries in all.

Llewellyn, Claire. *Growing Food* (First Look At Series). Milwaukee, Wisc.: Gareth Stevens Children's Books, 1991.
Introduction to gardening, farming, and harvesting.

MacLachlan, Patricia. *Sarah, Plain and Tall.* New York: Harper & Row, 1985.
Tells the story of a mail-order bride and her new prairie family. Also available on video.

MacLachlan, Patricia. *What You Know First.* New York: HarperCollins, 1995.
A young girl is sad about leaving their prairie farm.

Schlissel, Lillian. *Black Frontiers.* New York: Simon & Schuster Books for Young Readers, 1995.
Focuses on African Americans as cowboys, mountain men, soldiers, homesteaders, scouts, and more in the western frontier.

Stephen, R. J. *Farm Machinery* (Picture Library). New York: Franklin Watts, 1986.
Provides descriptions and pictures of modern farm equipment and the jobs they perform.

Turner, Ann. *Sewing Quilts.* New York: Macmillan Publishing, 1994.
A young girl thinks about the meanings behind the quilts she and her sister and mother sew.

Wilder, Laura Ingalls. *Little House on the Prairie.* New York: Harper & Row, 1935.
Classic story of a pioneer family. Also available on video.

Williams, Lucy. *The American West.* New York: Bookright Press, 1991.
Encompassed the many aspects of the westward movement of the pioneers. Could be used as a companion to *Pioneers* by Martin Sandler for parallel reading on an easier level.

Wright, Courtni, C. *Wagon Train.* New York: Holiday House, 1995.
Tells the story of an African-American family's wagon journey from Virginia to California in 1865.

Videos

Home at Last. Wonderworks Family Movie. Public Media Video, 1988.
Tells the story of an orphan boy who goes to live with a pioneer family in Nebraska. 60 minutes.

Indians of North America Video Collection. Bala Cynwood, Pa.: Schlessinger Video Productions, 1993.
A ten-volume set for grades 4 to 10, addressing Native American history, culture, and way of life today for
    tribes such as Comanche, Cherokee, Cheyenne, Iroquois, and Maya. 30 minutes each.

The Legend of Paul Bunyan and the Legend of John Henry. A Golden Book Video Classic. Racine, Wisc.: West-
    ern Publishing, 1992.
Animated illustrations of two classic tall tales. 25 minutes.

Little House on the Prairie. Goodtimes Home Video, 1989. 120 minutes.

Sarah, Plain and Tall. Random House Video, 1988. 30 minutes.

Shelley Duvall's Tall Tales and Legends: Johnny Appleseed, Pecos Bill, Darlin' Clementine, Little Miss Sure Shot.
    New York: Playhouse Video, 1989.
Somewhat humorous, nonanimated versions of tall tales. Approximately 50 minutes each.

The Story of Money

Betsy Maestro

NEW YORK: CLARION BOOKS, 1993

ABOUT THE BOOK

The Story of Money by Betsy Maestro is a detailed account of how the exchange of goods and services has changed over the course of human history. In the many centuries of human existence, we have moved from self-sufficiency, to trading and bartering, to using valuable objects as money, to minting precious metals as coins, to adopting official banknotes and alloy coins as currency, to buying on credit. Many maps and illustrations help to explain how this entire process took place over time.

Maestro concludes by stating that although the forms of money have changed dramatically throughout history, it was and always will be whatever people agree on at the time as a medium of exchange for goods and services.

INVESTIGATIONS

Investigative Themes

Currency and Coins
History of Money
Making/Spending/Saving Money
Trade and Barter
Coin Collecting (Numismatics)

Investigative Skills

bartering	bargaining
using maps	counting money
sequencing	observing
recording	graphing
weighing	making change
problem solving	comparing/contrasting/categorizing
planning	buying/selling

cooperation	budgeting
defining words	reading for information
writing stories	listening and speaking
thinking critically	reading/making charts and graphs
creative designing	using mathematics and calculators
hypothesizing	collaborative decision making

Investigative Materials

1 copy of *The Story of Money* for every three students
5 to 6 copies of *Pigs Will Be Pigs* by Amy Axelrod
supporting library books

10–20 magnifying glasses
real bills and coins for examination
play money
calculators for each student
index cards
round balloons, paper towel tubes, pipe cleaners (one for each student)
papier-mâché
old newspapers
scissors
tape, glue
glossy paint for piggy banks
bulletin board paper
markers, crayons, colored pencils, ink pads
large U.S. wall map
baby food jars/egg cartons for sorting
cotton balls, alcohol, toothpicks, old toothbrushes, vinegar, salt for cleaning
play/salt dough (see recipe)
5–6 rolling pins
scales
current business sections from newspaper
white paper cut to "dollar" size (approximately)
magazines for cutting
fliers from discount stores from Sunday newspapers
5–6 menus from different restaurants
pad of restaurant order forms used by waitresses when taking orders
7–10 rulers with centimeters and inches
large chart paper

New Words for *The Story of Money*

barter—the exchange of goods and services for other goods and services ($1.00)
circulate—to move from place to place, person to person ($5.00)
colonial—having to do with the thirteen original colonies that became the United States of America ($1.00)

counterfeit—an imitation intended to be passed off as genuine ($2.00)
currency—any form of money that is circulated and accepted in a country ($1.00)
foreign—from another nation or country ($1.00)
guarantee—a promise ($1.00)
ingot—lump of precious metal ($5.00)
merchant—a person who buys, sells, or trades goods ($2.00)
milling—tiny grooves made on the sides of coins to prevent forgery ($5.00)
mint—a place where money is made; the act of stamping metals to make coins ($1.00)
numismatics—the collecting and studying of coins and money ($6.00)
self-sufficient—able to live without outside help ($2.00)
surplus—an amount that is greater than needed ($1.00)

Investigations for Before Reading

New Words Investigation

Provide small groups of students with a list of new words and their "worth." Challenge them to find the definitions of as many words as they can within a given time frame from any available resource. (The amount of time will depend on the age and ability of your students.) When the time is up, they can trade in the correct definitions for their value in play money. They do not earn money for incorrect definitions or any words not defined. If all definitions are correct, the group can collect a maximum of $34.00. Then the group must spend the money, cooperatively agreeing on what to buy and then sharing what they purchase. You will need to have seven to ten different things for them to "buy" with their money such as jacks, a long jump rope, a Frisbee, balls, whatever would be desirable, nonconsumable, and could eventually be shared by the whole class during free time. Prices for each item will be inflated (i.e., a $34.00 jump rope, a $30.00 Frisbee, etc.) and will vary according to what you offer. The group that has made the most money should be allowed to buy first. After deciding on their purchase, each group should then figure out what their change should be, even though change cannot be spent. For more of a challenge, ask students to figure out sales tax and add it to the price of the item (total cannot exceed $34.00), then figure out the change. A free

time should follow at some point during the same day to allow students an opportunity to use what they purchased.

Simple Coin Investigation

To gain brief, yet concrete, exposure to "the real thing," provide small groups or pairs of students with one quarter, dime, nickel, and penny. Invite them to observe each coin's characteristics and record them on the Coin Characteristics Chart (see unit appendix). With the whole group, discuss the completed charts to form one large classroom chart that shows each coin's unique characteristics.

Small Change Investigation

Provide pairs of students with play money (100 pennies, 20 nickels, 10 dimes, 4 quarters, and $1.00) and an equal to sign (=) printed on an index card. Share the books *Dollars and Cents for Harriet* by Betsy Maestro and Giulio Maestro and *The Money Book* by Joan W. German about coins that equal $1.00. While slowly reading aloud, pause and allow students to manipulate the amounts mentioned in the text with play money. This will help students recognize the value of each coin and that equal amounts can be expressed with different coin combinations.

Also, share the book and/or video *Alexander, Who Used to Be Rich Last Sunday* by

Judith Viorst. Invite students to help Alexander keep track of the money he spends and loses throughout the story. Perhaps Alexander just needed a safe place to keep his money—see next activity.

Money-Keepers Investigation

Share *The Purse* by Kathy Caple. Discuss ways to keep, hold, or save money. Ask students to bring in things that they use to save or carry money in (i.e., purses, wallets, jars, boxes, banks, etc.) to share with the class on the following day.

Make piggy banks out of papier-mâché (see recipe in Main Appendix) using the following steps:

1.) Give each student a round balloon, a cardboard paper towel tube, scissors, tape, and newspaper.
2.) Blow up and tie the balloon.
3.) Spread out some of the newspaper to protect the work area.
4.) Cut five sections from the cardboard tube—one for a snout and four for feet—and attach them to the balloon with tape.
5.) Snip two extra pieces to make the ears and attach each piece to the balloon with tape.
6.) Cut short, thin strips of newspaper to dip into papier-mâché paste (premade).
7.) Dip each piece of newspaper into the paste and smooth off the excess with fingers so that it drips back into the paste container. Then smooth each piece onto the balloon.
8.) Cover the entire balloon (including the cardboard tube pieces) with newspaper pieces and papier-mâché and allow to dry.
9.) When completely dry, paint with a glossy color, add a curly pipe cleaner for a tail, and make a slit in the top to drop money into.

Upon completion of the piggy banks, share *The Gift* by Alaina Brodmann. Then ask students to write down a couple of ideas on a small slip of paper of what they would spend $5.00 on if they had it. They should put the slip of paper inside their new piggy bank and begin saving their change for the item(s) they wrote down. You could suggest keeping track of the money that goes into the bank on a little notebook because the bank will be destroyed once opened to count or collect the money inside.

Dollar Investigation

Share *The Go-Around Dollar* by Barbara Johnston Adams to discover some facts about our current $1.00 bill as the reader watches a single dollar bill change hands many times. Just for fun, students, as a class or in groups, could write similar fictional stories about another dollar bill that changes hands throughout a day's or week's time.

Provide pairs of students with a dollar bill and a magnifying glass for some close-up observation of the symbols and characteristics mentioned in *The Go-Around Dollar*.

Then for some measuring fun, instruct small groups of students to measure a dollar bill with inches and/or centimeters. Then use the dollar bill to measure objects in the classroom. For example, a desk may measure the length of five dollar bills. For a further challenge, students could then convert their dollar measurements to inches or centimeters.

Penny Tally

Ask each student to bring in five pennies for this investigation. Use tally marks to count the number of coins. Also, record the dates and tally the number of pennies with each date. Then, using the tally marks, make a class graph showing the dates of the coins brought in. Use the graph to find out which dates appear the least/most on the collected pennies. Ask students for possible explanations for these results.

Next, ask students to locate and observe the letters on their coins. Ask them to hypothesize as to the meaning of each letter. Record and tally the letters on each coin to find out which letters appear most/least frequently. Students can speculate as to the reasons for these results as well. A large wall map of the United States would be helpful in showing students where the mints are located (presently Denver and Philadelphia, although some may be from

San Francisco) and helping them to deduce that the letter that appears most often will most likely be from the closest mint.

You may want to ask students to contribute their pennies to the class jar to be used later for fund-raising moneys.

Parent/Child (Pretend) Spending Spree

Send home the "Window Shopping" Sheet (see unit appendix) with each student and possibly a calculator to give parents and children a chance to do some window shopping together. See parent instructions on sheet.

Investigations for During Reading

Class Collection

Provide small groups with different dictionaries and ask them to find definitions for the word "hobby" and the word "collection." Each group should share their definitions with the class to begin a discussion on the hobby of collecting. In the discussion make it clear that each collected piece is important to the collection and should not be removed for any reason. Share pages 60 and 61 on "Collecting Coins" from *Money* by Joe Cribb to find out how to collect, clean, record, and protect coins. Provide small groups of students with some old, well-worn, dull coins. Give each group toothpicks, alcohol and cotton balls, an old toothbrush, a magnifying glass, tape, and two small sheets of plain paper. Instruct groups to clean their coin, make a "rubbing" of it on one paper, and make an envelope out of the other for safe storage. Then cut out and tape the rubbing to the outside of the envelope. Students can give their coins a final shine with a vinegar and salt bath and dry with a tissue before placing inside the envelope.

Throughout the unit, invite students to look for and collect coins for observation. Provide a place in the classroom, such as a desk, shelf, or table, where coins can be observed with magnifying glasses. Provide small containers, such as baby food jars and/or a divided tray such as an egg carton, for classifying coins. Also, provide paper for rubbings and copies of the Coin Characteristics Chart for students to record the details of each coin (including who brought it in) added to the collection. Completed charts could be kept in a folder or notebook. Perhaps special permission may be obtained to clean and shine a very dirty or dull coin as it is added to the collection. Use the coins from above to start the collection. Periodically add some interesting ones of your own for students to examine.

Suggestions for Reading The Story of Money

In order to get the most understanding out of the book, I recommend that students read aloud in small groups, separating the reading into seven shorter sections and pausing for discussion and activities:

> pages 3–9 cover barter and trade
> pages 10–13 cover using objects of value for money
> pages 14–19 cover ancient coins of precious metals
> pages 20–23 cover the first paper money
> pages 24–31 cover the transition from European currency to American currency
> pages 32–35 cover minting and engraving
> pages 36–43 cover the concept of modern-day money around the world

These sections can be read on different days or back to back, depending upon the level of your readers. I suggest that reading take place in small groups, with students taking turns reading aloud. You may want to reread certain sections aloud to the class.

I also suggest beginning each day with an interesting fact from the back of the book, "Additional Information About Money" and an activity, brainteaser, or story from *Math Fun with Money Puzzlers* by Rose Wyler.

Trade and Barter

After reading pages 3–9, invite students to share stories of trades/barters that they have made recently (e.g., trading an apple for a friend's sandwich or trading baseball cards). This is to further the concept that successful trading/bartering entails satisfying the desires of both parties and is limited by what each party has to offer.

To gain some firsthand experience with the ideas of trading and bartering, invite students to set up a trading post in the classroom. It can be limited to books only and may be ongoing throughout the unit. Or it may take place on one day and students can decide what they would like to trade—books, baked goods, stickers, and so on. Be sure to inform parents about this "Trade and Barter Day" so that they are aware of the trading that will be going on.

This activity can be taken even further by preparing a marketplace in which trading/bartering takes place for the whole school or just for certain grades. It could include crafts, baked goods, collectible cards, books, toys, and anything else that students may want to trade. The marketplace could take place after school and would need to be well supervised. I would suggest that each participating student be accompanied by their parent during the actual trading, not to bargain for their child but to observe and only give advice if requested.

"Other" Money

After reading pages 10–13 about the types of objects used as money long ago, invite small groups of students to design a poster using chart paper or tagboard that illustrates at least five items that may have been used as money in the past. They can use examples from *The Story of Money,* or they can consult other books from the supporting library. The group should be prepared to present their poster to the class and provide possible reasons why each object was considered valuable at the time.

Another task for the group is to think about and discuss a world without money, and come to a consensus on one item in today's society that is considered valuable and could be used in place of money. The group should be prepared to share their choice with the class along with their reasons for choosing it. Once all of the groups have shared, hold a class discussion on the items presented and try to come to a consensus on one item that the whole class can agree on. The object here is not to just come up with one thing that everybody can agree on but to get students to think critically and make decisions based on reasoning.

Design Your Own Coin

After reading pages 14–19 about the world's first coins and the use of precious metals, invite students to create their own "precious" coins out of Play Dough (see recipe in the unit appendix). Students can work in small groups to make the dough. Once the dough is ready they can split up into pairs or choose to work independently. Their job is to design coins from the "precious" dough. Their task may include deciding what their coin is worth, finding a uniform cutting device to make each coin the same size, and choosing objects to make identifiable, meaningful stamps in each coin. Students may wish to examine several resources such as *Money* (Eyewitness Book) by Joe Cribb or *Coins and Currency* by Brenda Ralph Lewis or *Sold! The Origins of Money and Trade* by Buried Worlds to gather ideas for their coins. They should weigh each coin on a scale to see that each one is approximately the same weight. Allow coins to dry somewhat so that they can be passed around as each pair or individual shares their coin design with the class.

Share more information on actual early minting methods from *Sold! The Origins of Money and Trade,* pages 24–35.

Save some of the dough in an airtight container for the Counterfeit Investigation.

Design Your Own Bills

After reading pages 20–23 on the first paper money, share the book *Money, Money, Money* by Nancy Winslow Parker to examine the detailed artwork of the paper currency in the

United States. Afterward, invite students to design their own money out of paper using colored pencils, pens, markers, ink pads, scissors, dollar-size paper, and so on. Additional sources may be consulted for design ideas such as *Coins and Currency* by Brenda Ralph Lewis and *Money* (Eyewitness Book) by Joe Cribb. Students can work in pairs or individually in making several bills of equal value. As they work on their designs, they should consider, among other things, colors, sizes, shapes, and special stamps that would be meaningful to them and difficult for anyone else to copy. Each pair or individual should be prepared to share their design with the class. Save for the Counterfeit Investigation.

Making Money and Counterfeit Investigation

After reading pages 24–35, share the videos *Making Money* and *Magical Field Trip to the Denver Mint* that take students on informative journeys to a mint and a bureau of engraving to see how our money is really made. Afterward, share the counterfeiting sections from *Money, Money, Money* by Nancy Winslow Parker (pages 28 and 29) and *Stepping Through History: Money* by Peggy Burns (pages 21 and 22) to begin a discussion on counterfeiters, their crime/punishment, and how they attempt to copy currency.

After discussion, provide pairs of students or individuals with a magnifying glass and "money" made by classmates in previous activities. Their job is to closely examine each coin and/or bill and attempt to copy it exactly. The time you allot for this activity depends on your students' frustration level. Afterward, display the originals with the counterfeits and ask students to vote on the counterfeits that are most accurate.

After Reading Investigations

Investigate Foreign Exchange

Provide five groups of students with copies of one of the bills from pages 36 and 37 in *The Story of Money*. As a group, they should locate the country that their bill is from on a large wall map and attach it to the map. Invite each group to research another country's money. They can begin by looking in the back of *The Story of Money* and choosing a country. They will need to consult outside resources, such as encyclopedias and school and public library books, to find out what their chosen country's bills look like. Provide them with dollar-size paper on which they should complete a drawing imitating their country's currency. These dollar drawings should be attached to the wall map as well.

Share pages 28 and 29 from *Stepping Through History: Money* by Peggy Burns on how we exchange money with other countries. Using the exchange rate chart on page 29, calculators, and the What Would You Pay? sheet (see unit appendix), challenge students to convert U.S. dollars into foreign currency.

Next, provide students with the business sections from several newspapers. Ask them to locate the current foreign exchange information. Ask students how the exchange rate has changed since the one in the book was printed.

The Million Dollar Investigation

Share aloud the book *If You Made a Million* by David M. Schwartz. Using dollar-size paper and green markers, ask students to make 10,000 $100.00 bills. After figuring out what a $100.00 bill looks like, students should decide how the money will be printed, who will print what, how this new money will be counted (stacks of 100? 1,000?), and what would be the easiest way to keep track of what has been made.

Take a picture of your students with the "million dollars" and, if possible, enlarge it by photocopying. Use this picture as a cover illustration for a class book in which each student contributes one page that explains and illustrates what they would do with a real million dollars. Bind pages together to share with others.

Look for examples of checks and how they are made out in *If You Made a Million* by David M. Schwartz, *The Monster Money Book* by Loreen Leedy, and *The Story of Money* by Betsy Maestro. Then provide small groups of students with school supply catalogs to look through and find something that the school or class-room could use. Then each group should write an extralarge check (two pieces of $8\frac{1}{2}$ x 11 paper attached together lengthwise) to the cata-log company to "pay" for what they chose. I suggest doing an example of the basic check design on the chalkboard as the groups are working on their own. Students should use one color for the check design (the lines for the date, amounts, and signature) and another color for actually filling out the information on the check.

For individual experience in check writing, provide each student with a magazine to look through, find a picture of something that they would want to buy with some of their "mil-lion," and cut it out. They will need to decide how much they will pay and make/write a check for that amount using dollar-size paper. Then they should glue the picture and the check onto one piece of colored paper for display.

An "Interesting" Investigation

Share parts of resource books that deal with interest, such as *Stepping Through History: Money* by Peggy Burns or *If You Made a Mil-lion* by David M. Schwartz. Provide pairs of students with calculators and the You Owe … sheet (see unit appendix) to determine how much extra would be paid in interest in differ-ent situations such as banks, credit cards, or other lending companies.

Take a short field trip to a local bank. In-vite parents to join you to obtain information about how to open an account for their child. Before the trip, help each student to create one question to ask the banker. Students will hope-fully be able to discover where money is kept, how to open accounts, how much interest can be made with different accounts, and about banking careers. Upon returning from the bank, provide pairs of students with calculators and the You Made … sheet (see unit appendix) to determine how much money could be made in different situations.

Bargain Hunter's Delight

Prior to this activity, gather and look through several fliers from discount department stores (found in any major Sunday newspaper). Take note of similar items on sale at different stores. Then provide groups of students with the same fliers. Write the name of each store across the top of the chalkboard. Describe an item on sale and challenge students to locate the item and the price as quickly as they can, then record the price under the store's name. The group who writes the price first gets a point. The group who finds the best price gets a point as well. Be sure to keep track of all of the best prices to find out which store has more bargains.

What's for Dinner?

Provide groups of students with copies of *Pigs Will Be Pigs* by Amy Axelrod to read aloud together. Also, provide calculators, paper, and pencil for keeping track of who found money and how much and then adding all of the money found on the "money hunt." The an-swers as well as other questions can be found in the back of the book.

Using the menu in the book, ask students to combine other menu items and write them on a restaurant order form and add for the to-tal cost to the pigs, not exceeding $34.67. As-sume tax and tip are included. Students can figure out tax and tip separately for an addi-tional activity.

Provide each group with a menu from a different restaurant and invite them to make choices from the new restaurant, again writing them on a restaurant order form, still not ex-ceeding $34.67. Challenge students to find the restaurant that would give the pigs the most/ least food for their money.

Money Mural Timeline

Provide small groups of students with bulletin board paper, pencils, markers, and crayons. Using the information in *The Story of Money* and the timeline (page 30) of *Stepping Through History: Money* by Peggy Burns, assign each group a different time period and ask them to design a piece of a mural that depicts what was used for money during that time period and the people who used it. Put the pieces together to form one long timeline/mural.

Make Cash for Your Class

With the whole class, read aloud *How the Second Grade Got $8,205.50 to Visit the Statue of Liberty* by Nathan Zimmelman to introduce the concepts of expenses and profits. Also, view the video *Piggy Banks to Money Markets*. Brainstorm things that the students would like to do or buy, thinking about how much money would be required. Brainstorm ideas for things that students could do or sell to raise money. Students could make food to sell such as soft pretzels and mulled cider (see recipes in unit appendix). They could create crafts like wrapping paper, bird feeders, or floating candles. They could start spider plants from babies and sell them in water. They could have a garage sale. They could even offer a service such as a car wash. See resources such as *Making Cents: Every Kid's Guide to Money, How to Make It, What to Do with It* by Elizabeth Wilkinson and *Making Money* by Teena McDiarmid and *50 Nifty Ways to Earn Money* by Andrea Urton for many more ideas. Regardless of which ideas are chosen, it is important to keep track of expenses and profits and to repay any investors. Be sure to inform and include parents in your fund-raising efforts.

Once money has been raised, share *The Monster Money Book* by Loreen Leedy to introduce the idea of making a budget. As a class, make a budget like the one in the book to decide exactly what to do with the money. Once everyone agrees to the budget, try to involve students in the disbursement of funds as directed.

PARENT LETTER

Dear Parents,

During the next couple of weeks we will be exploring the wonderful world of money—how it began, how it's changed, and what we can do with it in our modern world. The book we will be using is *The Story of Money* by Betsy Maestro, which tells the whole story. It can be found at your local library along with other fascinating books about money.

Throughout our unit, your child will be learning about earning, spending and saving money, as well as designing and collecting it as a hobby. We will be working with play money, our own handmade money, and some real money. It would be most helpful if you could provide your child with some extra experience in the handling of real money at home at this time.

We invite you to share in our learning adventure by taking your child to a local store with the "Window Shopping" Sheet (attached) and joining us for our Trade and Barter Day on _____ at _____ as well as our fund-raising efforts toward the end of our study of money (more information on both will be coming your way soon). If you by chance collect coins and/or currency and would be willing to visit us to share some of your prized possessions, please let me know. Also, we will be in need of several odds and ends and ingredients that you may be able to send from home. Please check the attached "Wanted" sheet to see if you can help. We certainly do appreciate your assistance.

Sincerely,

$$$$$$$$$$$$

Parent/Child "Window Shopping" Sheet

Directions for parents: Visit a local department, discount, or toy store with your child where he or she can window shop for something that they could buy with $2.00, $5.00, $10.00, and $20.00. Assist them minimally in their decision making. Help them figure out the tax, total cost (and if they can, in fact, afford it with the given amount), and the change they would receive.

Directions for students: Take your parent, a pencil, a calculator, and this paper to a place you like to shop. Complete this sheet with your parent's help.

1.) If you had $2.00, what is one thing that you could buy?

Price _____ Tax _____ Total cost _____ Your change _____

2.) If you had $5.00, what is one thing that you could buy?

Price _____ Tax _____ Total cost _____ Your change _____

3.) If you had $10.00, what is one thing that you could buy?

Price _____ Tax _____ Total cost _____ Your change _____

4.) If you had $20.00, what is one thing that you could buy?

Price _____ Tax _____ Total cost _____ Your change _____

5.) Name one thing that you would really, really like to have and would be willing to save your money for.

Price _____ Tax _____ Total amount you need to save _____

Coin Characteristics Chart

front illustration/design (draw it)   back illustration/design (draw it)

(describe it) _____   (describe it) _____

_____   _____

_____   _____

Value _____   Color _____   Size _____

Weight _____   Date _____ Minted in _____

Coin Characteristics Chart

front illustration/design (draw it)   back illustration/design (draw it)

(describe it) _____   (describe it) _____

_____   _____

_____   _____

Value _____   Color _____   Size _____

Weight _____   Date _____ Minted in _____

Recipes

Mulled Cider

1 gallon apple cider
4 sticks cinnamon
2 tsp. ground nutmeg
2 tsp. whole cloves

Soft Pretzels

1.) Dissolve 1 T yeast in $\frac{1}{2}$ cup warm water
2.) Add 1 tsp. honey and 1 tsp. salt
3.) Add $1\frac{1}{3}$ cups flour
4.) Knead
5.) Form pretzels
6.) Brush with beaten egg and sprinkle with salt
7.) Bake 10 minutes at 425°F

Play Dough

$2\frac{1}{2}$ cups flour
$\frac{1}{2}$ cup salt
1 T cream of tartar
2 cups boiling water
3 T vegetable oil
1 pkg. Kool-Aid for color and scent

Mix dry ingredients. Add water and oil mixture, stir. Knead dough when cool.

What Would You Pay?

Name:_____

Date:_____

1.) A candy bar in the United States costs 50¢. What would you pay in schillings?

_____

2.) A shirt in the United States costs $10.00. What would you pay in yens?

_____

3.) A gallon of milk in the United States costs $2.59. What would you pay in drachmas?

_____

4.) A bottle of bubbles in the United States costs $1.00. What would you pay in Canadian dollars?

_____

5.) A pair of jeans in the United States costs $25.00. What would you pay in pesos?

_____

6.) A candle in the United States costs $5.00. What would you pay in pounds?

_____

7.) A hamburger in the United States costs $1.89. What would you pay in francs?

_____

8.) A blanket in the United States costs $15.00. What would you pay in marks?

_____

See page 29 in *Stepping Through History: Money* by Peggy Burns for an exchange rate chart.

You Owe ...

Name:_____

Date:_____

1.) If you borrowed $5,000 from the bank at a 15% interest rate to buy a car, how much interest would you owe? _____

_____

What would be the total amount that you would have to pay back? _____

2.) If you took out a student loan for $3,000 at a 9% interest rate, how much interest would you owe?

_____

_____

What would be the total amount that you would have to pay back? _____

3.) If you bought a new TV for $400 and charged it on your Visa card at a 21% interest rate, how much would the finance charge be on your bill? _____

_____

Now what is the total that you owe? _____

4.) If you borrowed $30 from your uncle to buy a puppy and he charged you 3% interest, how much interest would you owe? _____

_____

What would the total cost of the puppy be including interest? _____

You Made ...

Name:_____

Date:_____

1.) If you put $100 in a regular savings account with a 3% interest rate, how much interest would you have made in one period (three months)?_____

How much would you have made in one year (four periods)?_____

2.) If you put an additional $650 in the same account as above, how much interest would you have made in one period?_____

How much in one year?_____

3.) If you put $400 in a CD with a 5% interest rate, how much interest would you have made in one period?_____

How much in one year?_____

4.) If you bought a $50 U.S. savings bond with a 4% interest rate and if you wait to cash it in for seven years, how much interest would you have made?_____

What would be the total value of the bond?_____

5.) If you put $30 inside your piggy bank with a 0% interest rate, what would you have made at the end of one year without adding any more money?_____

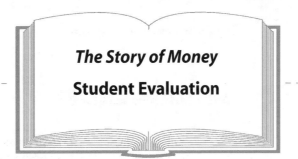

The Story of Money
Student Evaluation

Name:_____

1.) During the unit, I worked cooperatively in my groups

      not at all   sometimes   most of the time

2.) During the unit, I tried my best

      not at all   sometimes   most of the time

3.) During the unit, I completed

____ a Coin Characteristics Chart   ____ a "Window Shopping" Sheet

____ a piggy bank   ____ a small change investigation

____ a story   ____ a cleaning, rubbing, and recording

____ a trade or barter   ____ a coin for the class collection

____ an original coin design   ____ an original currency design

____ a foreign currency investigation   ____ a poster of things once used for money

____ a counterfeit coin/dollar money   ____ a check for a pretend purchase

____ a page for the million dollar book   ____ a money mural/timeline

____ 2 sheets on making/paying interest

4.) Something new that I learned about ancient buying/selling is:_____

_____

5.) Something new that I learned about making and designing money is:_____

_____

6.) Something new that I learned about earning or saving money is:_____

_____

7.) Something new that I learned about spending money is:_____

_____

8.) One thing that I worked on that I am especially proud of is: _____

_____

9.) My favorite things about this unit were:_____

_____

SUPPORTING LIBRARY

Adams, Barbara Johnston. *The Go-Around Dollar*. New York: Four Winds Press, 1992.
Tells the story of one dollar bill changing hands throughout a day while giving facts about U.S. dollar bills.

Adler, David A. *All Kinds of Money*. New York: Franklin Watts, 1984.
Discusses the history of money from primitive times to today.

Axelrod, Amy. *Pigs Will Be Pigs*. New York: Four Winds Press, Macmillan Publishing, 1994.
The story of a hungry pig family who searches the house for money to go out to eat.

Brodmann, Alaina. *The Gift*. New York: Simon & Schuster Books for Young Readers, 1993.
A young girl considers the many things she could buy with her birthday money.

Burns, Peggy. *Stepping Through History: Money*. New York: Thomson Learning, 1994.
Describes the history of trade and money from long ago to today.

Caple, Kathy. *The Purse*. Boston: Houghton Mifflin, 1986.
Katie earns money, spends it, and saves it.

Cribb, Joe. *Money* (Eyewitness Books). New York: Alfred A. Knopf, 1990.
Discusses old money and modern money from more than ten different countries. Includes sections on forgery, checks, and credit card and coin collecting.

Elkin, Benjamin. *Money* (A New True Book). Chicago: Childrens Press, 1983.
An easy-reader about basic money concepts.

German, Don. *Mattie's Money Tree*. Philadelphia: Westminster Press, 1984.
Mattie and Scott grow money on a tree and find themselves doing some interesting things with it. A beginning chapter book.

German, Joan W. *The Money Book*. New York: Elsevier/Nelson Books, 1981.
Describes the coins that can be combined to make a dollar. Includes simple problems for practice in making change.

Giff, Patricia Reilly. *Count Your Money with the Polk Street School*. New York: Yearling Books, 1994.
The Polk Street gang learns about money concepts and friendship. A beginning chapter book.

Hoban, Lillian. *Arthur's Funny Money*. New York: Harper & Row, 1981.
Violet and Arthur go into business together.

Leedy, Loreen. *The Monster Money Book*. New York: Holiday House, 1992.
A club looks at new members and how to spend dues collected.

Lewis, Brenda Ralph. *Coins and Currency* (Hobby Handbooks). New York: Random House, 1993.
Complete look at coin collecting and the history of money.

Maestro, Betsy, and Giulio Maestro. *Dollars and Cents for Harriet*. New York: Crown Publishers, 1988.
An elephant wants to buy a kite and needs to make money to buy it. She discovers six ways to make a dollar.

Manes, Stephen. *Make Four Million Dollars by Next Thursday.* New York: Bantam Books, 1991.
Jason starts following the advice of a get-rich-quick book. Chapter book.

Marshall, James. *Fox on the Job.* New York: Dial Books for Young Readers, 1988.
Fox tries to earn money for a new bike.

McDiarmid, Teena. *Making Money.* Milwaukee, Wisc.: Penworthy Publishing, 1988.
Discusses eighteen different ideas for kids to make money and includes a section to help them to evaluate their work.

Mitgutsch, Ali. *From Gold to Money.* Minneapolis, Minn.: Carolrhoda Books, 1985.
Describes in simple terms how bartering gave way to precious metals, which in turn gave way to alloy coins and paper money.

Parker, Nancy Winslow. *Money, Money, Money.* New York: HarperCollins, 1995.
Describes the artwork and symbols, their origin, and meaning on U.S. currency.

Schwartz, David M. *If You Made a Million.* New York: Lothrop, Lee & Shepard, 1989.
Describes earning, spending, and saving money in different combinations and forms.

Stanley, Diane. *Woe Is Moe.* New York: G. P. Putnam's Sons, 1995.
A factory worker wins a contest and gets rich but finds happiness with a true friend.

Stewart, Sarah. *The Money Tree.* New York: Farrar, Straus & Giroux, 1991.
A strange tree grows in Miss McGillicuddy's yard.

Urton, Andrea. *50 Nifty Ways to Earn Money.* Los Angeles: Lowell House Juvenile, 1993.
Describes fifty ways to make money. Includes a rating scale of difficulty for each job and specifies what is needed, how to prepare, and how to do each one.

Viorst, Judith. *Alexander, Who Used to Be Rich Last Sunday.* New York: Atheneum, 1978.
A boy receives $1.00 from his grandparents and hopes to save it but ends up spending or losing all of it.

Wilkinson, Elizabeth. *Making Cents: Every Kid's Guide to Money, How to Make It, What to Do with It.* Boston: Little, Brown, 1989.
Seasonal ideas for kids to make money including a business section.

Williams, Vera B. *A Chair for My Mother.* New York: Greenwillow Books, 1982.
A girl and her mother and grandmother save to buy a comfortable armchair.

Williams, Vera B. *Something Special for Me.* New York: Greenwillow Books, 1983.
Rosa has difficulty deciding on what to buy with the coins her mother and grandmother had saved.

Wyler, Rose. *Math Fun with Money Puzzlers.* New York: Julian Messner, Simon & Schuster, 1992.
An activities book with stories, games, brainteasers, and tricks about money.

Zimmelman, Nathan. *How the Second Grade Got $8,205.50 to Visit the Statue of Liberty.* Morton Grove, Ill.: Albert Whitman, 1992.
A class of second-graders make money for a class trip, keeping track of all of their expenses and profits.

Buried Worlds. *Sold! The Origins of Money and Trade.* Prepared by the Geography Department, University of Minnesota. Minneapolis, Minn.: Runestone Press, Lerner Publications, 1994.
Discusses many different aspects of money including its origin, history, how it was made and used, and how archeologists discover and use ancient money.

Videos

Alexander, Who Used to Be Rich Last Sunday. VanNuys, Calif.: Aims Media, 1990.
Based on the book by Judith Viorst, Alexander gets $5.00 from his grandparents and hopes to save it but ends up spending or losing it all. Not animated. Approximately 14 minutes.

Magical Field Trip to the Denver Mint. VanNuys, Calif.: Aims Media, 1988.
A magical cleaning lady takes three children on a field trip to the Denver Mint to see how quarters are made.

Making Money. Carlsbad, Calif.: Kidvision, Dave Hood Entertainment, 1995.
Professor Hoody "quantumtransports" to the engraving bureau in Washington, D.C. Discusses characteristics of U.S. paper money and shows the actual buildings that appear on the backs of bills. 28 minutes.

Piggy Banks to Money Markets. Newton, Mass.: Kidvidz, 1993.
Shows how kids can make money and how to use it once they've made it. 30 minutes.

Musical Instruments: Voyages of Discovery

Ken Moore

NEW YORK: SCHOLASTIC, 1993

ABOUT THE BOOK

Readers of *Musical Instruments: Voyages of Discovery* will take a journey back in time to discover the origins of musical instruments and some lasting cultural connections, myths, and beliefs associated with certain instruments. It also becomes clear that modern music is always changing as a result of new technology. Readers learn to distinguish between the main families of musical instruments, who makes them, and how these instruments are brought to life in the creation of different types of music. Overall, *Musical Instruments* helps the reader see that whether past or present, music has touched all of our lives with its sounds, its messages, and its wonder.

INVESTIGATIONS

Investigative Themes

Musical Instruments Past and Present
Music and Cultures
Making Sounds and Making Music
Production of Musical Instruments
Messages of Music
Famous Musicians and Composers

Investigative Skills

reading for information
comparing/contrasting
categorizing
creating music
performing experiments
note taking
making decisions
solving problems
thinking critically

researching
defining words
using maps
critiquing music
listening/speaking
writing
making charts and graphs
following directions

Investigative Materials

1 copy of *Musical Instruments* for every three students
Live Music Series by Elizabeth Sharma (six books)
supporting library books

large wall map of the world
removable stickers
tape/record player
recordings of individual instruments, jazz music, duets, ensembles, and symphony music
scores of orchestra music
white butcher/bulletin board paper
white and black construction paper
sandpaper, rocks, sticks, bottles, caps, buckets, etc.
alcohol and cotton balls
recorders or penny whistles (optional)
markers, crayons
tape, glue
supplies for simple sound experiments
examples of musical instruments and/or performers (i.e., anyone who has knowledge of an
     instrument that they can share, along with a performance of a simple song or two …
     unless, of course, you have free access to more professional performers!)

New Words for *Musical Instruments*

brass—instruments made from a long tube that opens out into a bell shape at the end; played by blowing air directly into a mouthpiece (e.g., trumpet, trombone, tuba)
composer—a person who writes a piece of music
conductor—the leader of an orchestra
ensemble—several musicians playing together
instrument—a tool used for making musical sounds
keyboard—any instrument with keys arranged like a piano's keys
lyrics—the words to a song
melody—combination of many different notes; a tune or a song
notes—single sounds made by an instrument
opera—musical theater; the performers sing all words
orchestra—a large group of performers on various musical instruments
percussion—instruments designed for rhythm; played by striking or scraping (e.g., drum, tambourine, triangle)
symphony—a musical composition in several parts written for an orchestra
synthesizer—an electronic instrument that can imitate every instrument
woodwinds—instruments that originally were made from wood; played by blowing wind through or into a hole (e.g., flute, saxophone, clarinet)

Investigations for Before Reading

Investigating New Words

Draw a large musical scale on white butcher paper and display on a wall. (See illustration below.) Write the definitions of the new words on the lines of the scales. Using the pattern, trace and cut out fifteen music notes from black construction paper. Write the words with white crayon on the black notes. Divide notes and distribute among groups of students who will cooperatively decide upon definitions using all available resources (*Musical Instruments,* dictionaries, supporting library, etc.). When they have agreed on the definition for each word, one member of the group tacks or tapes the note onto the wall scale next to its written definition. A melody could actually be created by playing the notes on the wall scale for those of you who are musically inclined.

Noise Minute

On scrap paper, ask students to list five ways that they could make noise. Then set a timer for one minute and ask students to make one of the noises that they listed. This illustrates the beginning of music—making sounds. Then, as a class, ask students to classify the sounds they made (and maybe some on their lists that they chose not to make) on a chalkboard chart. They should decide whether their noises were made by blowing; rubbing/plucking/scraping; rapping/tapping/shaking. Use these as headings for the chart. This introduces the concept of the different types of instrument families (wind,

string, percussion, respectively) and how their sounds are made. Headings on the chart can be changed to more formal names as each group is discussed. You may find a need for an "other" category that could become a place for "New Age sounds."

Sound Investigation

As an extension for the above activity, have students investigate sounds that they can make with primitive or unusual objects (i.e., sandpaper, rocks, a bottle, a can, sticks, a tin pail, etc.). Again, this illustrates early musical sounds. They can classify each of the objects as to how they are played and their instrument family by talking about them in small groups, writing the objects' names on a group Sound Investigation sheet (see unit appendix) and then passing them on to the next group for investigation.

Sound Fair

Depending upon the age of the children, this could be done in two different ways:

A.) Each student chooses a partner. Together they choose a sound experiment to share with the class. Give them time to prepare and gather materials from home. Half of the class can present or demonstrate their experiment on one day while the other half rotates among experiment stations. Then do the reverse on the following day.

B.) Choose several experiments for students to do independently or with the help of an adult (or older student) volunteer. Students in groups of three or four rotate to each available station every ten minutes or so. See Simple Sound Experiments in unit appendix.

Sound Notes

Provide students with materials to make a simple book to use throughout the unit to keep a record of music they hear around them:

sounds that they hear every day and sounds that they find particularly special or interesting. The books could be titled "I Heard It!" or "Sounds Around" or something else of their choosing. Their notes could be shared daily with a partner as a warm-up activity.

Where in the World?

Make sure that students have access to a large wall map of the world for reference throughout the unit. There will be references to many other countries in the world during the reading of *Musical Instruments*. Students can locate these countries on the wall map and mark them with removable stickers. This will illustrate that yesterday's and today's music exists everywhere in our world.

Prereading Investigation

Because *Musical Instruments* is full of interesting illustrations, flaps, overlays, and foldout parts, let students investigate these things beforehand. This way they can concentrate on the information being presented during reading.

Listening Center

Provide students with a variety of music to listen to and critique (see unit appendix) throughout the unit in a center for no more than three students at a time.

Investigations for During Reading

Suggestions for Reading Musical Instruments

Because the format of the book has similar layouts for each section, I recommend that the reading be varied. For example, the left side of each section could be read aloud by the teacher or individual students, then the right-hand side could be read in a cooperative group as it is conveniently divided into smaller parts to facilitate turn taking.

"Early Music" and "Music and Myth"

Discuss and recall the many purposes and meanings of early music. Ask students to list or draw some of the earliest instruments.

"Blowing"

Provide several examples of instruments that are played by blowing. Depending on the source of these instruments, you may invite children to investigate their own blowing techniques. Wipe the mouthpieces with alcohol after each child. After recalling the definitions for woodwind and brass instruments, students could classify each instrument accordingly. Then, in small groups, ask students to make illustrated attribute charts for woodwind instruments and

brass instruments. Students may need to refer to illustrations from additional resources before drawing their own.

This would be the perfect time to have guest performers share information and a song or two on several different wind instruments. If this is not possible, then listen to recordings of different wind instruments. If you do have guest performers, students should write thank-you notes promptly afterward.

This is also an excellent opportunity to introduce students to recorders or penny whistles if they are available. Provide them with a very simple song to practice and learn together. Give a miniperformance for the principal, office staff, or kitchen staff.

"Rubbing, Plucking, Scraping"

Provide students with several examples of stringed instruments to investigate. Guest performers could share more specifics about the playing of string instruments and a song or two. Again, if this is not possible, then provide recordings of different string instruments.

Share recordings of jazz guitar and acoustic guitar for children to compare. Talk about differences, similarities, and opinions in small groups.

Afterward, ask students in small groups to design an illustrated chart for stringed instruments.

"Rapping, Tapping, Shaking"

Provide students with as many different types of percussion instruments as you can find. An optimum amount would be one simple percussion instrument per student, such as two dowels for rhythm sticks, blocks wrapped in sandpaper, drums from plastic or cardboard containers, bells, gourd shakers, and so on. See *Making Music with Instruments You Make Yourself: Shake, Rattle and Roll* by Mike Jackson and *Sound and Music* by David Evans and Claudette Williams for more ideas for handmade percussion instruments. Students may be able to add to the selection by bringing percussion instruments from home. This should illustrate for students that there are more percussion instruments than any other kind. Students can investigate the many different sounds you can make with percussion instruments. Ask four or five students to play their instruments together and observe the combined sound. Trade instruments with others until the group creates a combined sound that they all like. Afterward, ask students in small groups to design illustrated attribute charts for percussion instruments.

Class Graph

Make a class graph by asking each student which family of instruments they found most appealing. Make another class graph by asking each student which family of instruments they thought was the most difficult to play. Compare the information of the two resulting graphs.

"Who Makes Musical Instruments?" and "The Birth of the Violin"

Share parts of *The Master Violinmaker* by Paul Fleisher. Invite students to comment on possible pros and cons of factory-made versus handmade instruments.

"Playing Together" and "The Orchestra and Conductor"

Listen to recordings of duets or ensembles and symphonies. Ask students to compare the char-

acteristics and possibly the instruments playing in the two selections using a Venn diagram. For example, both selections may have drums and brass but only one may have stringed instruments. Or one selection may be slow and soft and the other loud and fast.

Provide small groups of students with different scores of music to investigate. How many instruments are playing at once? What do all the symbols mean?

Look at the foldout page of the full orchestra. Ask students to count how many people play each instrument. Ask the following questions: Why are there so many of some and only a few of others? Why are they positioned in this particular way (certain instruments in front and others in back)? How many altogether? Help students figure out fractions or percentages of each instrument in regard to the whole orchestra. Invite students to create additional math problems that they can challenge another group with using the picture of the orchestra.

Make a tiny accordion book that tells five things that a conductor must do in leading an orchestra.

"The Piano, King of Instruments" and "New Sounds"

Divide the class into three groups. Arrange with the music teacher so that one group can investigate a piano inside and out and listen to a guest performer. The second group could listen to and evaluate recordings of pianists. A third group could be invited to investigate the sounds of a synthesizer or electric guitar with microphones and sound amplification. Groups should be rotated so all students can participate in each activity. Afterward, have a debriefing session with the whole group.

"The Voices of Music" and "Music as Companion"

Play recordings of the four pieces of music suggested in *Musical Instruments* to illustrate how music can send messages and evoke feelings in the listener. Play other pieces and ask students to guess or speculate as to the mood that each piece is trying to create. Include a variety of examples such as modern-day music, lullabies, blues, military music, and so on.

Talk about the "Sound Notes" that the students have been keeping and have them try to figure out how many times they hear music in a day? in a week? in a month? in a year? Have them estimate the amount of time music is part of their lives and imagine what our world would be like without music.

Investigations for After Reading

Field Trip

Investigate a local museum that offers a section of musical instruments. Or attend a live performance of a symphony in concert and ask students to critique what they hear (see unit appendix).

Which Instrument?

Play recordings of instruments previously heard by students and have them guess which instrument is being played. Offer a musical prize, such as a kazoo or a plastic flute, to those who guess the most correctly.

Silly Symphony

Invite students and their families to a silly symphony. They should create their own instruments at home to play in a creative orchestra. You may choose a familiar folk song such as "Bingo" for the orchestra to play along with. Each person should have their own instrument in order to perform, otherwise they can be part of the audience. There should be sections for the different types of instruments for the musicians to sit in (e.g., string, woodwind, percussion, brass). Children should help set a date and time, plan out and set up the sections, including how many seats will be needed (according to reservations by instrument type), who should conduct, what to bring for refreshments, and who will bring them.

Group Project

Students may select one of the six interest groups to participate in: voice, percussion, keyboards, brass, woodwinds, strings. Each group should have a volunteer adult leader for reading and guidance through the following activities:

A.) Share the corresponding book together from the Live Music Series by Elizabeth Sharma *(Brass. Keyboards. Percussion. Strings. The Voice. Woodwinds.)*

B.) As a group, select new and interesting key points to share with the class. Each member of the group should contribute in writing or drawing the information on a small poster and be prepared to report to the class.

C.) Hold a short performance using the corresponding type of instruments (professionally made or handmade). Or compare members belonging to the same family of instruments (real or pictures). Or demonstrate how to make an instrument that would belong in that particular family of instruments. For example, the percussion group would perform on, compare examples of, or make percussion instruments only.

Other Challenging Investigations

A.) Independently or with a partner, make a timeline of musical history using all available resources.

B.) Investigate the lives of Thomas Edison or Alexander Graham Bell. When did they live? What did they contribute to our world of sounds?

C.) Design a bulletin board using the information from the "People to Know" section (red pages) at the end of *Musical Instruments.* Use the library to find books on some of these people to read up on more fun facts.

D.) Independently read *Midori, Brilliant Violinist* by Charnan Simon. Write about six different things that happened in Midori's life that are different from your life. If you were Midori, how would you have felt during those six times? Is there anything that you like to do as much as Midori likes to play her violin? Write about it. Try to locate a Midori recording at your local library. Listen and critique.

E.) Independently read *The Master Violinmaker* by Paul Fleisher. Make a book showing the steps involved in making a violin by hand. Include an explanation as to why the best violins are made by hand. Or make a poster identifying all the parts of a violin. Then borrow a real violin and identify its parts for the class.

F.) Listen to a sound recording of *Peter and the Wolf*. Draw pictures to go with the story you hear.

PARENT LETTER

Dear Parents,

Next week we will begin an enlightening unit on music and sound based on the book *Musical Instruments: Voyages of Discovery* by Ken Moore. We will spend about three weeks discovering the origins of music and what makes music through reading books and listening and experimenting with sounds. We will also be making some of our own music and perhaps discovering some hidden talents.

We are looking for guest performers to share musical instruments and simple songs. If you would be willing or able to share your talents with us or know someone else who might be interested, please contact me as soon as you can.

Also, we will be in need of six parent volunteers to help with group projects during the last week of our unit. Each volunteer will be working with a small group of students and focusing on a particular family of instruments. Please see the attached "Wanted" sheet for days and times.

Mark your calendars! We would like to invite you and your family to participate in our Silly Symphony, which will take place on _____ from _____ to _____. Each attending member will need to make a musical instrument at home out of anything you can think of and bring it with you for the performance of a lifetime. Idea resources for making musical instruments will be available after school in our classroom. I will be sending home an official invitation soon. Please R.S.V.P. as soon as possible. There will also be audience space for those who wish to spectate only. Start thinking about your musical creations now!

Lastly, we will be taking a field trip to _____ on _____. We would love for you to join us. Look for the permission form coming your way soon. Please sign and return this form as soon as possible. Thank you.

Keep a song in your heart!

Simple Sound Experiments

1.) Balloon noises

Experiment with blowing up balloons and letting the air escape through the opening as you stretch it in different ways. Listen to the different sounds you can make with air and different-sized balloons.

2.) Bottle blowing

Experiment by blowing on different types of bottles. Listen for the tone and loudness made by different-sized bottles and varying amounts of air. Fill the bottles with varying amounts of water and listen for changes.

3.) Bottle xylophone

Experiment with about five bottles that are the same size and shape but filled with different amounts of liquid. Tap them gently with a spoon. Try to arrange them in the order of the sounds they make. Think about why they make different sounds.

4.) Rhythm

Experiment with a wooden spoon and several different-sized "drums" (pots, pans, buckets, cups, etc.). Try to stay in rhythm with a metronome. Think about why they sound different and what that would mean with real drums.

5.) Tone

Experiment with a piece of wood with ten nails nailed at varying heights in order from small to tall. Tap each nail with a fork. Think about why they sound different and what instrument each one is similar to.

6.) Rubber band guitar

Experiment with different-sized (thickness and length) rubber bands stretched over an open container such as a shoe box or cake pan. Try strumming them together with your fingers. Then try strumming with a quarter. Try doing the same with individual strings. Have a partner pull some strings tighter and observe the change in sound.

7.) Megaphones

Experiment with making megaphones out of tagboard. See how far away you can hear your friend's voice. Try making different-sized megaphones and seeing if size makes a difference in the distance.

8.) Sound test

Experiment with listening and trying to identify objects that a friend drops behind your back. See how many you can guess correctly. Find different items to do the same for your friend. Also, try blindfolding yourself and guessing which direction something was dropped. See what happens if you cover one ear and guess the direction.

9.) Sound travels

Experiment by putting a ticking watch or clock on a wooden table, pressing one ear against the tabletop, and covering the other ear. See if you can hear the ticking through the wood. See how far you can move away and still hear it. Try the same thing on a metal table to see if the ticking can still be heard or if it sounds different.

10.) Ringing glasses

Experiment with several wine glasses filled with varying amounts of water. Wet your finger and slide it around the rim of each glass until you hear a ringing sound. Think about why they might sound different.

For lots more experiments with sound and music, see suggestions for supporting books. Make copies of slips like the following example to help students stay focused on learning as they perform each experiment. They can be stapled together when they have finished with all experiments and sent home to share with parents.

Names in group: _____

Experiment

What did I learn from this experiment? _____

_____

Which experiment was most interesting? Why? _____

_____

What does this tell you about musical instruments?_____

_____

Sound Investigation

Names in group: _____

Record below the names of objects according to how you get it to poduce a sound.

rubbing/plucking/scraping	blowing	rapping/tapping/shaking	other

What type of musical instruments are played by rubbing, plucking, or scraping? _____

_____

What type of musical instruments are played by blowing? _____

_____

What type of musical instruments are played by rapping, tapping, or shaking? _____

_____

What musical instruments might fit in your "other" category? _____

_____

Music Note Pattern

Ideas for Enlisting Possible Guest Performers ...

parents

teachers

spouses

principals

chorus directors

high school students

yourself

neighbors

friends

music teachers

band leaders

orchestra leaders

What kinds of things should guest performers share? Here are some ideas to help them prepare:

- talk about instrument and how it is played
- play a simple song to demonstrate
- when and how they became interested in playing music
- how much they practice
- how long they have been playing
- how much do their instruments generally cost
- how do they take care of their instrument
- do they play alone or with other people
- how do they feel when they are playing
- what do they like best about being able to play
- what is their favorite music or song
- play another song for demonstration

Students may ask some of these questions, but your guest performers may appreciate knowing what they will be asked ahead of time.

Listening Center Music Critique

Name:_____

Date:_____

Title of music:_____

Type of music:_____

1.) Overall, I liked/disliked this music because _____
_____

2.) I thought that the mood of this music was _____
_____

3.) I could hear the following instruments being played: _____
_____

_____

4. I would recommend this music to _____ because _____
_____

Field Trip Symphony Critique

Name:_____

Date:_____

My thoughts on the first piece:_____

_____

• the second piece:_____

_____

• the third piece:_____

_____

• the fourth piece:_____

_____

• the fifth piece:_____

_____

• the conductor:_____

• the theater:_____

What instruments could you see?_____

_____

Overall opinion:_____

_____

Musical Instruments
Student Evaluation

Name:_____

1.) During the unit, I worked cooperatively with my groups

      not at all   sometimes   most of the time

2.) During the unit, I tried my best

      not at all   sometimes   most of the time

3.) During the unit, I completed

____ a graph   ____ a letter/note   ____ a poster

____ a critique   ____ a handmade instrument   ____ a chart

____ a sound journal   ____ a list   ____ several sounds

____ a map of the world   ____ an accordion book   ____ experiments

4.) Overall, my group project/presentation was

      a flop   okay   a success

5.) Something new that I learned about sound is:_____

_____

6.) Something new that I learned about music is:_____

_____

7.) Something new that I learned about myself is:_____

_____

8.) Something that I worked on that I am especially proud of is:_____

_____

9.) My favorite things about this unit were:_____

_____

SUPPORTING LIBRARY

Ardley, Neil. *Music* (Eyewitness Books). New York: Dorling Kindersley, 1989.
Provides description, pictures, and background on all types of musical instruments.

Ardley, Neil. *The Science Book of Sound.* New York: Harcourt Brace Jovanovich, 1991.
Provides simple experiments with sound and music.

Ardley, Neil. *Sound Waves to Music.* New York: Gloucester Press, 1990.
Provides many sound/music facts and simple experiments.

Caseley, Judith. *Ada Potato.* New York: Greenwillow Books, 1989.
Ada learns to play a violin and learns how to handle teasing from other children.

Catherall, Ed. *Exploring Sound.* Austin, Tex.: Steck-Vaughn, 1990.
Includes a variety of simple sound experiments.

Evans, David, and Claudette Williams. *Sound and Music.* New York: Dorling Kindersley, 1993.
Explains sounds and making simple instruments with children. Perfect for adapting for younger children
    and/or special needs.

Fleisher, Paul. *The Master Violinmaker.* New York: Houghton Mifflin, 1993.
Step-by-step construction of a handmade violin. Includes real photographs.

Foley, Patricia. *John and the Fiddler.* New York: Harper & Row Junior Books, 1990.
A boy and an old man share a common love for the violin and develop a special friendship. Easy chapter
    book.

Jackson, Mike. *Making Music: Shake, Rattle and Roll with Instruments You Make Yourself.* New York:
    HarperCollins, 1993.
Describes materials and how to make and play a variety of instruments.

Jennings, Terry. *Making Sounds* (Junior Science). New York: Gloucester Press, 1990.
Simply describes different types of sounds and experiments to try.

Kaner, Etta. *Sound Science.* Reading, Mass.: Addison-Wesley, 1991.
Offers more than forty experiments and activities with sound.

Kraus, Robert. *Musical Max.* New York: Simon & Schuster Books for Young Readers, 1990.
Max disturbs his neighbors with his musical talents.

Krull, Kathleen. *Lives of the Musicians: Good Times, Bad Times and What the Neighbors Thought.* New York:
    Harcourt Brace Jovanovich, 1993.
Stories of twenty different composers/musicians.

Ober, Hal. *How Music Came to the World.* Boston: Houghton Mifflin, 1994.
A retelling of a Mexican myth explaining the beginnings of music on Earth.

Paker, Josephine. *Music from Strings.* Brookfield Conn.: Millbrook Press, 1992.
Provides a close look at the string family including the piano, the guitar, the banjo, the harp, and so on.
    Also includes sections on orchestra, opera, and special tools.

Parsons, Alexandra. *Sound.* New York: Aladdin Books, Macmillan Publishing, 1993.
Provides simple and advanced experiments with sound and music.

Pillar, Marjorie. *Join the Band.* New York: HarperCollins, 1992.
A young flute player talks about the instruments in her school band and the preparation for a concert.

Rachlin, Ann. *Chopin* (Famous Children). New York: Barron's Educational Series, 1993.
Tells the story of Frederick Chopin as a child and how he became a famous composer. Also in the series: Bach, Brahms, Handel, Haydn, Mozart, Schumann, and Tchaikovsky.

Rediger, Pat. *Great African Americans in Music.* New York: Crabtree Publishing, 1996.
Provides thirteen profiles of well-known African-American performers/musicians, including Aretha Franklin, Janet Jackson, M. C. Hammer, and Ray Charles.

Sharma, Elizabeth. *Brass. Keyboards. Percussion. Strings. The Voice. Woodwinds* (Live Music Series). New York: Thomson Learning, 1993.
Includes photographs, easy-to-understand facts about the instruments, and directions for making home-made instruments.

Shipton, Alyn. *Brass. Keyboards and Electronic Music. Percussion. Singing. Strings. Woodwinds* (Exploring Music Series). Austin, Tex.: Steck-Vaughn, 1994.
Similar to Live Music Series above, but slightly more advanced.

Simon, Charnan. *Midori, Brilliant Violinist.* New York: Childrens Press, 1993.
A short biography of a famous child violinist.

Stevens, Bryna. *Handel and the Famous Sword Swallower of Halle.* New York: Philomel Books, 1990.
With the help of his aunt and a boy who swallowed a sword, young Handel becomes a famous musician despite his father's protests.

Storms, Jerry. *101 Music Games for Children.* Alameda, Calif.: Hunt, 1995.
Offers games that can be played with large or small groups to help develop skills such as listening, expression, and concentration. Great teacher resource.

Storms, Laura. *Careers with an Orchestra.* Minneapolis, Minn.: Lerner Publications, 1983.
Describes fifteen jobs connected with a symphony orchestra.

Tusa, Tricia. *Miranda.* New York: Macmillan Publishing, 1985.
Miranda plays her piano for everyone and then learns a new kind of music.

Walter, Margaret Pitts. *Ty's One Man Band.* New York: Four Winds Press, 1980.
Ty meets a man who fills the night with music using some unusual instruments.

Warner, Gertrude Chandler. *The Boxcar Children: The Mystery of the Stolen Music.* Morton Grove, Ill.: Albert Whitman, 1995.
An orchestra comes to town and the children look forward to meeting performers and making their own instruments. But then a valuable piece of old music is stolen. Great for reading aloud.

See your local library for their selection of sound recordings.

Be a Friend to Trees
(Let's-Read-and-Find-Out Science Book)
Patricia Lauber
New York: HarperCollins, 1994

About the Book

Be a Friend to Trees by Patricia Lauber provides a look at the wonderful world of trees and their importance to us. The processes of photosynthesis and the exchange of carbon dioxide and oxygen between trees and animals are discussed in understandable text with helpful diagrams. The reader learns that we use things made from trees every day of our lives as they provide food, air, shelter, and many other things for humans and other living creatures. The author concludes with suggestions for things we can do for our very important friends—trees.

Investigations

Investigative Themes

Interdependence of Plants and Animals
Ecology
Botany and the Study of Trees

Investigative Skills

working cooperatively
creating designs
planning
defining words
categorizing
observing
collecting
recording data
making maps
estimating

thinking critically
sequencing
making charts
writing stories
comparing/contrasting
listening/speaking
researching
drawing
writing letters
measuring

identifying
using numbers

making murals
reading for information

Investigative Materials

1 copy of *Be a Friend to Trees* for every three to four students
one spotter's guide for every three to four students
supporting library books

bulletin board paper—green, white, brown, red, orange, yellow
scissors
tape, glue
markers, crayons, colored pencils
magnifying glasses
package of small sticky notes (green would be perfect)
3 sheets of lined chart paper
large white construction paper for charts
poster board
circles of white paper (traced with a coffee can lid)
paints—watercolors, poster paint, acrylics
old wire hangers
art smocks
newspapers
old sponges
clay
sketch pads or clipboards
shovels, spades, buckets
ribbon

New Words for *Be a Friend to Trees*

carbon dioxide—a gas that humans breathe out and plants take in
chlorophyll—the green pigment (color) in plants
coniferous—cone-bearing evergreen
deciduous—shedding leaves each year
girth—the distance around the trunk of a tree
groundwater—water held in layers of rock and soil beneath the Earth's surface
lumber—wood cut and split for market
oxygen—a gas in our atmosphere that is necessary for animal life and is given off by green plants
recycle—to use again
roost—to settle down to sleep on a perch
sap—watery juice of plants
sapling—a young tree
seedling—a plant or tree grown from a seed
shelter—a place where something may live and be protected
timber—trees suitable for cutting and building

(*Note:* Prior to beginning the unit, do your own investigation of your school's neighborhood and park areas within walking distance. Take pictures of the trees that reside there for identification and classification purposes later in the unit. Also consider the season of the year. This unit is most appropriate for early fall when leaf specimens are readily available but not entirely crisp. On the other hand, spring/summer is a perfect time for students to focus on the seeds and flowers of trees.)

Investigations for Before Reading

New Words Investigation

Beforehand, prepare a bulletin board with a large trunk and bare branches of a deciduous tree. Share the poem/book *Trees* by Harry Behn to set the tone for entering the wonderful world of trees.

Then provide students in groups of three with a piece of green bulletin board paper, three pairs of scissors, and a list of new words. Each student may choose five words to define. Then, using all available resources, challenge each group to locate all fifteen definitions. Students who have defined their chosen five words should be encouraged to help others in their group. Once all fifteen words are defined, each group should join another group of three to discuss each word, come to a consensus, and, if needed, "adjust" each definition on the list. Once consensus is reached, each student should trace and cut out five of their hands from the green bulletin board paper to make leaves for the bare tree. Then the words and definitions should be neatly printed on the leaves. The left-over leaves (those that are not written on)

should be attached to the tree first. The word/definition leaves should be attached last so that they can be seen and referred to throughout the unit.

Investigate Tree Parts

Invite students to begin gathering tree parts such as leaves, twigs, blossoms, and seeds for examination. Remind students to invite their parents along and to gather specimens only from their own yards or in public parks unless they have permission from the property owner. In addition, remind students that needles from coniferous trees are also leaves and their pinecones hold their seeds, both of which are needed in this investigation/collection. Once a variety of specimens has been gathered, invite small groups of students to examine them carefully with magnifying glasses and hypothesize as to what information each specimen provides us about the tree. Everything can be saved and used for special collections once the students have more information for categorizing.

Investigations for During Reading

Suggestions for Reading Be a Friend to Trees

Students should read the book aloud in its entirety in small groups. I suggest that they read it a second time and possibly a third time, taking time to make the lists the author asks for on pages 8 and 10 and taking notes about things that are made from trees, types of trees, and tree life, as this information will be needed in the activities that follow.

Just a Tree?

Invite several students to draw and color a large class tree on bulletin board or chart paper. During reading (of the main title as well as the supporting library books), every time something made from a tree is discovered, a student should write it on a small sticky note and attach it to the tree. Pages 8 and 10 of *Be a Friend to Trees* invite the reader to make lists of the things around them that are made of wood and paper. These lists can begin the "sticky note tree." Students should spend time looking at the "sticky note tree" each day to see what has been added, not only to increase their knowledge but hopefully to avoid repetition. The end result will be an amazingly full tree that will clearly illustrate the number and variety of things that come from trees. Some of which may surprise you and your students!

Investigating Types of Trees

Make three large characteristics charts by writing the headings "Deciduous or Broad-Leaved Trees," "Coniferous Trees," and "Tropical Trees." Students should assign themselves to one type of tree. Then provide each group with one general book on trees and forests, such as *Tree* (Eyewitness Book) by David Burnie, *Trees* (Eyewitness Explorers) by Linda Gamlin, or *Floratorium* by Joanne Oppenheim, so that they may share corresponding sections to discover the characteristics and examples of each type of tree. Begin the three lists by inviting members of each group to contribute one characteristic at a time until all possible characteristics are recorded for each type of tree. Students could also list the different names of trees mentioned in each section in the same fashion.

Investigating Forests

Following the chart activity, provide the same three groups with paints, bulletin board paper, and the books *Ancient Ones* by Barbara Bash, *Temperate Forests* by Terry Jennings, and *Tropical Rainforests* by Jean Hamilton, all of which are about different types of forests. Students should pay special attention to the illustrations as they research their forest type. Then each group should be responsible for making part of a forest mural, with separate areas for deciduous, coniferous, and tropical forests. I suggest using watercolor and watered-down acrylic paints for an overlapping/full forest effect. This mural will be used with the "Investigating Tree Life" activity.

As a further extension for this activity, students can make a world wall map of forests by tracing a wall map of the world using bulletin board paper and color coding for forest types. Consult *Floratorium* by Joanne Oppenheim, *Temperate Forests* by Terry Jennings, or *Forests* by Chris Arvetis to obtain appropriate information in designing the map.

Investigating Tree Life

Share the poems "A Tree Place" (page 21) and "Forest Secrets" (page 40) from the book *A Tree Place and Other Poems* by Constance Levy to begin a discussion on the living things that inhabit trees. Also share *Woods and Forests* by John Norris Wood to challenge students' skills of observation.

As a class, identify creatures that were mentioned in the main title, the above poems, and the selections from the previous activity by making a list on the chalkboard. Arrange four or five small groups of students. Provide each of the groups with A Forest Is My Home sheet (see unit appendix), several circles of white paper (these can be traced using a coffee can), pencils and crayons or colored pencils, and a supporting library book that identifies specific creatures that live in, on, or around trees:

Once There Was a Tree by Natalia Romanova
Tree by David Burnie
Forest Life by Barbara Taylor
Tree Life by Kim Taylor
Tree Trunk Traffic by Bianca Lavies

Students should locate as many creatures as they can from within their resource, then draw and label each one on a white circle of paper. The circles should then be attached in the appropriate area of the forest mural that was completed in the previous activity. Each group should also briefly research one of the creatures using the A Forest Is My Home sheet and all available resources. They should be prepared to share their research with the class orally afterward.

Groups that have extra time could consult further resources for more creatures to add to the forest. Students may now wish to title the forest mural "Who Lives Here?" and add to it throughout the unit.

My Tree Notebook

Make a notebook for each student by providing them with the cover page (see unit appendix) and about twenty half sheets of blank white paper and stapling the pages together. Share the books *Have You Seen Trees?* by Joanne Oppenheim and *Hello Tree!* by Joanne Ryder and discuss the different ways that trees are special to us. Each student needs to select a tree in their yard or neighborhood that they can observe and record information on. Tree notebooks should be sent home with students. Then, throughout the unit, students should complete the following exercises with their tree:

- describe your tree in words
- draw three pictures of your tree: one in the evening, one in the morning, and one during rain, snow, or fog
- draw seeds or flowers if the timing is right
- a leaf rubbing
- a bark rubbing
- tree research; try to identify your tree's name by comparing a leaf specimen with a tree spotter's guide such as *Peterson's First Guide to Trees* by George A. Petrides
- measure the girth of the tree with a string, then measure the string
- estimate the height of the tree (see *Tree* by David Burnie, page 63; *Trees and Leaves* by Rosie Harlow and Gareth Morgan, page 5; *(Focus on) Trees* by Anita Ganeri, page 22; or *Trees* by Linda Gamlin, page 9 for methods in estimating tree height)
- listen to your tree; write down what kinds of sounds you hear
- investigate the creatures who live in your tree by looking closely at the branches and the bark of the trunk; try placing a light-colored sheet on the ground beneath the

tree, then shake a branch from above to observe what falls out of the tree. Look fast and write down and/or draw what you see
- leaf watch; select a healthy twig and tie a clear plastic bag over a few leaves; leave it alone and check it later or the next day for changes; record what you see (leaves will give off water vapor that condenses into droplets)
- provide a leaf specimen (attach to page with tape)
- your tree's history; interview someone who has watched the tree grow; try to find out how old the tree is and who planted the tree
- take care of your tree by loosening the soil around the trunk for better water absorption; bring buckets of water to your tree twice a week; estimate the number of buckets it likes to drink by pouring buckets near its trunk until the water begins to puddle up—that tells you that it has had enough
- sit and enjoy your tree; take a blanket and just sit under your tree for an hour or so and write down how you felt or what you thought about during this time
- write a thank-you note to your tree for what it has given and continues to give you

You may wish to give students one or two activities at a time orally or simply give them a written list of all the exercises. The information and/or pictures for each exercise should be completed on its own page and dated. At the end of the unit, students can bring their notebooks back to school to share with others. The class can figure out whose tree is the tallest, smallest, youngest, oldest, and so on. They can also learn who used the same type of tree (or even the same exact tree) and compare findings. This information could also be organized into different graphs.

Investigations for After Reading

Be a Friend to Trees—*Spread the Word!*

With the whole class, brainstorm things that could be added to the back section (pages 30–32) of *Be a Friend to Trees* and write each idea on the chalkboard. Invite each student to design a poster depicting one thing that anyone can do to protect or save a tree or a forest. Display the posters around your school.

Or make a mural that includes trees and people together entitled "A Forest of Good Advice." Each student can contribute an index card printed with one way to be a friend to a tree along with their name to attach to the forest.

Tree Art

Invite students to choose one or two of the following art projects:

A.) Leaf Printing—paint actual leaves of various shapes and sizes and press onto paper to make prints

B.) Twig Sculptures—collect dry, dead twigs and put them together with string and glue to create a sculpture

C.) Pinecone Printing—dip a variety of pinecones into paint and press or roll the painted cones on paper

D.) Sponge Painting—cut several old sponges into different tree shapes, dip into paint, and lightly press onto paper

E.) Growth Rings—use a brown marker to make circles within circles like a bullseye but with many more circles to create growth rings such as the ones that could be seen in the stump of a mature tree; then paint with water inside all of the circles to create a darker ring/lighter ring pattern (dark ring indicates summer growth; lighter ring indicates spring growth)

F.) Challenge Project—make a life-sized tree (sapling) by using a sturdy piece of board for a base, masking tape, newspaper, cardboard tubes from wrapping paper, wire hangers, and papier-mâché; paint trunk and branches; make paper leaves

Before beginning any of these "messy" projects, I recommend reviewing appropriate behaviors and your set up/clean up procedures. I also recommend the use of art smocks and newspapers to protect clothing and work areas.

Book Projects

Invite students to work with a partner on one or more of the following projects:

A.) Tree Poetry—read *Sky Tree* by Thomas Locker and *Trees* by Harry Behn; write a poem that tells about trees in some way; make a shape book using a tree pattern (see unit appendix) to write your poem in and illustrate

B.) A Tree for All Seasons—read *Sky Tree* by Thomas Locker and *How Do Apples Grow?* by Betsy Maestro; make a shape book using the unit appendix tree pattern; show how a deciduous fruit tree looks over a year of changing seasons; write about the changes that take place below each picture

C.) A Tree Has Enemies—find out about the enemies and problems that trees are faced with in the books *Trees* (Eyewitness Explorers) by Linda Gamlin and *Tree* (Eyewitness Book) by David Burnie; write about five to six of them in a minibook and illustrate

D.) Write a Sequel—read *The Lorax* by Dr. Seuss; make a minibook and write what might happen next if the story were to go on

E.) Tree Types—make a shape book of one of the three tree types … deciduous, coniferous, or tropical; pick a corresponding shape pattern from the unit appendix; trace and cut out pages; describe the tree type, then choose six trees to illustrate and label along with their leaf; use charts from previous activity for names of trees; consult spotter's guide for shapes, sizes, and leaf information

F.) A Tree Knows—read *The Tree That Would Not Die* by Ellen Levine and/or *A Trees Tale* by Lark Carrier; write about an old tree in your neighborhood and what it may have seen as it has grown (interview a grandparent or another elderly person who can describe what has gone on around the tree through the years or just make up your own story)

G.) Save the Rain Forests—read and research several different books about rain forests such as *Nature's Green Umbrella* by Gail Gibbons and *Tropical Rainforests* by Jean Hamilton, paying special attention to why they are important; make a minibook in the form of a letter saying why it is important to save the rain forests and what you can do to help; begin your book with Dear Mr. Hays and send your book/letter to:

Randall Hays, Director
Rainforest Action Network
450 Sansome Street, #700
San Francisco, CA 94111

Chart Projects

Invite students to work with a different partner to design one of the following charts:

A.) Flip Flap Chart—read *ABCedar* by George Ella Lyon; make the chart by folding a large piece of construction paper in half lengthwise; keeping the paper folded, make three perpendicular cuts up to the fold to end up with four flaps equally spaced; pick four trees that you both like the best; illustrate top flaps with trees of choice and label them; underneath each flap illustrate each tree's leaf. (See illustration below.)

B.) Size Chart—use "spotter's guide" in *(Focus on) Trees* by Anita Ganeri; make a chart showing drawings of ten different types of trees in order by height; label each tree with name and potential size

C.) Exchangeable Air—make a picture chart that shows the air exchange between animals and plants and the process of photosynthesis

D.) A Life Cycle—read *The Acorn's Story* by Valerie Greeley; make a flowchart showing the lifecycle of a tree

E.) Seeds on the Go!—use indices in the resource books (see supporting library) to research the ways in which seeds travel to replant themselves and make a picture chart with markers or real seeds that illustrates this information

F.) A Tree of Many Parts—using paints or markers make a poster-sized chart that shows the basic parts of any tree with each part clearly labeled

Cut or Not to Cut

Share *Timber!* by William Jaspersohn, *Giants in the Land* by Diana Appelbaum, *Song for the Ancient Forest* by Nancy Luenn, and *Rain Forest* by Helen Cowcher and discuss or debate the messages that these books are trying to get across. Students can voice their opinions and/or request information about this debate by writing letters to one of the following:

Barbara Dudley
Greenpeace USA
1436 U Street NW
Washington, DC 20009

Michael Fisher
Sierra Club
730 Polk Street
San Francisco, CA 94109

Andy Lipkis, President
Tree People
12601 Mulholland Drive
Beverly Hills, CA 90210

Children of the Green Earth
P.O. Box 95219
Seattle, WA 98145

Learning from Collections

Using specimens collected earlier, groups can look at:

Leaves—Categorize leaves by type, shape, simple or compound, color, and so on; sequence leaves by size or color; press leaf specimens between two sheets of paper and some heavy books (or between two sheets of waxed paper covered with old towels and heated with a hot iron to keep a more permanent collection).

Twigs—Look for leaf/bud scars and count them to see how old each twig is; look in indices of resource books (see supporting library) to find out more about them.

Flowers—Make a pressed flower chart on poster board, labeling each with the tree's name and possibly the fruit that will follow blossoms.

Tree Walk

Take students (and parents) on a walk in the neighborhood surrounding the school. Allow students to choose their own groups of three and give each group one of the pictures you took at the beginning of the unit, some clay, a tree spotter's guide, such as *Peterson's First Guide to Trees* by George A. Petrides, and a parent. Provide each student with a sketch pad or a clipboard with three sheets of paper and a pencil. On the first page, students should look for the tree in the picture and, once found, decide what type of tree it is. Then they should identify the tree's name using the spotter's guide, draw the tree itself, and label it.

Each group should examine the bark of a variety of trees and make prints of two different barks by pressing clay onto the tree trunk and peeling it off. After the walk they need to carry their "clay bark" carefully back to school for examination, comparison, and sequencing according to bumpiness (age).

If possible, the walk should end up at a place such as a park that has a variety of trees reasonably close together. On the second page of paper, students should sketch or make a picture map of a chosen area and try to identify some of the trees on the map.

Students should spend time just quietly looking around in order to make as many observations as they can in regard to the trees and wildlife in the area. On the third page, they should record anything unusual they see as well as any questions they have for a discussion upon returning to the classroom. They should also be encouraged to collect any specimens that they find on the ground to add to the class collections.

Plant a Tree

First obtain permission to plant a tree on school grounds. Determine what types of tree would do well in the designated area and the cost of each. I suggest calling a greenhouse or tree nursery for advice. Then invite your students to help decide what kind of tree to plant by offering them the available and affordable choices. Groups can research the choices further to find out about their characteristics and share with the class. Hold a vote with majority ruling. Once decided, you and your students (and possibly your principal and parent/teacher group) will need to figure out how you will raise the money to pay for it. (See moneymaking ideas from *The Story of Money* unit appendix.) If possible, take some students with you to select the actual tree; however, you may need to arrange to have the tree delivered.

When the planting day comes, have several small shovels or spades for digging and buckets for watering the new tree on hand so that everyone may participate in some way. Many new trees come with directions for planting. Make several copies and invite students to read them aloud and follow them precisely. When the tree has been successfully planted in the ground, celebrate your good deed by tying a big, colorful ribbon around its trunk and having a picnic lunch around it to keep it company on its first day in its new home.

PARENT LETTER

Dear Parents,

We shall soon begin an invigorating hike into the world of trees. The book we will be using, *Be a Friend to Trees* by Patricia Lauber, will guide us as we investigate different types of trees, how they grow, where they grow, who lives among them, and the many uses we have for trees. Don't be surprised if your child suddenly becomes interested in the landscaping in your neighborhood. Welcome this interest by helping your child find out as much as they can about any nearby trees. Assist them in collecting specimens of tree parts such as leaves, twigs, seeds, and so on, keeping in mind not to trespass on others' property and not to harm any tree. Also, help your child in selecting one tree to use for completing "My Tree Notebook" at home throughout the unit.

As part of learning about trees we will be going on a "Tree Walk" on _____ at _____. We would love to have you join us in admiring and identifying the trees in our neighborhood. A permission slip will follow soon. We will also plant a tree of our own on _____ at _____. If you are able to join us please bring along buckets and/or planting tools, a blanket, and a picnic lunch for you and your child. We will picnic "under" our newly planted tree in celebration of its new home. If you cannot join us but would still like to help out, please see the attached "Wanted" sheet for other unit project materials. Thank you!

Hug a tree today!

Deciduous Tree Pattern

Coniferous Tree Pattern

Tropical Tree Pattern

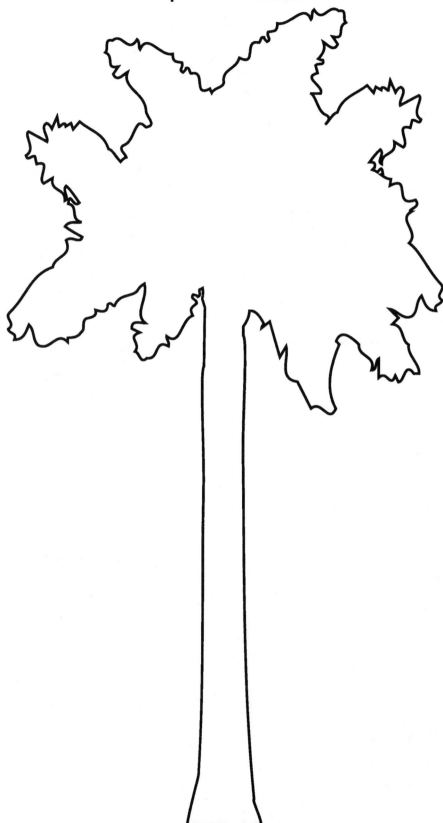

A Forest Is My Home

(A brief research report)

Names:_____

Name of forest creature:_____

Description:_____

_____

_____

The type of forest that is "home":_____

Two ways that this creature needs the trees in the forest:_____

_____

_____

Other interesting facts about this creature:_____

_____

_____

_____

My Tree Notebook

_____

My Tree Notebook

_____

Be a Friend to Trees

Student Evaluation

Name: _____

1.) During the unit, I worked cooperatively in my groups

        not at all   sometimes   most of the time

2.) During the unit, I tried my best

        not at all   sometimes   most of the time

3.) During the unit, I completed

____ a forest mural   ____ a minibook   ____ a chart project
____ a tree notebook   ____ a letter   ____ a tree art project
____ a picture map   ____ a tree type chart   ____ a "Be a Friend" poster
____ a tree sketch   ____ a clay bark specimen   ____ a forest life sharing

I also contributed to:
____ class specimen collections   ____ "Just a tree?"
____ tree selection, planting, and care

4.) Something new that I learned about trees is: _____

_____

5.) Something new that I learned about forests is: _____

_____

6.) Something new that I learned about creatures of the trees is: _____

_____

7.) Something that I worked on that I am especially proud of is: _____

_____

8.) My favorite things about this unit were: _____

_____

9.) One thing that I can do to be a friend to trees is: _____

_____

Supporting Library

(*Note:* There are so many wonderful resources currently available on rain forests, that an entire unit could be devoted to rain forests alone. Therefore, I have only referenced a few that I personally liked in order to briefly include rain forests in this unit on trees but not cover it in depth.)

Annatta, Ivan. *Trees* (The Child's World). Chicago: Encyclopaedia Britannica Educational Corp., 1993.
Focuses on twelve varieties of trees and their special features.

Appelbaum, Diana. *Giants in the Land.* Boston: Houghton Mifflin, 1993.
The story of the giant pines that once were abundant and how they were cut for the masts of English sailing ships.

Arnosky, Jim. *Crinkleroot's Guide to Knowing Trees.* New York: Bradbury Press, 1992.
An old character introduces the reader to a variety of his old and new friends.

Arvetis, Chris. *Forests* (Where Are We? Series). Rand McNally, 1993.
An introduction to different types of forests, where they are, and the creatures who live there.

Baker, Jeannie. *Where the Forest Meets the Sea.* New York: Scholastic, 1987.
A boy and his father visit an old-growth forest.

Bash, Barbara. *Ancient Ones.* San Francisco: Sierra Club Books for Children, 1994.
Discusses the web of life within an old-growth forest.

Bash, Barbara. *Tree of Life.* Boston: Little, Brown, 1989.
Describes the life cycle of the baobab tree on the African savannah.

Behn, Harry. *Trees.* New York: Henry Holt, 1949, 1992.
A poem that celebrates trees and all that they provide us.

Bunting, Eve. *Someday a Tree.* New York: Clarion Books, 1993.
A girl and her family and neighbors try to save an old oak tree from dying of poison and pollution.

Burnie, David. *Tree* (Eyewitness Books). New York: Alfred A. Knopf, 1988.
Provides in-depth information about trees, their parts, wildlife, enemies, lumbering, and more.

Carrier, Lark. *A Tree's Tale.* New York: Dial Books for Young Readers, 1996.
The story of a 400-year-old oak "path" tree that saw many changes in its life.

Coombes, Allen J. *Trees: A Visual Guide to More than 500 Species of Trees from Around the World.* New York: Dorling Kindersley, 1992.
A guide for identifying trees.

Cowcher, Helen. *Rain Forest.* New York: Scholastic, 1988.
Animals of the rain forest escape disaster but wonder how long the trees will remain to protect them.

Dorros, Arthur. *Rain Forest Secrets.* New York: Scholastic, 1990.
Discusses the variety of plants and animals that live together in the rain forests.

Gamlin, Linda. *Trees* (Eyewitness Explorers). New York: Dorling Kindersley, 1993.
Describes types of trees, their parts, uses, and what gives them life.

Ganeri, Anita. *(Focus On) Trees.* New York: Gloucester Press, 1992.
Provides abundant information on trees. Includes activities, a spotter's guide, and a glossary.

Garelick, May, and Barbara Brenner. *The Tremendous Tree Book.* New York: Four Winds Press, 1979.
A unique and simple celebration of trees.

Gibbons, Gail. *Nature's Green Umbrella.* New York: Morrow Junior Books, 1994.
Discusses characteristics of tropical rain forests and their importance to mankind.

Greeley, Valerie. *The Acorn's Story.* New York: Macmillan Publishing, 1994.
Tells the story of an acorn becoming an oak tree, living, and dying.

Hamilton, Jean. *Tropical Rainforests.* Parsippany, N.J.: Silver Burdett Press, 1995.
Discusses many different aspects of tropical rain forests. Includes photographs, questions/answers, and addresses to write for more information.

Harlow, Rosie, and Gareth Morgan. *Trees and Leaves* (Fun with Science). New York: Warwick Press, 1991.
Provides information along with numerous projects and games.

Jaspersohn, William. *Timber!* Boston: Little, Brown, 1996.
Describes how trees are cut for lumber and turned into wood products.

Jennings, Terry. *Temperate Forests* (Exploring Our World). Danbury, Conn.: Grolier Educational Corp., 1992.
Describes temperate forests of the world including types of trees, their life cycles, where they grow, and how they are cut and used.

Jeunesse, Gallimard. *The Tree* (A First Discovery Book). New York: Scholastic, 1989.
See-through pages help to illustrate the changes that a tree may go through during the seasons.

Lavies, Bianca. *Tree Trunk Traffic.* New York: E. P. Dutton, 1989.
Discusses the creatures that live in and around an old maple tree.

Levine, Ellen. *The Tree That Would Not Die.* New York: Scholastic, 1995.
A 500-year-old oak tree in Austin, Texas, tells of the history it has seen during its lifetime.

Levy, Constance. *A Tree Place and Other Poems.* New York: Margaret K. McElderry Books/Macmillan Publishing, 1994.
A collection of forty nature poems.

Locker, Thomas. *Sky Tree.* New York: HarperCollins, 1995.
Paintings show how one tree changes with the sky, the weather, and the seasons.

Luenn, Nancy. *Song for the Ancient Forest.* New York: Atheneum, 1993.
Raven, a trickster in Native American legends, finds someone who will listen to his song for the trees.

Lyon, George Ella. *ABCedar: An Alphabet Book of Trees.* New York: Orchard Books/Franklin Watts, 1989.
Shows a tree, its relative height, its leaves, and fruits or seeds for each letter of the alphabet.

Maestro, Betsy. *How Do Apples Grow?* (Let's-Read-and-Find-Out Science Book). New York: HarperCollins, 1992.
Explains the seasonal changes of an apple tree from bud to edible fruit.

Maestro, Betsy. *Why Do Leaves Change Color?* (Let's-Read-and-Find-Out Science Book). New York: HarperCollins, 1994.
Explains why and how leaves change colors and fall from deciduous trees.

Muller, Gerda. *Around the Oak.* New York: Dutton Children's Books, 1994.
Children go through the seasons with a very old oak tree. Includes sections on different plants and creatures that live in the forest surrounding the oak.

Oppenheim, Joanne. *Floratorium.* New York: Bantam Books, 1994.
Provides information about the plant world through a tour of a botanical museum.

Oppenheim, Joanne. *Have You Seen Trees?* New York: Scholastic, 1995.
Describes in rhyme different types of trees that change with the seasons.

Petrides, George A. *Peterson's First Guide to Trees.* Boston: Houghton Mifflin, 1993.
A guide for identifying trees.

Pluckrose, Henry. *Trees* (Walkabout Series). Chicago: Childrens Press, 1994.
Provides a brief introduction to trees with photographs.

Richardson, Joy. *Trees* (Picture Science). New York: Franklin Watts, 1993.
A simple introduction to trees and how they grow.

Romanova, Natalia. *Once There Was a Tree.* New York: Dial Books, 1985.
A tree stump gives different things to different creatures as does the new tree that grows in its place.

Ryder, Joanne. *Hello Tree!* New York: Lodestar Books, 1991.
Describes how trees can be special. Easy reading.

Ryder, Joanne. *Jaguar in the Rainforest* (Just for a Day Series). New York: Morrow Junior Books, 1996.
The reader becomes a jaguar in his rain forest habitat for a day.

Seuss, Dr. *The Lorax.* New York: Random House, 1971.
The Lorax speaks for the trees and the creatures when the careless Once-ler pollutes the area.

Simon, Seymour. *Wildfires.* New York: Morrow Junior Books, 1996.
Discusses fire as something that is part of the cycles of nature.

Taylor, Barbara. *Forest Life* (Look Closer). New York: Dorling Kindersley, 1993.
Describes plants and animals who live in forests including fungi, weasel, owl, and giant wood wasp.

Taylor, Kim. *Tree Life* (Look Closer). New York: Dorling Kindersley, 1992.
Describes a variety of creatures who reside in or around trees including a marmoset, a gecko, and a tree frog.

Waters, Gregory J. (expert reader). *Trees and Forests* (Scholastic Voyages of Discovery Series). New York: Scholastic, 1995.
Explains numerous aspects of trees and different types of forests, including how trees began, who lives among them, and their future.

Wiggers, Raymond. *Picture Guide to Tree Leaves.* New York: Franklin Watts, 1991.
A guide for identifying trees.

Wood, John Norris. *Woods and Forests* (Nature Hide and Seek Series). New York: Alfred A. Knopf, 1993.
Reader can search for hidden pictures of many different kinds of forest animals in several types of woodland.

Video

Totally Tropical Rainforest (*National Geographic*'s Really Wild Animals Series). Burbank, Calif.: Columbia Tristar Home Video, 1994.
Explores a variety of plants and animals within a tropical rain forest with music and an animated globe named "Spin."

Main Appendix

READING RESPONSE TO FICTION

Name:_____

Date:_____

Today I read the book:_____

The author:_____

The illustrator:_____

I chose this book because:_____

_____

This book was about:_____

_____

_____

_____

_____

Things I liked about this book:_____

_____

Things I did not like about this book:_____

_____

Things that I wondered about after reading this book:_____

_____

I would/would not (circle one) recommend this book to a friend because:_____

_____

READING RESPONSE TO NONFICTION

Name:_____

Date:_____

Today I read the book:_____

The author:_____

The illustrator/photographer:_____

I chose this book because:_____

_____

I learned something new by reading this book. I learned that:_____

_____

_____

Things I liked about this book:_____

_____

_____

Things I did not like about this book:_____

_____

_____

I would/would not (circle one) recommend this book to a friend because:_____

_____

_____

FIELD TRIP PERMISSION

Yippee! We're going on a field trip!

Our class is going on a field trip to:_____

On: _____

Leaving at:_____

Returning at:_____

Special Instructions _____

_____

_____

– –

My child _____ has my permission to go with the class

on the field trip to _____ on _____.

I will/will not (please circle one) be going along.

Signed:_____

Please complete and return to school as soon as possible. Thank you!

Recipe for Papier-Mâché Paste

$1/_2$ cup flour
2 cups water

Heat and stir constantly until thick. Pour into container. When cool, cover to keep from drying out.

Wanted

Supplies:
(Donations)

Volunteers

_____

For:_____

_____

Date:_____

_____

Day:_____

_____

Times:_____

_____

For:_____

_____

Date :_____

(For Loan Only)

Day:_____

_____

Times:_____

_____

For:_____

_____

Date:_____

_____

Day:_____

_____

Times:_____

Parents, if you are able to donate or lend any of the above materials for our unit projects, please send them as soon as possible. Also, if you are willing to donate some of your valuable time, please fill out the form below, send it back to me, and I will call you to confirm. As always, please call me if you have any questions. Thank you!

Child's name:_____

Parent's name: _____

YES! I can help! I would like to volunteer for _____ on

_____ (day and date) from _____ to _____.

YOU'RE INVITED

For: _____

Where: _____

When: _____

Special instructions: _____

_____

- -

Please send R.S.V.P. below by _____ .

Child's name: _____

Parent's name: _____

_____YES, I plan to attend   _____ NO, I do not plan to attend

Number attending: _____

Signed: _____

Compare/Contrast Report

Title of book:_____

Author:_____

Title of second version (or video):_____

Author:_____

Things that were the same:_____

_____

_____

_____

Things that were different:_____

_____

_____

_____

Which version did you like better?_____

Why?_____

_____

_____

Name:_____

VENN DIAGRAM

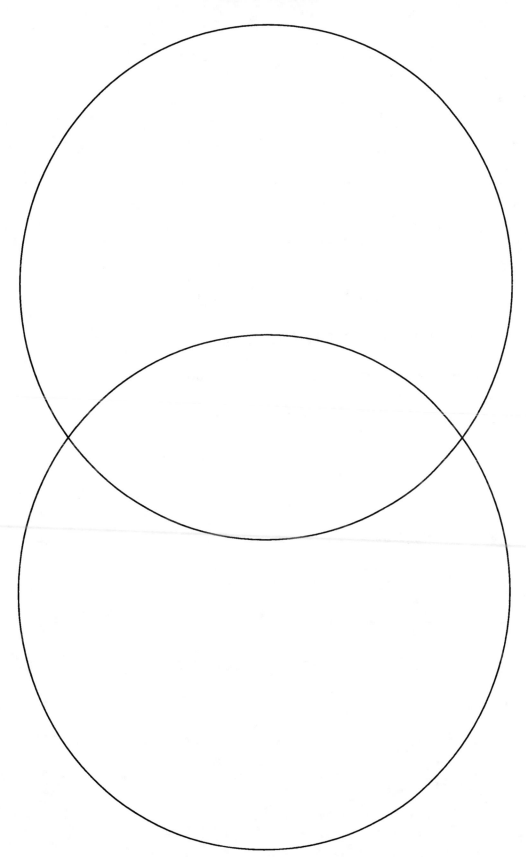

PRESENTATION CHECKLIST

To be used by audience when evaluating group presentations.

Group members:_____

_____

_____

Topic:_____

_____ each member contributed to the presentation

_____ group was organized and prepared

_____ group was enthusiastic about their presentation

_____ group provided adequate and accurate information

_____ group used loud, clear voices during the presentation

Other comments or suggestions:_____

_____

_____

_____

GROUP EVALUATION

To be discussed and agreed upon by all members following a group activity.
Cut on dotted lines. Each member take a copy for their folder.

- -

Names of group members: _____

_____

Date: _____

_____ Today our group worked very well together.
_____ Today our group worked fairly well together.   (check one)
_____ Today our group did not work well together.

Because _____

_____

- -

Names of group members: _____

_____

Date: _____

_____ Today our group worked very well together.
_____ Today our group worked fairly well together.   (check one)
_____ Today our group did not work well together.

Because _____

_____

- -

Names of group members: _____

_____

Date: _____

_____ Today our group worked very well together.
_____ Today our group worked fairly well together.   (check one)
_____ Today our group did not work well together.

Because _____

_____

COOPERATION CHECKLIST

To be filled out by person observing cooperative group interactions.

Names in group: _____

_____

_____

_____ heads together

_____ quiet voices

_____ taking turns

_____ listening to each other

_____ helping each other

_____ encouraging others

_____ all members are participating

_____ following directions

_____ staying on task

UNIT EVALUATION

For (name of unit): _____

1.) Students' reactions, in general, to the topic and related projects and activities were

      negative/unexcited   satisfactory   positive/very excited

2.) The level of student involvement within groups was

      low   average   high

3.) The level of parent involvement was

      low   average   high

4.) Appropriateness in meeting individual needs

      not very/more adaptations needed   satisfactory   very appropriate

5.) Students' demonstration of learning through investigative activities and projects

      below expectations   satisfactory   above expectations

6.) Which investigations seemed most effective and why? _____

_____

_____

Which seemed least effective and why? _____

_____

_____

7.) As per students' evaluations, did the majority of students learn new things in each different theme area? _____

_____

8.) As per students' evaluations, what did they enjoy the most about the unit? _____

_____

9.) Thoughts for teaching this unit next time: _____

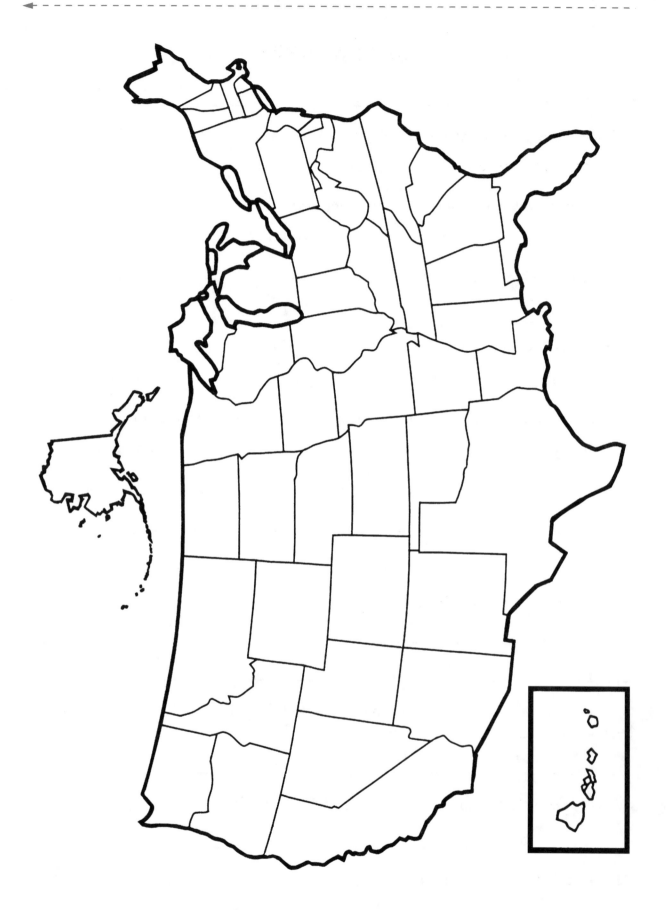

Copyright © 1998 Laura Turner Pullis, *Information Investigation*, Fulcrum Publishing (800) 992-2908, www.fulcrum-resources.com.

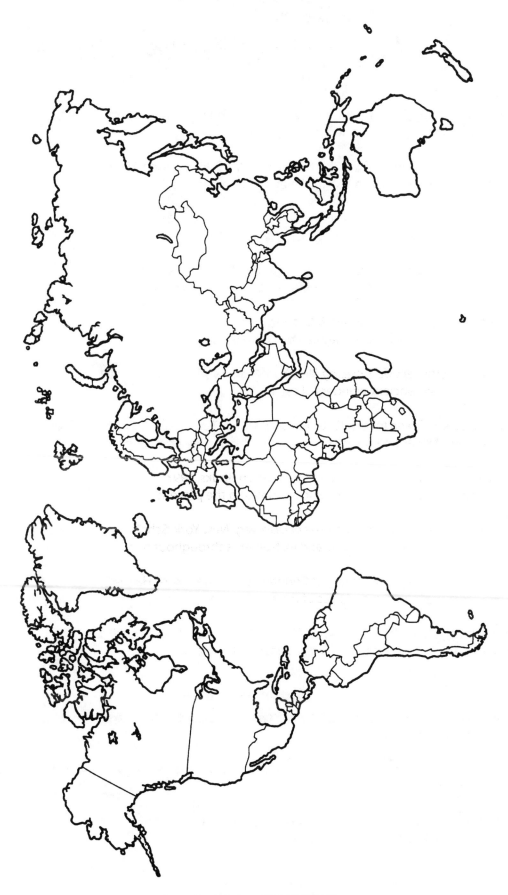

Copyright © 1998 Laura Turner Pullis, *Information Investigation*, Fulcrum Publishing (800) 992-2908, www.fulcrum-resources.com.

Bibliography of Featured Titles

Burns, Peggy. *Stepping Through History: The Mail.* New York: Thomson Learning, 1995.
A historical account of the postal service.

Cherry, Lynne. *A River Ran Wild.* New York: Harcourt Brace Jovanovich, 1992.
An environmental history of the Nashua River in Massachusetts.

Cole, Joanna. *The Magic School Bus: Inside the Human Body.* New York: Scholastic, 1989.
Ms. Frizzle takes her class on a field trip inside Arnold's body.

Gibbons, Gail. *Caves and Caverns.* New York: Harcourt Brace, 1993.
Discusses different types of caves, their formations, and the creatures within.

Heller, Ruth. *Color.* New York: Putnam & Grosset, 1995.
A unique look at colors and how they can be combined and applied.

Krupp, Robin Rector. *Let's Go Traveling.* New York: Morrow Junior Books, 1992.
A young tourist visits ancient wonders of the world.

Lauber, Patricia. *Be a Friend to Trees* (Let's-Read-and-Find-Out Science Book). New York: HarperCollins, 1994.
Discusses types of trees and the many important things they provide for us.

Maestro, Betsy. *The Story of Money.* New York: Clarion Books, 1993.
Describes the history of money from ancient times to the present.

Moore, Ken. *Musical Instruments: Voyages of Discovery.* New York: Scholastic, 1993.
Describes the development of music and instruments throughout history.

Sandler, Martin W. *Pioneers* (A Library of Congress Book). New York: HarperCollins, 1994.
A rich history of the journeys and lives of the early pioneers.

Thomson, Peggy. *Siggy's Spaghetti Works.* New York: Tambourine Books, 1993.
Children take an informative tour of Siggy's spaghetti factory.

Other Resources

Green, Pamela. *A Matter of Fact: Using Factual Texts in the Classroom.* Armadale, Victoria Australia: Eleanor Curtain Publishing, 1992.

Johnson, David W., Roger T. Johnson, and Edythe Johnson Holubec. *Cooperation in the Classroom.* Edina, Minn.: Interaction Book Company, 1991.

Lepscky, Ibi. *Pablo Picasso.* New York: Barron's Educational Series, 1984.
Describes the childhood of the famous artist.